Cambodia
YEAR ZERO

Cambodia
YEAR

ZERO

FRANÇOIS PONCHAUD

Translated from the French by Nancy Amphoux

HOLT, RINEHART and WINSTON   NEW YORK

Library of Congress Cataloging in Publication Data

Ponchaud, François (date)
  Cambodia: year zero

  Translation of Cambodge année zéro.
  1. Cambodia—History—1975.
DS554.8.P6613   1978   959.6'04   77-15204
ISBN: 0-03-040306-5

Designer: A. Christopher Simon

Printed in the United States of America

10   9   8   7   6   5   4   3   2   1

TO THE LEPER-KING

He suffered more
from his subjects' diseases
than from his own,
for it is the people's pain
that makes the pain of kings
and not their own.

STELE OF JAYAVARMAN VII
(1183–1201) (The Leper-King)

CONTENTS

PREFACE

"The seventeenth of April 1975, a glorious date in the history of Kampuchea,[1] has ushered in an era more remarkable than the age of the Angkors."[2]

A page in the history of Cambodia has certainly been turned. But it is hard to decipher the writing on the new page that began in April 1975, for since "liberation" the country has withdrawn behind a wall of silence. What has happened, and what is happening now in Cambodia, the land of the enigmatic smile?

I lived there for ten years, from November 8, 1965, to May 8, 1975, five years in the kingdom of Cambodia under Prince Sihanouk and five in the first republic, under Lon Nol. My last three weeks were spent in Democratic Kampuchea, certainly not long enough for me to say I know it well.

As a missionary working for the Catholic community I spent my first three years studying the Khmer language, the Buddhist religion, and the customs of the country. Then I was sent out to different places in the rural districts and towns. The years passed, and the country became as dear to me as my native soil. During the final years of the war I was living in Phnom Penh, in charge of a Khmer translation committee and a student hostel.

---

[1] Kampuchea is Cambodia. Both names are used in this text, as in other French and English writings, although the new authorities presumably prefer the former.

[2] A slogan often repeated over Radio Phnom Penh, e.g., September 9, 1975.

In July 1975, three months after the change of regime, a Cambodian friend in Paris handed me a long letter he had just received from a friend who had recently crossed the Cambodian frontier into Thailand. His description of his homeland was grim indeed. I couldn't believe my eyes: with such sincerity and re-strained grief that no deception could be possible, he wrote of dreadful things, of deportations, massacres and forced labor. I had supposed that calm would be restored once the inevitable postrevolutionary upheavals had subsided, and the peasant com-mon sense of the peaceable Khmers would soften the rigors of revolution. Apparently, this was by no means the case.

After that, I wanted to find out, I tried to understand. There were two pitfalls to avoid: excessive mistrust and systematic criticism of the new regime, and blind infatuation with a revolu-tion which many, like myself, had longed to see. I pored over the official documents issued by the government in Phnom Penh, trying to grasp the sense of this revolution and its objectives. The Kampuchean diplomatic mission in Paris possessed very little material, so I began listening to the daily broadcasts of the official voice of Kampuchea, Radio Phnom Penh.

Upon their arrival in Thailand or Vietnam (or, for a few, in France), the refugees, too, told the tale of their lives in Demo-cratic Kampuchea. In addition to many conversations with the refugees, I collected some hundred written accounts.[3] I analyzed

---

[3] I have made use of the accounts of ninety-four Khmer refugees, seventy-seven in Thailand, and seventeen in Vietnam. Thirty-two wrote their stories in Khmer. The accounts totaled 303 pages. The authors of this body of testimony were five women and eighty-nine men, including ten students, eight officers, seven ordinary soldiers, five civil servants, four primary schoolteachers, four Khmer Rouge, three bonzes, three pharmacists, three noncommissioned officers, two doctors, two fishermen, two secondary schoolteachers, two office employees, two mechanics, a policeman, a customs officer, a provincial guard, a court clerk, a prince, a truck driver, a ware-houseman, and a shopkeeper. The accounts of refugees in Thailand and France have been checked by personal interview with the authors. In addition to this body of testimony by people from relatively literate backgrounds who know how to read and write, the book also reflects hundreds of interviews with refugees who could do neither and were questioned directly in Khmer by the author. Most of these came from the laboring classes. For obvious reasons, the names of witnesses quoted here have been changed.

and checked these with care, comparing them with each other and also with the statements made by Radio Phnom Penh.

It is hard to grasp the sense of a revolution without placing it within the historical, social, and political context in which it arose; and it is virtually impossible to write its history if one is looking at it from outside. What kind of account of the French Revolution could have been written by an observer sitting in Belgium or on the far side of the Rhine! But in our day, communications have changed.

In this case, official statements and the refugees' accounts are all we have to go on. Yet despite their relative inadequacy, they enable us to bore a small hole in the wall of silence erected by the authorities in Kampuchea. But the future alone can bear out, clarify, or contradict some of the assertions made today.

After relating my personal experience of conditions in Phnom Penh between April 17 and May 6, when I left the city, I have used the refugees' statements to attempt to show what life in the countryside was like during that same period and the months that followed. Next, an analysis of the "Voice of Democratic Kampuchea" provides a somewhat clearer picture of the new Cambodia's revolutionary aims for society, individuals, and culture. And last, a brief summary of the historic and social context in which the Khmer revolutionary movement took form throws some light on recent events.

This book will undoubtedly raise more questions than it settles. History alone can give the right answers, by putting present events into a broader perspective.

—FRANÇOIS PONCHAUD
Paris, October 23, 1976

AUTHOR'S NOTE FOR THE
ENGLISH TRANSLATION

On March 31, 1977, *The New York Review of Books* published an account of my book under the signature of Jean Lacouture,[1] which provoked considerable reaction in all circles concerned about Asia and the future of socialism. With the responsible attitude and precision of thought that are so characteristic of him, Noam Chomsky then embarked upon a polemical exchange with Robert Silvers, Editor of the *NYR*, and with Jean Lacouture, leading to the publication by the latter of a rectification of his initial account.[2] Mr. Chomsky was of the opinion that Jean Lacouture had substantially distorted the evidence I had offered, and, considering my book to be "serious and worth reading, as distinct from much of the commentary it has elicited,"[3] he wrote me a personal letter on October 19, 1977, in which he drew my attention to the way it was being misused by antirevolutionary propagandists. He has made it my duty to "stem the flood of lies" about Cambodia—particularly, according to him, those propagated by Anthony Paul and John Barron in "Murder of a Gentle Land."

---

[1] "The Bloodiest Revolution," *NYR* (March 31, 1977), pp. 9–10.

[2] "Cambodia—Corrections," *NYR* (May 26, 1977), p. 46.

[3] Noam Chomsky and Edward S. Herman, "Distortions at Fourth Hand," *The Nation* (June 25, 1977), pp. 7–9.

Mr. Gareth Porter[4] also criticized my book very sharply during a congressional hearing on the subject of human rights in Cambodia,[5] and argued that I was trying to convince people that Cambodia was drowned in a sea of blood after the departure of the last American diplomats. He denied that a general policy of purge was put into effect and considered that the tragedy through which the Khmer people are now living should mainly be attributed to the American bombings. He censured me for lacking a critical approach in my use of the refugee accounts, on the ground that they were not credible because the refugees were deliberately trying to blacken the regime they had fled.

In the beginning, I was not opposed to the Khmer revolution: having lived with the Cambodian peasants from 1965 to 1970, I was painfully aware of their exploitation at the hands of the administration under the corrupt Sihanouk regime. From 1970 to 1975 I shared the lives of the poor in the suburbs of Phnom Penh under the Lon Nol regime. From the tens of thousands of refugees who fled the "liberated" zones in 1973, I learned of the harshness of the revolutionary regime, but I regarded it as a transitory necessity imposed by the war. So I welcomed the revolutionaries' victory as the only possible means of bringing Cambodia out of its misery. But after making a careful and full study of the broadcasts of Radio Phnom Penh and the refugees' testimony relating to 1975 and 1976, I was compelled to conclude, against my will, that the Khmer revolution is irrefutably the bloodiest of our century. A year after the publication of my book I can unfortunately find no reason to alter my judgment.

I am an exegete by training and profession; I have long been accustomed to applying the methods of source criticism to a body of reported events in order to elicit the historical truth from them. The first precaution I took was to look for the context of the refugees' stories and to see how they should be interpreted. These people had been traumatized by the cyclone that had swept

----

[4] Mr. Porter is coauthor, with George C. Hildebrand, of the book *Cambodia: Starvation and Revolution* (New York: Monthly Review Press, 1977).

[5] U.S., Congress, House, Subcommittee on International Organization of the Committee on International Relations, *Human Rights in Cambodia*, 95th Cong., 1st sess., May 3, 1977, pp. 19–33.

through their society, by the loss of those closest to them, and, in some cases, by the loss of their privileges and by the new necessity of performing hard work with their hands. They labored and suffered, and often they could not see the sense of their work and their suffering. Radio and official documents enable us, on the outside, to see what the revolution was aiming at, which made such sacrifices necessary.

I was also careful to see that the refugees whose accounts I used came from a wide range of backgrounds: if testimony from places as far-flung as Vietnam, Laos, and Thailand (and recently Malaysia and Singapore) concurred, then there was some likelihood of the reported information being true. Thailand, of course, was where most of them went, and the majority came from the provinces near that frontier—Battambang, Pailin, Siem Reap, Oddar Mean Chey. Quite a few came from farther away, though —Kompong Thom, Pursat, Kompong Chhnang, Koh Kong, Kompong Som, Takeo, Kampot, and even Phnom Penh or Kandal—in 1976, at least. Among the few hundred refugees who escaped the country in 1977, only three came from east of the Mekong, one from Koh Sothin, near Kompong Cham, and two from Kratie. The regions near the Vietnamese border, on the other hand, such as Stung Treng, Ratanakiri, Mondulkiri, and Prey Veng, have yielded no secrets, and the only detailed information I have been able to hear about them is that furnished by the state radio.

In weighing the value of each refugee's testimony, his personality has been taken into account; I was instinctively suspicious of people who had "revelations" to make and came bearing sensational tidings. I also mistrusted those who spoke French and those who came from the wealthier classes, who had lost too much under the new regime. I was mainly interested in ordinary people, army privates, peasants, and laborers, who could neither read nor write nor analyze what they had seen but whose illiterate memories could supply exact details. True, fifty-six refugees wrote me the story of their lives under the new regime (and thirty-five more have done so since my book came out, making 322 more pages of manuscript); these are the accounts of relatively well-off people, and they were transmitted by friends of mine in Thailand. But I myself met with most of the refugees quoted in the book.

In my work with the refugees in France I have met thousands of persons from every level of society. Before I completed my book I never gave any refugee the smallest sum of money or help in other form, so that the lure of a payment could not distort the facts. All I took to them was my friendship and my sympathy for unhappy human beings. Only two people ever asked me for money after an interview; and they proved to be among the least worthy of credit!

The accounts of refugees are indeed to be used with great care, and it is indeed regrettable that one cannot verify the accuracy of their statements on the spot; but the exodus of over one hundred thousand persons is a fact, and a bulky one, that raises enough questions in itself.

Furthermore, the courage of the many public figures in America and elsewhere who rose up to defend human rights in Cambodia between 1970 and 1975 is indeed worthy of praise; but the self-slaughter of the Khmer people, which is taking place at this moment, must be denounced no less vehemently. We cannot make use of the deaths of millions of Khmers to defend our own theories or projects for society. Beyond all doubt, we, the French and the Americans, bear part of the responsibility for the Cambodian drama. The total annihilation of the country's economic infrastructure by five years of war accounts for another share of the tragedy. But accusing foreigners cannot acquit the present leaders of Kampuchea: their inflexible ideology has led them to invent a radically new kind of man in a radically new society. A fascinating revolution for all who aspire to a new social order. A terrifying one for all who have any respect for human beings.

May this book provide a modest contribution to the search for truth about the events in Cambodia. And may the Khmer people live to see the dawn of an age of peace and happiness.

—FRANÇOIS PONCHAUD
Paris, September 20, 1977

PHNOM PENH

CHRUOY CHANG
WAR

Mekong

To Prek Phneuv

Lambert
Stadium

French
Embassy

Khmero-Japanese Bridge
of Friendship

Calmette
Hospital

Tonle Sap

TUOL KAUK

Bœung Kak

Phnom Hotel

Bishop's
Residence

Cathedral

Ministry of Information

Railroad Station

Monorom Hotel

Market

To Pochentong

T O E K   L O A K

Bonzes Hospital

Sokun Mean
Bon St.

Royal Palace

Norodom Boulevard

Monivong Boulevard

Olympic Stadium

Independence
Monument

T U O L   T O M P O U N G

CHAMCAR MON

Bassac

N

To Saigon

Monivong Bridge

To Takmau

MILE
0   1

KILOMETER
0

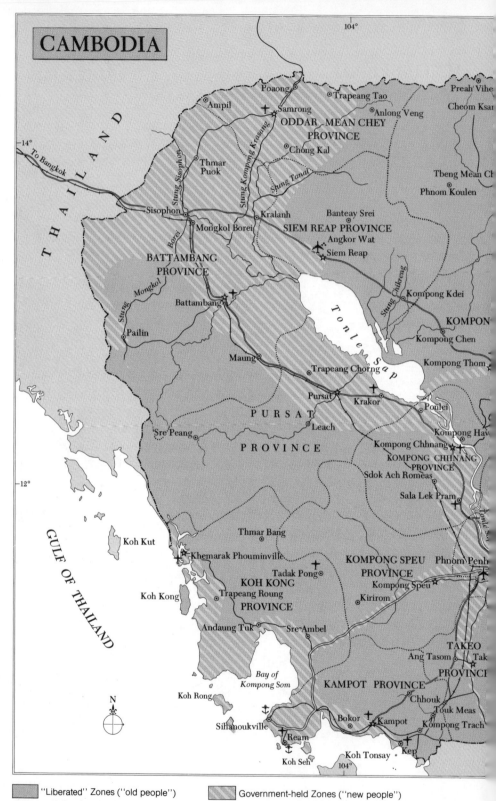

CAMBODIA

104°

To Bangkok

Poaong
Ampil
Trapeang Tao
Preah Vihe
Samrong
Anlong Veng
Cheom Ksar
**ODDAR MEAN CHEY
PROVINCE**
14°
Chong Kal
THAILAND
Thmar
Puok
Tbeng Mean Ch
Phnom Koulen
Sisophon
Kralanh
Banteay Srei
Mongkol Borei
SIEM REAP PROVINCE
Angkor Wat
**BATTAMBANG
PROVINCE**
Siem Reap
Kompong Kdei
Battambang
KOMPON
Pailin
Kompong Chen
Maung
T o n l e   S a p
Trapeang Chorng
Kompong Thom
Pursat
Krakor
Ponlei
P U R S A T
Sre Peang
Leach
Kompong Hav
P R O V I N C E
Kompong Chhnang
12°
**KOMPONG CHHNANG
PROVINCE**
Sdok Ach Romeas
Sala Lek Pram
GULF OF THAILAND
Koh Kut
Thmar Bang
Khemarak Phouminville
KOMPONG SPEU
Phnom Penh
PROVINCE
Tadak Pong
Koh Kong
KOH KONG
Trapeang Roung
Kompong Speu
Kirirom
PROVINCE
Andaung Tuk
Sre Ambel
TAKEO
Ang Tasom
Tak
PROVINCE
*Bay of
Kompong Som*
KAMPOT PROVINCE
Koh Rong
Chhouk
Touk Meas
Bokor
Kampot
Kompong Trach
Sihanoukville
Ream
Kep
Koh Tonsay
Koh Seh
104°
N

☐ "Liberated" Zones ("old people")   ☐ Government-held Zones ("new people")

Areas of Cambodia liberated (May 1972) by the People's National Liberation Armed Forces of Kampuchea;
the situation remained virtually unchanged until April 17, 1975

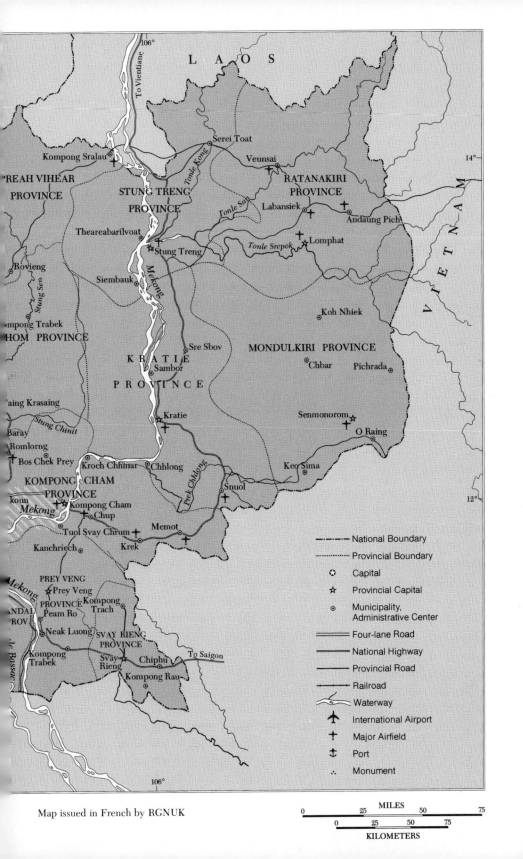

L A O S

106°

To Vientiane

14°

Kompong Sralau

Serei Toat

Veunsai

PREAH VIHEAR
PROVINCE

STUNG TRENG
PROVINCE

RATANAKIRI
PROVINCE

Tonle Kong

Theareabarilvoat

Labansiek

Andaung Pich

Tonle San

Stung Treng

Lomphat

Tonle Srepok

Rovieng

Siembauk

Stung Sen

Mekong

mpong Trabek

HOM PROVINCE

Koh Nhiek

Sre Sbov

MONDULKIRI PROVINCE

K R A T I E

Sambor

Chbar

Pichrada

P R O V I N C E

aing Krasaing

Stung Chinit

Baray

Kratie

Senmonorom

Romlorng

O Raing

Bos Chek Prey

Kroch Chhmar

Chhlong

Keo Sima

Prek Chhlong

KOMPONG CHAM
PROVINCE

Snuol

koun

Mekong

Kompong Cham

Chup

12°

Tuol Svay Chrum

Memot

Kanchriech

Krek

PREY VENG

Prey Veng

Kompong
Trach

PROVINCE

Peam Ro

NDAL

ROV

Neak Luong

SVAY RIENG
PROVINCE

Kompong
Trabek

Svay
Rieng

Chiphu

To Saigon

Mekong

Kompong Rau

106°

VIETNAM

Jr. Bassac

—·—·— National Boundary
············· Provincial Boundary
⊙ Capital
☆ Provincial Capital
⊙ Municipality,
   Administrative Center
═══ Four-lane Road
─── National Highway
─── Provincial Road
—┼— Railroad
〰 Waterway
✈ International Airport
✝ Major Airfield
⚓ Port
∴ Monument

Map issued in French by RGNUK

MILES
0   25   50   75

0   25   50   75
KILOMETERS

Cambodia
YEAR ZERO

ONE

"The Glorious Seventeenth of April"

It had been a very bad night. At regular intervals, the macabre whine of 107-mm rockets and 105-mm shells tore through the stillness and damp that are typical of nights at the end of the dry season. About five hundred shells had wailed over our heads and exploded noisily and haphazardly in teeming Phnom Penh. My colleagues and I had sat up with the International Red Cross team, acting as interpreters for the townspeople who were flocking into the shelter area hastily set up in the Phnom—the big hotel for foreigners.

Since evening, tens of thousands of inhabitants from the northern suburbs had been pouring into the center of the capital carrying meager bundles of personal treasures; they had drawn faces and frightened eyes. "They're at Kilometer 6!" "They're at Kilometer 4!" "They" were the Khmer Rouge, and the name alone struck terror.

On January 1, 1975, at exactly 1:00 A.M., "they" had begun their all-out offensive against Phnom Penh. Every revolutionary cannon, north, east, south, and west, began firing at exactly the same moment, while the republican generals were ushering in the Western New Year at a well-watered party. Every day thereafter, the corset had grown a little tighter: "they" got a foothold on the banks of the Mekong facing Phnom Penh and clung to it despite the combined efforts of government aviation and artillery to dislodge them. Since February "they" had occupied the riverbanks below Phnom Penh, cutting the umbilical cord along which supplies and ammunition were brought to the town. Then the Americans started flying in forty DC-8s and C-130s every day, taking considerable risks to deliver rice to the besieged townspeople and weapons to the troops defending them.

Rumors were eddying about on all sides: "They're terribly cruel." "They kill any soldiers they capture, and their families too." "They take people away to the forest."

We didn't give too much credence to these statements, supposing them to be the product of government propaganda. Khmers were Khmers, we thought; they would never go to such extremes with their own countrymen. Victory was within their grasp: what psychological advantage could they gain by taking wanton reprisals? Yet I met one woman from Arey Ksach on the opposite shore of the Mekong, who had climbed a tree when she heard the Khmer Rouge were coming and was so terror-stricken by what she saw beneath her—children torn limb from limb or impaled— that she preferred to let her legs be eaten off by giant red ants, rather than come down again. Surely she was exaggerating? Maybe; but one doesn't allow one's legs to be eaten off for an illusion!

April 13 marked the traditional Khmer New Year, the end of the Year of the Tiger and beginning of the Year of the Hare, and everyone was trying to guess what the new year would bring. Many people felt that an era was about to end, but refused to worry about it. For instance, the students in the hostel I was running had organized a party with all the traditional Khmer games and dances, and it was I, the European, who found their preparations somewhat inappropriate to the circumstances. The government had declared a state of emergency, forbidden all merrymaking, and ordered all places of business to remain open on New Year's Day. But it is hard to kill a tradition. Even my secretary said to me, privately, "This government is just as bad as the Khmer Rouge, it has no respect for our religious traditions!"

Around nine on the morning of Monday, April 14, the end came: a government army plane dropped two bombs on the Phnom Penh republican army headquarters only minutes after it was vacated by the chiefs who had been holding an emergency session there. The explosions instantly put a stop to all festivities. A twenty-four-hour curfew was proclaimed but could not be enforced because groups of refugees, into which large numbers of deserting soldiers from the routed republican army were mingling, came pouring in from all sides, preventing reinforcements from moving up to the front. What remained of the army tried to hold the refugees back on the outskirts of town, but in vain. Around 10:00 A.M. we learned that the revolutionaries had cut the road linking Phnom Penh to the airport, which was only six miles away. Rockets began raining down on the city, setting up waves of panic and terror.

On Tuesday, April 15, another turn of the screw. Huge fires swept through the outlying districts, consuming fuel reserves in the north, a sandal factory in the northwest. On the morning of the sixteenth another curfew was proclaimed, this one for forty-eight hours. Everybody knew the situation was critical: in the north "they" had reached Kilometer 6; to the south they had crossed the Monivong Bridge; in the west they were at the city gates near the Bonzes' Hospital. Around 6:00 P.M. we learned that the government troops had abandoned the northern front, and armored tanks were falling back to muster near the French embassy. Burning factories reddened the sky to the south, munitions depots were exploding in the west.

The International Red Cross delegation had been hoping to save civilian lives by setting up a shelter zone in the Phnom Hotel. On the afternoon of April 16, after long opposition, the government finally agreed. Prince Sihanouk, in Peking, had not responded to the appeal, but the Red Cross decided to act, anyway, well aware how fragile was the haven it could offer.

By dawn, April 17, the team was submerged by a tidal wave of refugees and could take no more. Suddenly, around 7:30 A.M., the streams of people dried up and gave way to eerie silence. The

armored tanks standing in firing position near the French embassy moved toward the city center and assembled in front of the
cathedral and Descartes *lycée* with their guns pointing north.
From the bishop's residence facing the Phnom Hotel, my friends
and I watched a group forming outside the French embassy—
could this be the Khmer Rouge asking France to act as go-
between in the negotiations for the surrender of the government
army?

A few moments later a group of men in black detached themselves from the main body—long-haired young men surrounding
a mysterious moon-faced man, unarmed, wearing a black polo
shirt. We assumed he was a Khmer Rouge emissary come to
negotiate the surrender. The people in the houses on Monivong
Boulevard, along which the little procession was moving, ven-
tured out onto the sidewalks and then, relieved to see the conquerors enter without bloodshed, sent up a timid cheer.

When the man in black drew close to the Phnom Hotel, a few
of the tanks stationed about fifty yards away moved off deeper
into town as though to continue fighting, while the remainder ran
up white flags. Their crews got down and ran to meet the conquerors, applauding and embracing them. The mysterious man,
cheered on by the thin crowd, climbed into one of the tanks,
turned it toward the center of town, and was met by heavy
machine-gun fire. He bravely dismounted and set off, on foot and
unarmed, to meet the soldiers, who lowered their weapons at the
sound of his voice alone. Then came a great surge of joy: the war
was over at last, people began hugging and kissing each other.
We, the foreign onlookers, were utterly amazed. Could this be the
end of the fierce fratricidal war lasting five long years, in the
course of which neither side had ever given quarter? Were these
men, looking so well fed, and so few in number, the dreaded
revolutionary troops? Our amazement grew when we saw two
jeeps drive up—bearing officers no doubt—flying flags showing a
cross potent on a red-and-blue field—an unlikely flag for Khmer
Rouge.

Soon, small groups of young Khmers, hardly into their teens,
began moving silently into town from all sides. They were dressed
all in black, wearing black Chinese caps and Ho Chi Minh

sandals—soles cut out of old tires fastened to the feet with rubber thongs. Hung about them were Chinese grenades; B-40s (anti-tank explosives); AK-47s, the famous Chinese assault guns, and strange clips and loaders dangled from their chests. They looked bewildered, on the verge of collapse, utterly remote from the people's jubilation. They alone did not seem happy. Curiously unlike the previous group.

But who was that first group? Later, we learned that the man in the black polo shirt was Hem Keth Dara, the son of a republican general who was a former minister of the interior. He was accompanied by about two hundred men, mostly students. They were acting for General Lon Non, the brother of Lon Nol, ex-president of the Khmer Republic, and their idea was to snatch the victory from the Khmer Rouge by disarming the government forces ahead of them and setting up a new government to replace the dying one of Long Boret, who was then premier. They called themselves the Monatio or National Movement, and at first the Khmer Rouge themselves could not make out who they were.

Around 9:30 Keth Dara reached the ministry of information and introduced himself as commander in chief of the Khmer Rouge. The place was almost deserted. The radio, which had been silent since the previous day, began broadcasting a little military music. Then, all employees of the ministry were ordered to return to their posts at once. About 10:00, Samdech Sangh Huot That, patriarch of the Buddhist community, was asked to appeal to the people to remain calm: "The war is over, we are among brothers! Stay quietly in your homes!" A few moments later General Mey Si Chan, head of the third bureau of the general staff of the republican armed forces, ordered all officers, noncommissioned officers, and regular troops of the three armies to cease fighting, for "negotiations are in progress." The war was, indeed, over.

An almost physical sense of relief led to general rejoicing. No more rockets to fear; no more blind slaughter; no more compulsory military service; no more of this rotten, loathed regime that didn't even pay its soldiers; no more food rationing because of the blockade. At last, the peasants could go back and cultivate their rice paddies. The thousands of refugees who had poured into town during the preceding days delightedly turned back to the homes they had fled for fear of the fighting. Military trucks sped past, flying white flags and honking their horns nonstop. The government troops they were transporting were cheered as though they were the ones who had won the war! A few journalists and members of the Red Cross who had climbed onto an M-113 (armored troop transport) were hailed by the crowd as though they too were the victors.

All through this explosion of joy—the "village *fête*"[1] foretold by Prince Sihanouk—the little men in black continued to move quietly into the city. Working in small groups, they took over intersections, appropriated tanks and other military vehicles, collected weapons, and forced government troops of all ranks to remove their uniforms. The village *fête* soon subsided into confused alarm, followed by consternation and a sinking dread. The little men in black were now absolute masters of all traffic. Every car was being exhaustively searched, and the initially irate drivers soon realized their error and raised their hands, trembling. I had a physical sensation that a slab of lead had suddenly fallen on the city.

Around one in the afternoon I received a phone call from the students' hostel: could we take in the sick and injured from Preah Ket Mealea Hospital who had just been told to evacuate the premises? This was the biggest civilian hospital in town, but it contained a fair number of injured soldiers as well. "You decide, do whatever you think is best."

A few moments later a hallucinatory spectacle began. Thousands of the sick and wounded were abandoning the city. The strongest dragged pitifully along, others were carried by friends, and some were lying on beds pushed by their families with their plasma and IV bumping alongside. I shall never forget one cripple who had neither hands nor feet, writhing along the ground

---

[1] In reply to frequent charges in the American press that Cambodia would drown in a sea of blood if the revolutionaries came to power, Prince Sihanouk, in exile in Peking at the time, said that if the foreigners left the country, the Khmers on both sides would join together in a great village celebration (*fête*), the traditional Cambodian way of marking any major event.

like a severed worm, or a weeping father carrying his ten-year-old daughter wrapped in a sheet tied round his neck like a sling, or the man with his foot dangling at the end of a leg to which it was attached by nothing but the skin. "Can I spend the evening and night here with you?" he asked. "No, you know it's not possible, you must leave as quickly as you can." Refusing shelter to the sick and injured makes one feel one has lost one's last shred of human dignity. That is how the first evacuees left, about twenty thousand of them.

Then, after the sick and wounded, we witnessed the departure of the entire population of Phnom Penh. Before noon, the little men in black were going around to every door in the district: "You must leave quickly. The Americans are going to bomb the city. Go ten or twelve miles away, don't take much with you, don't bother to lock up, we'll take care of everything until you get back. You'll return in two or three days, as soon as we've cleaned up the city." So the people of Phnom Penh, carrying a few clothes and a little rice, went out into the country. There was nothing very brutal about this first evacuation, a few shots in the air were enough to make up the minds of the unwilling. Benumbed by the nightlong bombardment, relieved by such a bloodless cease-fire, the people would have done anything to keep on the good side of their conquerors.

All afternoon we witnessed this pitiful exodus, from the bishop's residence, where ten or so priests had assembled. The poor people carried nothing but shrunken bundles. One mother came past with a load on her head and one infant in her arm, dragging one or two more tearful children; the members of other families took turns carrying an aged grandfather or bedridden grandmother. More prosperous folks had crammed their cars full of supplies and treasure, but it was forbidden to start up the motors, so they were pushing the vehicles out of town on foot. About 5:00 P.M. several students from the hostel, my secretary and his wife and their three young children, and several other friends came up to bid me a wordless farewell.

People living on the northern side of town were forced to go northward, those in the south had to go to the south and those living in the west marched westward, all with the single objective of getting out of town and into the country by the shortest route.

For several months we had been sheltering a poor family who had fled to escape the fighting. The father had enlisted to make sure that his family would receive at least some rice, and was now on some battlefield; nobody knew where. The mother had been at the maternity hospital since the previous day and had just given birth to a baby girl. Sok, their twelve-year-old son, had stayed behind to look after his two younger brothers. When the evacuation order came he wanted to rejoin his mother and baby sister, but that was impossible because the maternity hospital was on the south side of town and the boys were on the north. We gave him a bicycle and some food and he went away to the north in tears with his two little brothers.

Around 4:00 P.M. a car moved along Monivong Boulevard broadcasting a general evacuation order. "The people who have taken refuge in the Phnom Hotel and all foreign personnel must be off the premises before 5:00 P.M." For the thousand refugees there, and the Red Cross team, this meant total panic: where to go? The foreigners wanted to head for the French embassy, but the Khmers kept imploring, "Don't leave us alone!" The hotel was evacuated in indescribable disorder, and all equipment and medicine was left behind. The foreigners were admitted to the French embassy, and many Khmers sneaked in by climbing over the walls.

During the afternoon various teams of Khmer Rouge stopped at the bishop's residence, some affable, others surly and aggressive: "Why haven't you gone yet?" "But we're French!" "That doesn't matter, the Americans are going to bomb the city. Hurry up!" We sat tight, and nobody forced us to go, so we were able to observe what was happening inside the town.

The young revolutionaries who were having their first taste of a new world showed a predilection for its gaudier aspects. They took special delight in one particular gadget, the ball-point pen with a click-in tip. One of them asked me for one, but all I had was the ordinary throwaway kind. He waved his gun at me angrily and it took all my knowledge of the Khmer language to convince him that I really did not possess any of the other type. Some went around with four or five wristwatches on one arm, and one showed me his shiny nickel-plated surgical kit. At least once every hour, some soldier turned up to "borrow" something, a motorbike or bicycle. For them, after all, the entire contents of the city were "war plunder."

What struck me most was the arrival, around 6:00 P.M., of a company of revolutionary troops from the front. These men in black moved along in Indian file, treading softly, their faces worn and expressionless, speaking not a word and surrounded by a deathly silence. Only the last man in line seemed alive: his head was high and his glance keen, one hand was raised, holding a pistol pointing skyward, his finger on the trigger. He was the brains, all the rest were well-disciplined followers.

There were many groups of *neary*, too, young women fighters, oblivious of their femininity, even more resolute than their masculine comrades; everything about them expressed icy determination.

Around seven a unit of Khmer Rouge entered our garden and moved into one of the outbuildings. At first they contemplated the hideous aliens—ourselves—with sharp disapproval. Gradually, with the aid of a few sentences in Khmer, we managed to strike up an acquaintance. They turned out to be fine fellows from the provinces of Kompong Thom and Siem Reap who belonged to the people's militia and had been sent up as reinforcements for the capture of Phnom Penh. "Do you know Helene's mother?" their leader asked me. "Of course I do, her husband is a friend of mine, he lives just around the corner." "Well, I am the brother of Helene's mother. I'll go say hello to her tomorrow!" Tomorrow would be too late, though, because Helene's mother had taken the road out of town, like everybody else. We spent the night talking to these soldiers. Visibly, no ideology had yet affected their reactions, which were those of the peasants we had known before. They hated nobody and had no very clear idea what they were fighting for. They had been promised an age of happiness, which was going to begin immediately after the capture of Phnom Penh.

The long night wore on; suddenly they decided that they wanted to learn how to drive the abandoned cars that were littered all around. What a great new toy! But many of the cars refused to go any farther than the row of trees edging the boulevard, because these guerrillas had had little experience with steering wheels. Earlier in the day we had often heard the army trucks protesting under the hands of their new drivers, who tried to jam the accelerator down to the floorboard without shifting out of first or change gears without using the clutch.

At seven on the morning of April 18, the head of the unit quartered in the bishop's residence asked me to drive his group to the railroad station, where he was to relieve somebody else. "Gladly!" It was a terrific stroke of luck, a chance to see what was going on in the center of town. With my old Ami 6 (a small Citroën) loaded to the gills, I drove past the station—which was only a hundred yards away—and on along Monivong Boulevard, Sokun Mean Bon Street, and Norodom Boulevard to Independence Monument and the royal palace. As we went, I acted as guide to my passengers: "There's the marketplace, that is the home of ex-Premier Long Boret, that's Independence Monument." "Where does the queen live?" Surprised by the question, I pointed out the royal residence, near the monument. They were gaping in wonderment. The sight had a very different effect on me. During the half hour I had been driving, I had seen nothing but desolation: abandoned cars, rubbish and litter everywhere, and above all, a dead city. From time to time I saw more small groups of people trudging along with their bundles over their shoulders. The Khmer Rouge, few in number, were doggedly smashing the grilles across the doors of the Chinese merchants' shops and hurling television sets, tin cans, and refrigerators pell-mell into the middle of the street. When I reached the royal palace I was intending to drive along the bank of the Tonle Sap and take a look at the port. "Stop, soldiers!" The voice of the unit leader beside me was suddenly filled with fear: in front of us, a handful of government troops were still holding out, firing their last shots. A little farther on, outside the ministry of information, the Khmer Rouge were eliminating another pocket of resistance. My passengers got out there and were sharply reprimanded for turning up so late. It was more my fault than theirs.

After this, several more patrols came to the bishop's residence and urged us to leave as quickly as possible. The French government had a week earlier recognized the RGNUK, Royal Government of National Union of Kampuchea (or GRUNK, *Gouvernement royal d'union nationale du Kampuchéa*), so we thought we would receive special treatment and decided to sit still and await further developments. But at 10:00 A.M. a more aggressive patrol arrived and left us no choice: it was get out or smell gunpowder. So we went, to the French embassy.

The embassy stood in a large square measuring more than one hundred meters on a side and containing three two-story buildings. The consulate, near the main entrance, housed the embassy staff; the former planters and colonists had assembled in the hall in the central wing; and farther away, in the ambassador's quarters, were the staffs from the U.N., the Red Cross, and Calmette Hospital, and journalists from various countries. About a thousand Khmers, Chinese, and Vietnamese had taken refuge in the extensive grounds. There was no room for our group indoors, so we set up camp under a bamboo thicket.

The atmosphere was not particularly festive. How long would we have to stay here: a week, a month, a year? Wild optimism rapidly gave way to black pessimism. Some of the Khmers were already beginning to wonder if they had been wise to seek refuge in the embassy. Jean Dyrac, French vice-consul and the only representative of the French government in Phnom Penh, sent several requests to meet with someone of authority in the new government, but to no avail. "We have no leaders," was all he was told. Several groups of revolutionaries tried to force the embassy gates when they first arrived in town, looking for the hideous Americans who must be lurking inside. It took all our powers of persuasion to make them understand the meaning of *extraterritoriality*.

That vice-consul had already seen a good deal of action in his lifetime: he fought against Franco with the International Brigade; he fought with the French Resistance against the Germans, who captured and tortured him; then he fought in the Indochina expeditionary force to Laos and Cambodia, where he met his Laotian wife. When his military career ended he entered the administration, and was appointed consul of France in Phnom Penh in 1974.

It was a curious embassy, the one in Phnom Penh. The French
government, unable to decide upon a policy toward the new
republic, had recalled its ambassador for consultation in 1970.
Then, following a diplomatic *faux pas* on the part of the government of the Khmer Republic, which changed its ambassador to
Paris without notifying the French government beforehand, the
post had been left vacant. Routine business was handled by a
chargé d'affaires, later replaced by an interim *chargé d'affaires*. In
March 1975 the interim *chargé d'affaires* also went back to
France, leaving complete responsibility for the embassy in the
hands of the consul, who, because of diplomatic protocol, was
demoted to vice-consul. France recognized the revolutionary
government—hoping that would put it on good terms with the
new regime—only a week before the fall of Phnom Penh. So here
was the vice-consul in charge of everything, and in a very tense
situation. On the morning of April 17, in a burst of chivalrous
generosity, he had opened the embassy doors to anyone who
wanted to come. Then, either acting on orders from Paris or
seeing for himself what an extremely precarious position he was
in, he found himself forced to close the embassy to anyone of
Cambodian origin. One old man of noble bearing came up to
request asylum, and the duty officer told him no. Without further
ado, the old man proceeded on his way. That was Prince Monireth,
a companion-in-arms of Jean Dyrac, whom France had set aside
in 1941 to put his nephew, young Norodom Sihanouk, on the
throne.

On the morning of the nineteenth, three high-ranking persons
in the new regime finally turned up outside the embassy gates.
"We wish to speak to the representative of France." The moment
they were taken to see the vice-consul, they laid down an ultimatum which had to be met before any negotiations could begin:
"Expel the traitors from the embassy; then we can discuss what
is to be done with the foreigners." The "traitors" were a few well-
known figures who had asked for political asylum: Ung Bun Hor,
president of the national assembly; Luong Nal, minister of health;
Princess Mam Monivann, the Laotian wife of Prince Sihanouk;
and Prince Sisowath Sirik Matak, a cousin of Prince Sihanouk,
who was one of the chief instigators of the *coup d'état* of March

18, 1970, the brains of the republican regime, and one of the "seven traitors" sentenced to death by the Khmer Rouge. "But they have asked France for political asylum, and the French embassy is inviolable ground!" replied the despairing diplomat. "We are the masters in our own country, this land belongs to us. In a revolutionary war there is no such thing as extraterritoriality and no privileges. It's up to you: either the traitors come out or we'll come in after them, and in that case we won't answer for anything!" That was clear enough. The vice-consul had no choice but to comply with the conquerors' demand, if he wanted to save the lives of the French and foreign nationals.

The "traitors" had been informed of the ultimatum. Prince Sirik Matak had been expecting it. With great dignity, he thanked France for her hospitality, shook hands with the French staff, and left, with his companions in misfortune, to surrender to the Khmer Rouge who were waiting for them with a jeep and a GMC. "My only mistake was to have trusted the Americans," he had written a few days before in an open letter to President Ford. He made another when he turned to the French embassy for refuge. Mr. Dyrac accompanied his guests to the gate, where his emotions got the better of him. He stood leaning his head against one of the pillars, with tears streaming down his face, and he kept saying, "We are no longer men."

Later that afternoon we had a little diversion: four fair-haired men and three women were ushered into the embassy with their hands tied behind their backs and the barrels of Khmer Rouge guns trained upon them. They were the diplomats of the Soviet Union and East Germany. The Soviets had put up big posters in French on the doors of their nearby embassy, reading: "We are Communists, we are your brothers. Come forward with a French-speaking interpreter." The young Khmer Rouge had looked at the posters, presumably without understanding a word, and then forced open the doors using Soviet B-40s! Once inside, they searched out the diplomats and led them to the embassy refrigerator, from which they removed some eggs and broke them under the Russians' noses. The Soviets had no idea what this gesture meant: implicitly, it accused them of revisionism—a true Communist, a Khmer, does not eat eggs; he puts a hen on them to hatch them so he can eat the chickens later, at a meal shared with his fellows.

Throughout their compulsory residence in the French embassy and the journey that ended our stay in Cambodia, the Soviet diplomats made poor salesmen for the egalitarian and fraternal ideals they were supposed to personify. They kept to themselves, never mixed with their fellow prisoners, and refused to share their food supplies.

The East German diplomat, graying and fifty with a face seamed by deep wrinkles, made no secret of his displeasure. He had taken the very last commercial flight into Phnom Penh on April 12, just to be on hand for the victory of his revolutionary brothers. "My father a Communist, a Communist myself, a former officer of the Wehrmacht, once I was made a prisoner by the French and now I'm a prisoner with the French. They'll pay for this!"

Two French teachers and their wives turned up a few days later. One of the men, a bearded chemistry teacher and member of the French Communist party, fancied himself a revolutionary militant; the other was a mathematics teacher who spoke Khmer fairly fluently and had donned a Khmer Rouge uniform for the occasion. But they were treated no better than the rest of the foreigners, because you can't play make-believe revolutionary with people who are making a real revolution. Led into the embassy *manu militari*, they had taken care to load their personal belongings into a GMC beforehand.

On April 20, two Khmer Rouge leaders asked to see all the Cambodians, Chinese, and Vietnamese in the embassy. The day before, several Khmers had already decided to join the general exodus from the capital. "His Excellency Khieu Samphan would have liked to greet you in person," one of the leaders said, "but he is too busy. We welcome you all in the name of the Revolution. However, you are our brothers and you must join the rest of the population in rebuilding our country."

The Khmer Rouge laid down specific rules for members of mixed marriages: if the husband was French and the wife Khmer, she could remain in the embassy with her husband; if the husband was Khmer and the wife French, he had to leave and share the lot of his fellow countrymen, but his French wife and children could follow him or not as they pleased. Two couples chose the latter solution, and the wives went with their husbands for better or worse. Fifteen more opted for a painful parting: "Stay with the children," the husbands said, "look after their education. Don't be discouraged, we'll come back to you soon." Few had any illusions about this parting, however, and it is a fact that despite the tireless efforts of their French wives, not a single Khmer husband has succeeded in rejoining his family.

The vice-consul tried to play for time. He even recorded some fictitious marriages and issued a few last-minute passports; but he could do no more. He had decided to cooperate with the conquerors in order to avoid unpleasant surveillance inside the embassy, which would undoubtedly have cost several Khmer and foreign refugees their lives. He has been criticized for failing to get more people out of Kampuchea and for breaking up families; but what else could he do? It's too easy to rewrite history the morning after.

Around 10:00 A.M., a pitiful column of about eight hundred people walked quietly through the embassy gates to an unknown future. I can still see two little old women, apparently alone in the world, leaning against each other for support as they tottered away. I can still see one hundred and fifty FULRO mountaineers, men and women who had fought the Saigon regime, the Vietcong in Vietnam, and the Khmer Rouge in Cambodia to defend their territory.[2] They had counted on France, and she had let them down. They marched away sorrowfully but with their heads high. Y Bam, founder of the movement, and Colonel Y Bun Suor, their chief, led the way.

There were also a number of officers, ministers, and engineers among the Khmers leaving the embassy. One Khmer pharmacist

---

[2] FULRO is the *Front uni de libération des races opprimées* (United Liberation Front of Oppressed Races), an armed mountaineers' movement whose objective was to achieve some form of autonomy for the Indochinese high plateaus.

was in the group; he escaped to Vietnam in June 1975, and told what happened after their departure.

We were taken to the Lambert Stadium, two hundred meters from the embassy. There we went through a preliminary "processing": the Khmer Rouge asked us to state our identities and write our names on one of three lists: military, civil servants, people. Then the officers like Major Tanh Chea and Colonel Y Bun Suor, and high-ranking officials like Dy Bellon, Dy Ballen, and Phlek Phuon were taken away in trucks. The rest of us moved into the huts built around the edges of the stadium by officers' families and spent the night with the rats, sleeping on wooden platforms.

The next morning the Khmer Rouge came back and called out some more names from a list they had ready, and took them away. Then they told us to go north and set to work building the country. We pointed out that the people of Phnom Penh already had a long head start on us, and they provided trucks to drive us as far as Prek Phneuv, where we joined the bulk of the capital's population. The attitudes of the Khmer Rouge varied enormously from one to the next, and we got the impression that their orders were not very specific.

This left about six hundred foreigners inside the embassy. From time to time some French family would turn up, having gone off with the rest of the population and been brought back by the Khmer Rouge. Toward the end of our stay there, four hundred Pakistani nationals were also sent to the embassy and joined the group—or rather tried to, for some of the Europeans, who thought that they were the greatest victims of the revolution, had no time for anyone but themselves. They were used to living in Cambodia in the kind of comfort they enjoyed in their home countries, and they were finding this enforced residence rather trying, the diet a trifle spartan, and the hygienic conditions far from ideal. Those who had lived with the peasants didn't complain much, but they were in the minority. The Khmer Rouge treated the aliens very decently. They did their best to make our compulsory internment as painless as possible: we were never subjected to searches or surveillance, and in addition to water and rice they supplied us with beer and cigarettes, and brought us live pigs to slaughter. Knowing how frugal their own diet was, it was hard not to appreciate the worth of these gifts.

Nevertheless, the cruelty of family partings, the collapse of a universe, and anxiety as to what the future would bring kept our morale on the low side. But the ordeal of the Europeans could not be compared with what the evacuees had to live through. International opinion, however, had focused on the former, whose plight was considered catastrophic, and so the fate of the Khmer population faded into the background.

What was actually going on in Phnom Penh during the three weeks we spent inside the embassy? From our observation post we could see little, and our contacts with Khmers of any political persuasion were very limited. During the first few days we saw groups of stragglers leaving for the country. After the virtually complete evacuation of the center of town on April 17, the outlying districts were next, including Tuol Kauk, which we could see to the west of the embassy. At first, the people in that district were sent westward toward Kompong Speu, but at the end of the dry season the water shortage there was acute, so the columns of evacuees headed north, down the dike road which runs alongside the embassy. At the end of a few days, all civilian population movement ceased.

It was common to hear shooting and see thick columns of smoke rising in the sky, for there were a few scattered pockets of diehards in different parts of the capital—especially the Olympic Stadium, which had been a major military center during the republic. These pockets were eliminated within a few days, however, for their defenders soon ran out of water, food, and, in some cases, ammunition. Any isolated shots were part of the systematic cleanup of the city, which had to be emptied of its inhabitants. The water mains were turned off and the electricity cut in most areas to make sure that no one could survive. A few terrified souls were still huddling in their attics. One Frenchman, who had a Chinese wife, hid in a sort of closet for ten days with his family and collected the water that fell when the rains began. When he couldn't stand it any longer he emerged, and suffered no worse harm than the rest of his family, most of whom had French papers and were allowed into the embassy. Some of those who stayed in Phnom Penh died, of course, but then so did some of the Khmer Rouge: after a week in hiding, one man in the Gravelle

Foundation[3] had gone crazy with fear and shot the first Khmer who entered his house, before being killed himself.

We listened to the NUFK (National United Front of Kampuchea) radio broadcasts but none of them gave us precise information about what was going on in the rest of the country. A long speech by Khieu Samphan was rebroadcast many times, stating the main objectives of the revolution, and revolutionary songs marked the hours. We were excited to hear an announcement that there would be three days of festivities before the opening of the third People's Representative Assembly on April 24, but we observed little merrymaking in Phnom Penh, for by that time the city's entire population had been evacuated. All we saw were a few insignificant streamers celebrating "the glorious victory of April seventeenth and the extraordinary revolution of Kampuchea."

The question that kept coming to the forefront of our minds with painful insistence was, why had the Khmer Rouge done this? Why had the victors evacuated 2.5 million of their fellow countrymen? When had there been another event of this kind, as appalling as this, and one that had taken all observers so much by surprise? The deportation of the Jews from Babylon? The capture of Carthage, or Titus overcoming Jerusalem? The deportation of millions of Russians to Siberia at the end of the last world war? Whatever happened, this deportation would certainly mean hundreds of thousands of deaths. The ailing and aged, the children, and the large numbers of refugees who had been seriously undernourished for several months could hardly be expected to survive the miles of forced marches or the intensity of the sun, which was approaching its zenith. So what was the reason for this hecatomb?

If you think of the accumulated artistic and cultural wealth, the capital in buildings and furnishings of a city with a population of six hundred thousand (which was that of Phnom Penh

---

[3] A state charity for Eurasian families abandoned by France. It consisted of a group of primitive buildings in which a number of Eurasian families were housed.

before the 1970 war), you will have no trouble imagining the waste and spoilage entailed in such an exodus. To that wealth should be added the complete technical infrastructure, now useless, required to operate a modern capital city.

The evacuation has been justified by some on tactical grounds: the revolutionary soldiers were too few to keep effective control of an abnormally overpopulated capital. And everyone knows that cities afford ideal hiding places for the opponents of any regime, especially one just getting started. Emptying the town was a means of shattering traditional frameworks, mixing the entire population together indiscriminately and thereby cutting off any possibility of structured opposition. Ieng Sary, deputy premier of the RGNUK, did indeed advance reasons of security as a justification for the evacuation of Phnom Penh:

> We had discovered an enemy document revealing the details of a secret politico-military plan of the American CIA and the Lon Nol regime to stir up trouble after our victory. This plan had three parts:
> (1) Once in power, we would be unable to feed the population, so the enemy would foment disturbances by means of agents infiltrating the people.
> (2) Many of Lon Nol's troops who had surrendered were actually hiding weapons and had plans to attack us after our victory in Phnom Penh.
> (3) They intended to corrupt our troops and weaken their fighting spirit with girls, alcohol, and money."[4]

According to the young Khmer Rouge we met, the object of this all-out cleanup of Phnom Penh was to unearth secreted weapons and "enemies." And it was true enough, people were plotting against the new regime. There was a rumor that Long Boret; Op Kim Ang; Hang Tung Hak; General Ieng Chhong, chief of aviation; General Van Sarandy, chief of the navy; General Tran Vanphamuon; Sak Susakhan, an ephemeral chief of state; and Prince Sirik Matak had long since agreed to ask Prince Sihanouk to return to Phnom Penh. On a trip to Algiers Long

---

[4] Interview with James Pringle, *Bulletin du GRUNK*, no. 220b/75 (September 4, 1975), pp. 12–13.

Boret had asked President Boumedienne to approach the prince and urge him to come home; through the International Red Cross he had wired Peking, on April 16, in an attempt to set up last-ditch negotiations. Prince Sirik Matak was to wait for his cousin Sihanouk in Phnom Penh; one of them would take charge of domestic affairs and the other of foreign policy. The CIA was said to have agreed to this scheme. General Lon Non, meanwhile, was supposedly banking on the hypothetical support of the USSR, and this had led to the tragicomic interlude of General Hem Keth Dara.

But even without conspiracies to uncover, the revolutionaries would have had a hard time running the city. In March 1975, when the situation was worsening daily, we had been thinking very much along the same lines as Ieng Sary: how could the revolutionaries feed the population without help from some foreign power? Hunger would soon drive the people into rebellion against the new regime.

And, again according to Ieng Sary, the prospect of famine was the prime motivation for the evacuation:

We had estimated the population of Phnom Penh at two million, but we found almost three million people in the city when we entered it. The Americans had been bringing thirty to forty thousand tons of food into Phnom Penh daily. We had no means of transporting such quantities of supplies to the capital. So the population had to go where the food was. We had to feed that population and at the same time preserve our independence and our dignity without asking for help from any other country.[5]

Even this reason, however, given as the essential one, is not fully convincing: included in this population of over 2.5 million were more than 1.5 million peasants who had fled the fighting during the previous five years. Most had crowded into the homes of relatives and friends and were living in poverty. Several hundred thousand more had put up shacks on the outskirts of the

---

[5] *Bulletin du GRUNK*, pp. 12–13.

capital or were herded into refugee camps where conditions were appalling. Famished and idle, living in dread of being mobilized and sent to the front, and exploited by every official, they were all eager enough to return to their homes without being forced to go. There, within a few months, they would have been able to provide for themselves again. As for the native population of Phnom Penh, the stocks of rice accumulated in the capital during the previous weeks might have fed it for two months, with careful rationing. Also, several thousand tons of rice lay rotting in the port of Kompong Som (Sihanoukville) during the first months after the revolution.

So we must look elsewhere for an explanation of the deportation from Phnom Penh. The official reasons certainly had something to do with the decision to clear the city, but they do not seem sufficient. The deeper reason was an ideological one, as we later saw clearly when we learned that the provincial towns, villages, and even isolated farms in the countryside had also been emptied of their inhabitants.

The evacuation of Phnom Penh follows traditional Khmer revolutionary practice: ever since 1972 the guerrilla fighters had been sending all the inhabitants of the villages and towns they occupied into the forest to live, often burning their homes so they would have nothing to come back for. A massive, total operation such as this reflects a new concept of society, in which there is no place even for the idea of a city. The towns of Cambodia had grown up around marketplaces; Phnom Penh itself owed its expansion to French colonialism, Chinese commerce, and the bureaucracy of the monarchy, followed by that of the republic. All this had to be swept away and an egalitarian rural society put in its place.

On the morning of April 18 a political official explained this to me: "The city is bad, for there is money in the city. People can be reformed, but not cities. By sweating to clear the land, sowing and harvesting crops, men will learn the real value of things. Man has to know that he is born from a grain of rice!" Another official used similar terms: "In Phnom Penh you eat rice but you don't grow it. You should go to the country, where you can eat the rice you have grown." So the new man must invent a new art of living, in which work in the fields will take the place of the regenerating fountain of youth.

I come of peasant stock myself, and lived with the Khmer peasants for five years, so I listened to such language with a sympathetic ear: at last, the urban profiteers, the civil servants and the rich, even the students in the hostel I had been running, were going to learn the value of work in the fields, at which it was all too easy for them to sneer. At last the peasant, with all his subtlety hidden beneath his rough rural shell, would be treated as the equal of the white-collar worker who had been exploiting him with impunity. At last Cambodia was going to throw away the gadgets of a consumer society that created more needs than it satisfied. In short, this return to the land would make the Khmers into Khmers again.

But was that any reason for such suicidal haste? For imposing on the workers themselves a remedy so radical that they could only sink from poverty to total indigence; or for condemning so many of the old and weak and ill to certain death? Here one can look in vain for the slightest trace of that oriental wisdom with its great respect for time—a factor we in the West have been accused of neglecting all too often. The good of the people was not the goal of the evacuation of Phnom Penh: its aim was to prove a theory that had been worked out in the abstract without the slightest regard for human factors.

TWO

"Woe Unto the Defeated!"

On April 23, I was on duty as interpreter at the embassy gates. A Khmer Rouge official whose job was to locate foreigners informed me that ten French people had been found thirteen kilometers to the north and had to be brought back. This gave me an opportunity to get out of Phnom Penh six days after the revolutionaries' victory. The inner suburbs on Highway 5, leading north to the Thai border, were totally deserted. Not a soul in the Russey Keo district or around Kilometer 6, which had been heavily overpopulated before. A few homes were charred remains, the doors of others had been smashed in, the lanes were heaped with litter; a few Khmer Rouge were searching for recalcitrant lingerers, and dogs and swine were nosing about for food. Beginning at Kilometer 9 the houses were no longer completely empty but their inhabitants had made preparations for imminent departure. Between Kilometer 10 and Kilometer 13, the farthest I went from the city, there were hundreds of thousands of people blanketing the paddies, camping along the roadside or in the ruins of villages leveled by the war. No doubt there had never been such a crowd

at the market of Prek Phneuv, twelve kilometers outside Phnom
Penh. Our car could only creep through the dense human mass,
and I recognized several friends, both Khmer and Chinese. They
looked as though disaster had struck, and they made covert signs
of recognition, glancing fearfully at the guards sitting beside me.
The accounts of many Khmers who lived through the deportation
from Phnom Penh are filled with the same anguish. I personally
saw no dead bodies either in Phnom Penh or outside the town,
but the deportees were haunted by visions of death.

One group of women in charge of an orphanage were told to go
north. When they reached Vietnam in November 1975 they re-
counted the nightmare they had lived through:

About three on the afternoon of April 17 we were ordered to leave
the orphanage immediately. Young soldiers aimed their guns at us, telling
us to hurry. In our haste we left the house almost empty-handed, even
forgetting to take any rice, pots and pans, or fish. After a few hundred
yards we could go no farther. It was a stupefying sight, a human flood
pouring out of the city, some people pushing their cars, others their
overladen motorcycles or bicycles overflowing with bundles, and others
behind little homemade carts. Most were on foot, like us, and heavily
laden. The sun was fierce but we were so dazed we hardly minded it.
Children were crying, some were lost and searching vainly for their
parents. The worst part of the whole march was the stopping and
starting: there was such a crowd that we could never go forward more
than a few yards at a time before we had to stop again. Sometimes the
Khmer Rouge fired into the air to scare us and make us go faster. We
nearly died of fright when there was a burst of machine-gun fire just
beside us.

By evening that day we had reached Kilometer 4, in Russey Keo, and
slept in an abandoned house. We begged a little rice because the children's stomachs and our own were crying famine. The people on the
road with us were kind and helped each other out. The next morning
at dawn shots were fired and we got back on the road in a hurry. The
crowd was as dense as ever. When we got to Kilometer 5 we were very
frightened by the sight of several corpses lying by the roadside. Their
hands were tied behind their backs and nobody dared go near them.
People were saying they were the leaders of the former government,
but we didn't know them so we could not say if it was true. A little
farther on, ten more bodies were lying in front of the door outside the
Pepsi-Cola factory; the Khmer Rouge said they were soldiers, traitors.
People were allowed to take as much Pepsi-Cola as they wanted, but

we were too afraid of the dead men to go any closer. At Kilometer 6 the crowd surged into the Catholic Relief depot [an American charity] to take things. The Khmer Rouge let everyone take as much as he could carry: "They were imperialist goods and so they should be used to serve the people." We took rice, pots, and mats, which were precious to us afterward.

That night we were still not very far from Phnom Penh. We had only gone a few kilometers, and very slowly, because the road was so full of people. That slow pace was more exhausting than a quick march would have been. That night our bed was the dusty earth and our roof the sky. The next day, near Kilometer 10, we were terrified: there were several corpses in military uniform lying in the road, but the Khmer Rouge trucks had driven back and forth over them and flattened them completely. All you could see was the shape of their bodies. We were terribly disturbed by that sight.

After several days on the road these women reached Prek Kdam, about thirty kilometers from Phnom Penh, where the Khmer Rouge put them on board a launch that took them another fifteen kilometers to the north.

Suon Phal, nineteen years old, escaped to Thailand on May 4, 1976; this is his account:

I was in my last year at the Boeung Kak *lycée* in Phnom Penh. My family and I left the city and took the road to Prek Phneuv. Along the way I saw Khmer Rouge soldiers waiting in groups of three or four; they searched people and took their watches, radios, glasses, gold, and precious stones. Some even took 500-riel bills and threw them in the air, saying, "The revolutionary Angkar[1] has put an end to money." We had great difficulty making any headway because of the enormous crowd leaving town and also because some Khmer Rouge kept firing shots to scare us. Many people died on that march: the hospital patients who had been driven out, the women who gave birth on the road, the war casualties. We reached Vat Kak on April 25; along the way we saw many dead bodies scattered about everywhere—even in the pagodas—and the stench that came from them was almost unbearable.

Sam Suon, a twenty-six-year-old employee of the national import-export company, escaped to Thailand in July 1975 and is now in France. He tells what happened on the southern side of town:

---

1 "The Organization," both party and state.

The Khmer Rouge shepherded the deportees quietly along, without too much brutality. However, the food problem began that very first evening of April 17. The answer to every request for food was always the same: "Ask the Angkar!" People heard it so often that they started asking, "But who is the Angkar?" The Khmer Rouge answered, "It's every one of you! You must figure out for yourselves how to find something to eat." At that, several people lost all hope. Kong Sam Oeun, a very famous film star in Cambodia, was crying with rage; all he had left was one suit of clothes and his Mercedes! Some people tried to argue with the Khmer Rouge—a druggist, in particular. The Khmer Rouge cut off his head right in front of me and left the body lying in the road. Nobody dared to touch it for fear of reprisals. Many students who had shown dissatisfaction had their hands tied behind their backs and disappeared, taken away by the Khmer Rouge.

On the morning of the eighteenth the Khmer Rouge announced that everyone could go back to the village where he was born; a great many of the refugees set off for Neak Luong, secretly hoping to cross into Vietnam. Others turned back to Phnom Penh and recrossed the Monivong Bridge, which was soon closed to civilians. I wanted to go to Takmau but wasn't allowed to because there were already too many people in that area, so I was sent to Bek Chan, and then to Prek Kdam.

"We reached Phnom Penh Thmey [an extension of Phnom Penh in the west] around 6:00 P.M. on that April seventeenth," reports You Kim Lanh, a technician employed by Cambodian Electricity who fled to Thailand (Camp Aranh) in April 1976 and is now in France.

Here and there we could see the bodies of villagers who had been killed by the Khmer Rouge, presumably because they didn't want to leave their homes.

On April 19, at ten in the morning, I saw the Khmer Rouge arrest about twenty young men with long hair; they shot them before our eyes. Everybody was terrified and had their hair cut at once, even in the middle of the night.

When we got to Ang Long Kagnanh [10 kilometers from Phnom Penh] the road was blocked by Khmer Rouge who searched us, tore off wristwatches, and took away radios, necklaces, and gold rings. They told us the Angkar needed them and was only borrowing the jewels for a while but would give them back later. From there we were made to turn back to Highway 5. We reached Prek Phneuv on April 25 . . .

On every road leading out of the capital the revolutionaries adopted the same methods. "At Vat Kak," Suon Phal says, "I saw a Khmer Rouge writing down the names of officers, important officials, and notables. He said the Khmer Rouge were going to take them to the city to help the Angkar. In the group they took away I recognized Hang Tung Hak, Pan Sothi [both former ministers], Phi Thien Lay, Uk Yon, Ly Chae [a lawyer], Si Tek [major in the engineer corps], Sisowath Suong Chivin, and many more officers whose names I didn't know."

Mam Sarun reached Camp Kap Choeung in Thailand on February 15, 1976, and is still in that country. A captain, he was in command of a battalion in the Neak Luong region. When his base was invaded on April 1 he refused to surrender and took his battalion through the Khmer Rouge lines toward Prey Veng, which he reached on April 15. After the fall of Phnom Penh he again refused to surrender, changed to civilian dress, crossed the Mekong at Dey Eth, and went in search of his family.

I found my family near Kieng Svay pagoda on April 27, and we stayed there over a month. Behind the pagoda the Khmer Rouge had written an order on a big blackboard: "All officers from the rank of second lieutenant up must register here, in order to return to Phnom Penh. Professors, students, and schoolteachers must also give their names, but will leave later." Every day I saw many officers come up and sign their names. They were separated from the rest of the people and given plenty of rice; their families stayed inside the pagoda but didn't get much to eat. Then they were taken away and never seen again. Among them I recognized General Chlay Lay, General Pen Rada, Colonel Neang San, Lieutenant Colonel Nhong Chan Sovat, Colonel Kauk Ol, and many others.

Seng Huot, twenty-eight years old and a teacher, who escaped to Thailand in late February 1976, gives an account of the same procedure being employed on the road to Kompong Speu:

At Kambaul [fifteen kilometers from Phnom Penh] on Highway 4, the Khmer Rouge emptied cars and took all objects of value: watches, radios, tape recorders, etcetera. All along the road they were searching for pilots and teachers and every sort of weapon, drugs, batteries. The sorting center was at Kompong Kantuot; civilians were allowed to pass but the military were led away, and shots were heard soon afterward.

"At Prek Phneuv," You Kim Lanh says, "a loudspeaker car was inviting all officers, civil servants, ministers, members of parliament, and technicians to return to Phnom Penh to work with the Angkar. I returned with other technicians from Cambodian Electricity."

At the French embassy, we saw some trucks loaded with men and women returning to Phnom Penh. At first we thought they were revolutionary officials or peasants brought in to repopulate the city. However, on the afternoon of May 5 when I left the embassy to check the water reserves of the nearby French technical mission, I met a Khmer lady doctor whom I knew well, Oum Sameth. I was amazed when she told me that the Khmer Rouge had asked all senior officers to return to Phnom Penh "to organize the country." To get back to the capital she had passed herself off as the wife of her cousin, who was a colonel.

You Kim Lanh gives further details:

We were all taken to the ministry of information; there, we had to write our autobiographies before being sent to the Monorom Hotel, which was the headquarters of the "special forces." While I was in the hotel I saw more than two hundred of Lon Nol's officers brought in. They were taken away again the same night, for an unknown destination.

Every day the Khmer Rouge brought in another hundred or more people, mostly officers. Among them I recognized General Am Rong, the former government spokesman on military questions; Colonel Ly Teck; and Tep Chieu Kheng (former minister of information and ex-editor in chief of the newspaper *Dépêche du cambodge*). One after another they all disappeared, and always at night. I knew a few of the Khmer Rouge at the Monorom Hotel, Met [Comrade] Hok in particular, who was the nephew of Touch Kim, the former governor of the National Bank; and Met Sonn, commander of the special forces brigade. I asked them what had happened to the people who disappeared from the hotel. The answer was: "We kill them all because they're traitors and deserve to be shot!" Since I had seen the sick or invalid soldiers in Hospital 701 massacred with my own eyes, I am sure they were telling the truth.

So many accounts contain similar statements that it can safely be affirmed that the revolutionaries had simply decided to kill off the bulk of the former civilian and military establishment in the hours following the capture of Phnom Penh.

The decision took effect immediately, on April 17. Early in the
afternoon, when anxiety was beginning to steal over the inhabitants of Phnom Penh, the radio, which had been virtually silent
since the Monatio's misleading affirmations that morning, broadcast the first statement by the new authorities:

> This is the National United Front of Kampuchea. We are in the
> ministry of information. The northern, southern, eastern, and western
> fronts and the Monatio[2] have shaken hands in Phnom Penh. We have
> conquered by arms and not by negotiation. Samdech Sangh, venerable
> patriarch of the Buddhist community, and General Lon Non are standing
> beside us. We order all ministers and generals to come to the ministry
> of information at once to organize the country. Long live the courageous
> and extraordinary People's National Liberation Armed Forces of Kam-
> puchea! Long live the extraordinary revolution of Kampuchea!

The imperious tone and new vocabulary implied a firm decision. Many officers did not obey this injunction, however, but put
on civilian dress and sank into the anonymity of the crowd. A
few, though, did as they had been told and presented themselves
at the ministry of information, desiring to "organize the country"
with the new authorities. Among them were General Chim
Chuon, Lon Nol's right arm, who was held to be one of the most
corrupt officers of the republic. There were others who had no
illusions as to the fate in store for them: two brothers who had
dual French-Cambodian nationality, generals Paul and Aimé
Litaye Suon, donned their best dress-uniforms, pinned on all their
decorations, and went to the new authorities; in a somewhat be-
lated act of bravura, they refused to run away and determined to
end their careers with honor.

Long Boret, the ex-premier, was late for his appointment at the
ministry. He had believed in the Americans' promises until the
end, and only now realized that all was lost. A few days before, he
had been in the Philippines with Lon Nol, who was abandoning his
post as president of the republic, and could have stayed away;
but he didn't think the end would come so soon. On the morning

---

[2] Why this mention of the Monatio? Perhaps to establish a reassuring continuity
with the A.M. broadcast.

of April 12 he could have left with the American diplomats, but refused, letting General So Kham Koy, the chief of state, go in his place. "I am not a mercenary," he told Gunther Dean, the United States ambassador, who openly invited him to come with him. On the morning of April 17 he also could have fled on board a helicopter, as did many other ministers and generals, but he stayed at his post although there was a price on his head. During the day he tried several times to get to the ministry of information, but in vain, because the young Khmer Rouge patrols did not recognize him and would not let him through. Then he telephoned and told them to come and get him, he was tired and worn out and defeated. He shook hands with the other people present, and paused for a long moment holding the hand of General Hem Keth Dara and looking at him in silent reproach for that morning's attempt to overturn his government. After a few polite noises, the Khmer Rouge led all these generals and ministers away to the Angkar Leu (Higher Organization), which, in the revolutionary parlance with which we had long been familiar, meant death.

In the takeover of Phnom Penh, nothing was left to chance: the military occupation of the town, evacuation of its population, and liquidation of its former civilian and military leaders were all part of a precise, preestablished plan. The revolutionaries had rightly counted on their republican compatriots' naïveté and failure to grasp the situation, and so they were able to decapitate the entire political and military structure of the former regime.

Woe unto the defeated! who had been too ready to believe it would be possible to come to terms with their fellow Khmers, and many of whom were paying for their credulity with their lives. Not all were opposed to the idea of working for the new regime. Most had no clearer views about a social system than they had about politics, and in obedience to the best Khmer tradition they were perfectly prepared to serve their new masters, to "bend with the breeze" as the Khmer saying goes.

The best among them were disgusted by the corruption of the republic and longed to see a more just system, but had no idea how to translate their longings into realities. Several believed, no doubt, that the revolutionaries would need them and were considering whether they might not take a hand in the new regime, even after their privileges had been abolished. They never dreamed their careers would end as they did. Besides, the revolutionaries had proclaimed again and again that they were only interested in the "seven traitors" whose death sentences were irrevocable: Lon Nol, Long Boret, Prince Sisowath Sirik Matak, General Sosthenes Fernandez, ex–commander in chief of the armed forces; In Tam, a popular former premier; Cheng Heng, president of the parliament after the deposition of Prince Sihanouk and chief of state until 1972, and Son Ngoc Thanh, a sworn enemy of Prince Sihanouk, former leader of the American-run Khmers Serey (Free Khmers),[3] and government adviser. Two of them went to their deaths, the rest fled the country. The list of traitors had grown somewhat longer in recent months, but it still contained a relatively small number of known figures. This list was meant for international public consumption, and reflected only a fraction of the revolutionaries' real plans.

The systematic cleanup continued as the days went by. Civilian and military officials were methodically eliminated from the national community, the cities were "swept clean of their enemies." They were also purged of everything that had come from the West. You Kim Lanh describes the process:

> I spent a month in Phnom Penh working with the Khmer Rouge. I had to search all the houses and collect any rice left in them, and stock up the medicine from all the pharmacies. We loaded everything onto boats run by Vietnamese crews. Now and then a fire broke out in the city, but we did nothing to put it out. Sometimes the Khmer Rouge had us tear down wooden houses and pile up the beams and boards.

Yen Savannary, a teacher who fled to Thailand around mid-October, confirms this report indirectly:

---

[3] An armed opposition group to Prince Sihanouk, chiefly recruited from the Khmer minority in Cochin China by the CIA; under the leadership of Son Ngoc Thanh, they carried out several commando operations along the Khmero-Thai frontier.

Beginning in late April there was steady two-way truck traffic on Highway 1 to Saigon; they were transporting radios, motorcycles and other small motor vehicles of all sorts, bicycles, packaged medicines, and weapons of every description. Near Neak Luong around two hundred vehicles were waiting to cross the Mekong, among them Mercedes and Peugeot 404s. There were also three or four 105-mm cannons and three trucks full of medicine. Apparently it was all going to Vietnam.

Lao Bun Thai, a twenty-three-year-old mechanic who also fled the country in October 1975, says that until mid-May he was employed transporting furniture, television sets, refrigerators, and other household appliances to an enormous bonfire about a dozen kilometers north of the capital near the Stung Kambot dike.

I saw several trucks, filled to the roof with books, going past the embassy to the north. I also saw the books from the cathedral library burning on the lawn. The library of the French Far-Eastern School a few hundred meters from the embassy was disposed of in the same way on the morning of May 5, but there was little of value left in it, for the most important volumes had been sent to safety in France.

One Pakistani staying in the French embassy told how the Khmer Rouge had broken into his shop; they stole nothing, but grabbed pairs of scissors and began slashing the bolts of cloth. A druggist added that young revolutionary soldiers had broken every bottle and vial in his shop.

This behavior was not motivated by a desire for or envy of riches but by a fierce determination to do away with everything reminiscent of the West. After the euphoria of the first few days, when the soldiers had been seduced by the glitter of a civilization they were seeing for the first time, they returned to their chosen path of austerity and renunciation. Like Noah, the revolutionaries were led astray by the power of liquor, which they found in plenty in the capital immediately after their victory, but the regime soon put them back on the straight and narrow.

Emptied of its population and despoiled of its goods, Phnom Penh, capital of Cambodia since 1865, pearl of Southeast Asia with its wide shady avenues, has become a ghost town and is gradually being reclaimed by the forest. Many lawns have been planted with banana trees so as not to lose an inch of precious ground.

Several refugees have come through Phnom Penh in recent months, and they estimate that there are fewer than twenty thousand people in the city now, all of them Khmer Rouge and their families. Workers live in the outskirts near their factories but are not allowed inside the city. Unmarried Khmer Rouge live separately, men on one side of the street and women on the other. The ministries of the revolutionary government operate with skeleton staffs, most of whom do not even have offices.

The nine diplomatic delegations accredited to Phnom Penh in June 1977 (China, North Korea, Cuba, Vietnam, Laos, Romania, Yugoslavia, Egypt, and Albania) do not find life easy there.[4] One assumes that apart from a few high-ranking Chinese or Korean officials, diplomats cannot leave their embassies. A jeep brings them their meals three times a day. They have no entertainment, no staff to wait on them, and they do their own laundry. Every other Friday a Chinese CCAC plane enables them to snatch a breath of fresh air and freedom in Peking. Since September 1976, they have also been able to use the newly opened air service between Phnom Penh and Hanoi, and a service has been running between Phnom Penh and Vientiane since August 1977. A single four-page newspaper, in Khmer, called *Padevath* [Revolution], comes out every two weeks and publishes nothing but news relating to the construction of the country.

Phnom Penh the corrupt has become virtuous and spartan.

---

[4] Since June 1977 the Albanian delegation has closed its doors. The Cuban delegation has also left, but diplomatic relations continue.

THREE

The Overturned Basket

On the evening of April 27 the atmosphere inside the embassy was more relaxed: three Khmer Rouge emissaries had come to make arrangements for the repatriation of all foreigners. The few thousand persons involved would be driven by truck to the Thai border, and the first convoy would leave on the morning of April 30. The negotiations had been rather sticky: the vice-consul had suggested that France send a few planes to repatriate her nationals and the other aliens, but was met with a categorical refusal. Yet we knew that it was safe for aircraft to land at Phnom Penh airport, for we had seen two Chinese planes resembling Boeing 707s land since the liberation of the city. For the first time, Met Nhem, vice-chairman of the northern district of the capital and official in charge of foreigners, showed his temper. With bloodshot eyes, as though stung by some dreadful insult, he retorted, in tones that left no room for discussion, "We have our own resources! Consider yourselves fortunate that we are letting you go. We could perfectly well have disposed of you otherwise!" The insinuation was plain: we were troublemakers who had not obeyed the Angkar's order to all foreigners to leave Cambodia in March 1975, when Prince Sihanouk, in a statement made in Peking, said that he would not answer for anybody's life. If the new authorities deigned to let us live and even convey us to the frontier it was out of the kindness of their hearts, and here we were offending them by showing contempt for their means of transport and lacking confidence in their abilities. The fear that the foreigners might see things from the air that were better left hidden was undoubtedly not the main reason for this journey by truck. A trek of four hundred and fifty kilometers overland was more dangerous than a quick airview. Besides, the Khmer Rouge must have known that American spy-planes had been flying back and forth overhead at high altitudes since April 17. The new authorities said they had nothing to hide. And true enough, we were not searched before we left; everyone was allowed to take away whatever he wanted, even rolls of film shot after the liberation. Nor was this rather primitive form of travel a kind of vengeance, one last jab at the unwanted aliens. Once again, ideology would seem to have been the main consideration: the new Kampuchea was counting on its own strength alone and wanted nothing from anybody. The Khmer Rouge refused all forms of foreign help, regarding it as unjustifiable interference in their domestic affairs and an insult to the country's independence and sovereignty.

This policy of self-sufficiency is borne out by another significant reaction in the same period. The reply given to the UNICEF representative, when he offered his organization's assistance in caring for Khmer children, was, "Our Angkar has everything it needs." The French government had loaded a Transal plane with medicine to be exchanged for the release of its nationals. It sat waiting in Bangkok for several weeks but was never given permission to land. Kampuchea could treat its own sick without help from anyone else.

On the morning of April 30, twenty-five trucks, half of them American GMCs from the former government army and the other half Chinese Molotovas, drew up before the embassy to carry about five hundred people to the frontier. The non-French and their families had been given priority. After three and a half days of heat and rain on the road they crossed the border at Poipet.

The second convoy left on the morning of May 6. On the strength of their experience with the first convoy the Khmer Rouge advised us to take food, tarpaulins, and hats. "I felt sorry for the French, they had a hard time," one driver told me after the first convoy. The departure was delayed by the evacuation of the embassy archives and by a few French diehards who did not want to leave. Around six o'clock the vice-consul handed over the embassy keys to Met Nhem and gave him a list of some twenty French nationals who were still unaccounted for. He thanked the Angkar for its considerate treatment of the foreigners and expressed his hope that diplomatic relations would soon be established between France and the new Kampuchea. Met Nhem, his even-tempered self again, apologized for the inconvenience inflicted upon the foreigners; they must understand, it was wartime. Soon, once the country was "organized," the foreigners would be able to return.

Instead of heading north by the shortest route, both convoys started off westward along Highway 4. We went through the western suburbs of Phnom Penh, where some areas had been burned, then we caught a glimpse of the airport, where a few carcasses of incinerated planes were lying on the field. At the city limits the roadsides were littered with abandoned cars, their doors open, some overturned. The tires had been removed from others, to make Ho Chi Minh sandals, which adhere to the foot, are silent, cost nothing and last forever: the ideal revolutionary footgear. The outskirts of every town looked the same, like a car-cemetery. In the new Cambodia there was no place for the automobile, the gadget of Western consumer society and symbol of inequality among classes.

After seventeen kilometers we reached Thnal Totung. The village had long since been razed to the ground; there was nothing left standing but a few brick walls and concrete stairs, rising despairingly to meet an empty sky. The famous sugar palms, characteristic features of the Cambodian landscape, had mostly been decapitated by government bombardments or burned by napalm. It was a dead landscape, showing no trace of human life.

Turning obliquely to the north, the convoy continued along roads which took us into an area that had been "liberated" for several years. There, people were working: more than a thousand young people were building a dike, and in another place bonzes were repairing a bridge. These villages were different from the traditional Khmer hamlet: the houses stood at ground level in the Sino-Vietnamese style, and not on stilts, as was the Khmer custom. The fields were covered with yams, a crop cultivated by the Vietcong, for the yam is a fast-growing plant and the food it provides can be easily carried by guerrillas. The people were smiling in the true Khmer fashion. Along the roadsides, we saw a few empty bomb craters, vestiges of the dreadful American air warfare. At noon we stopped by the side of a little pool near a pagoda. The villagers came to see us; apparently no one had tried to keep them away. We talked about their lives, about war and peace. They were curious to see the different races traveling in our convoy. They gaped when I showed them an American journalist —they presumably imagined he would be an ogre with huge fangs. "What was the worst part of the war?" I asked. "The bombardments!" "Which ones, the B-52s?" "No, we weren't very worried by them because we could hear them coming and hide in our trenches and wait. Sometimes it was terrible when the bombing was very close, but most of the time they were bombing the forests, where there was nobody. But the 'Lap Kats'[1] did much more damage; they flew almost at ground level and we couldn't see them coming. They dropped napalm bombs on the villages and killed a lot of people." "Are you happy now that the war is finally over?" "Of course, now we're going to be able to live like normal people and not have to hide anymore."

We drove on under a leaden sky to Amleang, which had been the revolutionaries' command post for many years but which, oddly enough, had never been bombed. Then we went through

---

[1] Peasant abbreviation of "Slap Kats" or "sawed-off wings," referring to the government air force T-28s.

miles and miles of forest. Around five o'clock we came upon several thousand oxcarts; they belonged to the peasants of the region,
who had either fled to Kompong Chhnang or had been living in
the provincial capital and were now being sent elsewhere, taking
their most precious belongings with them—their oxen, carts, a
few cooking utensils, and clothes. The expressions on some of
their faces turned my blood to ice: their skins were sun-scorched,
their features drawn with fatigue, and their look was one of un-
fathomable distress. Plainly, their universe had crumbled beneath
their feet and they didn't understand what was happening to
them.

Night was about to fall when, as though by chance, our convoy
made a lengthy pause at Romeas, near a huge cemetery where
thousands of revolutionary fighters were buried—we had to be
persuaded, as if we needed to be, that the war had been hard on
their side too. After a hair-raising crossing of a railway bridge we
came to a good road and drove quickly toward Kompong
Chhnang, which we reached about eight in the evening. The
Organization had provided a fairly substantial meal for all the
foreigners, and we slept in what had formerly been the provincial
prefecture.

Kompong Chhnang, the "stewpot riverbank," took its name
from the pottery works in the town. Before the 1970 war it had
been a small provincial capital with some ten thousand inhabitants.
Peasants fleeing the fighting had gradually swollen their ranks,
and around 1973 many more came as refugees from the "liberated" zones. Now they had gone back to live under the regime
they had tried to escape. As far as we could make out at our
arrival and departure, the city was deserted. So not only Phnom
Penh, but Kompong Chhnang as well had been completely
emptied.

Back on the road at dawn, we continued to meet the same
desolation everywhere: nobody in any of the towns, villages, or
isolated hamlets in the countryside.

About eleven we reached Pursat, another provincial capital: it
was also deserted. We must have been entering a different military region, for we changed vehicles, drivers and leaders there,
abandoning the GMCs and Molotovas for buses driven by sol-

diers who were older than the previous group. Met Nhem turned over his command to Met Vichhai, committee chairman of the town of Battambang. The authorities were extremely generous and handed out more than enough food and fruit. "If you want to pick any fruit, don't hesitate," the drivers told us. "From now on the trees belong to everybody." But there was nobody left in the rows of houses standing in their orchards on either side of the road.

That evening, after going through Maung, another major town which had been totally destroyed by the fighting at the beginning of 1975, we reached Battambang, the second largest city in Cambodia. A car-cemetery greeted us a few kilometers outside the town, and inside there was no spark of life. We asked the chief of the convoy for permission to spend the night in the marketplace, and were refused without explanation.

All the way to the frontier, which we reached around nine the next morning, the desert continued: Thmar Kaul, Mongkol Borei, Sisophon, Poipet—so many more ghost towns. Now and then we saw clouds of black smoke rising in the distant countryside, and we supposed it came from burning villages. Even the rice paddies were deserted, although it was the beginning of May, when the cultivation should have been finishing. In the whole of this rice-growing region I saw only two tractors at work.

Where were all the people who used to live in these parts? From many refugee accounts we can reconstruct the sequence of events in the provinces. For the sake of brevity, I shall quote from only a few, relating to two towns: Battambang, which lay on our route, and Pailin, eighty kilometers farther west.

Battambang was the capital of the rice granary formed by the vast black-earth flatlands surrounding it. A river, the Stung Sangker, comes down from the Pailin mountains, bringing water and giving access to the Great Lake. The town is linked to Phnom Penh by a railway, which had been cut for several years between Pursat and Kompong Chhnang, and by Highway 5, which had been closed to traffic since 1973. It would have been possible to reopen the road, except that some generals, influential stockholders in the numerous airlines serving the town, found it to their advantage to make sure the road was kept closed by "en-

emies." The population, which was around forty thousand before
the war, had almost trebled, especially in the last few months,
under the pressure of the *purs et durs*[2] revolutionaries who were
terrorizing the countryside and forcing people to flee. Many of
the refugees from that period, moreover, had crossed the border
into nearby Thailand.

Chea Sambath was a student in Battambang. Like most young
people he was simply waiting for the war to end, without any
definite political ideas and without taking sides. War was something for politicians, and even more for the Americans who had
started it all! He dispassionately relates his experience:

Around noon on April 17 we learned that Phnom Penh had been
taken. Everybody rejoiced to think that there would be peace again,
and hoped to see the light of a new justice shining at last. Around
5:00 P.M. a helicopter landed at the airport; I thought it was a Khmer
Rouge leader coming so I went to see, but it was a local dignitary
evacuating his family. A little later, around six o'clock, a number of
Khmer Rouge came and marched three times around the marketplace,
followed by a cheering crowd. We were surprised because they didn't
talk or shout and didn't look at all happy to have won the war. That
night we enjoyed ourselves, singing and dancing like at the New Year,
celebrating the return of peace. But the Khmer Rouge wouldn't mingle
with us. Why not?

On April 18 the people in Battambang were delighted, because food
prices went down by order of the Khmer Rouge. A kilogram of pork
cost only 12 riels instead of 300, which was the price the day before,
and rice cost 3 riels a kilo instead of 150, and salt only 1 riel. Chinese
soup and coffee were 1 riel too. There was a stampede, everybody trying
to buy as much as he could. The shopkeepers were tearing their hair
because they were losing so much money. People could hardly buy and
sell because they all had lots of 500-riel bills but hardly any of 1, 5, 10,
20, or 50 riels, which were the only kind allowed. Meanwhile, loudspeaker cars drove through the streets asking people to return to their
native villages; but it wasn't an order. Many of the newly arrived
refugees left, but the people of Battambang stayed put. That night,
however, we began to worry because the "Voice of America" announced
that Phnom Penh had been completely evacuated. Would the same thing
happen to us?

---

2 "Pure and hard" or "tough," a term much employed in the past, sometimes
derisively, by and about French leftist movements—Tr.

The sequel to this civilian account is provided by the reports of many soldiers. Phal Somnang, a captain, has this to add:

On April 17, around eleven o'clock, Radio Phnom Penh, speaking in the name of the chief of staff, ordered all Khmer Republic troops to lay down their arms. Although they heard the order, the troops around Battambang went on fighting until about 6:00 P.M., or in other words until the chief of staff of the third military region himself ordered us to cease fighting and return to our camps. The Khmer Rouge troops then took possession of the different posts, beginning with the radio; then the liberators, of whom there were very few, entered Battambang.

Colonel Leng Raoul had taken command, replacing General Sek Sam Iet, the governor of the town, who had disappeared at 2:00 P.M. At nine o'clock, he issued the following order over the Battambang regional radio: "We ask all officers, noncommissioned officers, and regular soldiers to remain calm. Assemble your arms and bind them into parcels which you are to bring, without fail, to the command post of the third region before 8:00 A.M. tomorrow, April 18. You will then assemble in front of the prefecture to receive further orders."

Throughout the night, Radio Battambang appealed for union; first, it was the voice of a Khmer Rouge, then Colonel Leng Raoul, telling us we were to assemble the following morning; sometimes they said in front of the prefecture, sometimes it was in front of the university. On the morning of the eighteenth the soldiers turned up outside the prefecture, but it was pointless, because nobody gave any further orders. The Khmer Rouge had just taken over and were forming a central committee with the provincial civilian and military authorities.

At 2:00 P.M. on April 19, the Khmer Rouge leaders ordered the committee to assemble all the military, some on the grounds of the prefecture and the rest in the psychological warfare barracks. When everybody was there, they marched to the university. There they were divided into three groups: the officers had to go to the Sar Hoeur primary school, the noncommissioned officers to the Eap Kuth primary school, and the ordinary soldiers to the Battambang *lycée*.

On the twentieth and twenty-first we saw heavy trucks removing the soldiers from the *lycée:* nine trucks went on the twentieth and seven on the twenty-first. They left at night, crossed the Stung Sangker, and headed west.[3]

At 1:00 P.M. on April 23, Colonel Leng Raoul, speaking on behalf of the central committee, took the list of officers and called them by name, telling them they were going to welcome Prince Sihanouk in Phnom

---

[3] These soldiers were sent to a prison camp in the region of Phnom Sampeou, where most of them died of hunger or by summary execution.

Penh. Those who had been called left the Sar Hoeur school and marched to the prefecture. When they got there, Colonel Leng Raoul told them, "You have fifteen minutes to return home, put on your dress uniforms with all your decorations, and take a few personal belongings!" When they all returned, a Khmer Rouge leader named So Kor was standing, all in black, with lieutenant colonels Sisowath Kossarak and Chap Vong, and he had the list in his hands.

Six trucks were waiting outside the prefecture. When the roll call ended, all the officers shouldered their bags and moved off to the trucks in rows. Some of the officers' wives were watching us anxiously, others were weeping. At 1:30 the trucks drove off in single file, with a jeep and a Land Rover full of Khmer Rouge leading the march. At the rear was an open truck containing about forty armed Khmer Rouge. The six trucks drove slowly, about thirty kilometers an hour, along Highway 5. We were all very quiet. After a short time the trucks turned off on a track leading to Phnom Thippadey. At the crossroads we saw two 30-mm mortars, a 60, and an 81, and about thirty armed Khmer Rouge. Five hundred meters farther on, we saw a large number of Khmer Rouge hiding in the ditches alongside the road. The trucks stopped in front of two 30-mm mortars which were pointing south. There were two 60-mm mortars as well, also aimed toward the south.

A Khmer Rouge came out of the forest and ordered us to get out. While we were picking up our bags he said, "You don't need to take anything with you, we're only stopping for a moment." So we got down and sat in groups, and the trucks drove off. I whispered to the companions sitting near me, "They've brought us here to massacre us all! Watch out!" Some stared in amazement, others pulled statuettes of the Buddha from their pockets and began kissing them.

About fifteen minutes after we had left the trucks, we heard a dozen Chinese AK-47 shots. I thought, This time it's the end. Here is death. I tried to get out of sight and run away. The sound of the automatic guns was the signal for action by the Prince of Death. The servants of the Prince of Death, hiding along the road and in the forest, all armed, began to send a rain of fire down upon us. Smoke rose up in thick clouds and we couldn't see anything. There was an infernal racket, like seven thunderclaps at once. I lay flat on the ground, then got up and ran south. I hadn't gone more than a hundred meters when two balls flew my way and hit me in the right arm, tearing through my jacket and burning the flesh. They were like sticks of incense burning in honor of the Prince of Death. But his servants did not cut the thread of my life.

I looked back: my friends were falling on all sides, some were running, but fell, mowed down; others got up to run again but could not escape the talons of Death. The Khmer Rouge were using arms of every caliber. All my comrades lost their lives except three: Major Phim Uon and two others whose names I don't know. All four of us were slightly wounded.

The Khmer Rouge soldiers kept firing in our direction, so we scattered. I dived into a thicket of reeds and lay there without making a sound, about four kilometers from the scene of the massacre. I was winded, overwhelmed, in despair. The noise of firing went on behind me. Night came down over the mountain, clouds covered the sky, but I was still stifling as though I was in a nightmare. I kept calling upon the Compassionate. . . .

Phal Somnang fled to Thailand on February 17, 1976. Major Phim Uon, his companion in misfortune, reached Thailand before him, in October 1975, and gave a similar account, adding that rich civilians of Battambang such as Khy Seng Ho, the director of the sawmills, and Ho Tong Hanh, a wealthy merchant, had also been invited to welcome Prince Sihanouk. Major Phim Uon was more seriously wounded than his comrade and became a monk at the Po Veal pagoda in Battambang for the duration of his convalescence. After reaching Thailand he returned to fight the Khmer Rouge and was killed in an ambush near Snoeung in May 1976.

This massacre of the Battambang officers is confirmed by a large number of independent witnesses. The first to speak of it to me was Sam Suon, who came from Phnom Penh. He had gone through the area a week after the event and saw heaps of swollen corpses in fatigues.

"They were officers," he said.

"How do you know they were officers?"

"Because you could see their bars!"

Another refugee, Kim Sanh, a warrant officer from Battambang, had donned civilian dress and joined the officers' families and technicians who left by train on April 27, 1975, to repair the railway. All stopped at the Phnom Thippadey station, where they slept for two nights. On the evening of the second day a *neary* he knew advised him not to stay with the officers' families because it might be dangerous. So he set out by night, traveling along the railroad ties with about fifteen other men. About three or four hundred meters from the station they came upon the site of the massacre. Kim Sanh crossed the frontier on August 19.

In September 1975, Yen Savannary, from Phnom Penh, was working near Phnom Thippadey. Traveling in a truck on Trunk

Road 64 he saw large piles of bones, and expressed surprise. A
Khmer Rouge told him, "They are the bones of the Battambang
officers; we told them they were going to meet Prince Sihanouk
and we killed them all. There are only six truckloads here, but
there are eight more on Trunk Road 54."

But to return to Battambang.

"On the evening of April 23," reports Sanet, a thirty-five-year-
old mechanic,

the Khmer Rouge told the noncommissioned officers that they were to go
for retraining and could choose the place, either Siem Reap or Phnom
Penh. Ten trucks were waiting for those who chose Siem Reap, and each
carried about thirty men. When they reached Thmar Kaul, about thirty
kilometers north of Battambang, they stopped, because that was the
headquarters of the higher authorities. They got out at a hamlet called
Bat Kang, about a kilometer from Thmar Kaul; their hands were tied
behind their backs and they were simply shot down. Many people saw
their bodies, for they were piled along the sides of Highway 5, which is
a very busy road.

"On April 24," Chea Sambath says,

around six o'clock, loudspeaker cars ordered the civilian population to
leave Battambang within three hours. Anyone caught in the city after
that would be killed. Even the dogs would be shot. So I left, taking a
few things with me, and headed north toward Sisophon. The road was
swarming with people, some on cycles and some on foot, all going
northward. Many bodies were rotting along the sides of the road, un-
burned and unburied. I suppose they were victims who fell in the final
battles. At Thmar Kaul there were hundreds of bodies lying by the roadside with their hands tied behind their backs. I learned later that they
were the noncommissioned officers from Battambang who were supposedly going for retraining. Then I went on north as far as Ta Kong,
and then to Phnom Thom, where I stayed four months. Near Phnom
Thom, at the place called Mechbar [a Khmero-Japanese experimental
farm], I saw many more bodies.

According to a large number of witnesses this farm was the
scene of atrocious happenings: hundreds if not thousands of soldiers were executed there. In particular, an entire company was

massacred, with their wives. The children stood by crying as their parents were shot before their eyes. "Why are you crying over enemies?" they were asked. "If you don't stop we'll kill you too." So Vichea, an agricultural technician from Sisophon, had gone into the country west of Mongkol Borei; he says that around April 26 he met some people coming from the Mechbar farm: "I asked questions of the people coming back from there, but they couldn't talk. They were sick; I don't know what was wrong with them but they couldn't talk."

The civilian population was ordered to go ten kilometers away from the national highways, and was immediately redistributed among the villages of zones which had been "liberated" some time before. And the town of Battambang became another ghost town, totally deserted. The only signs of human life came from the rice paddies and suburban factories, which were working day and night. One refugee who went to cut down some trees inside the Battambang hospital grounds in August 1975 said that the banks of the Stung Sangker were littered with furniture dragged out of the houses and abandoned to the weather. "That furniture represents class and therefore it must disappear," the cadres said.

Similar and equally detailed accounts of events during the change of regime could be quoted about Mongkol Borei, Sisophon, O Chreuv, or any of the towns and villages along Highway 5. So that was the explanation of the ghostly emptiness that had chilled our hearts as we drove through the region—one of the wealthiest and most populous of Cambodia.

Had the same thing happened in the towns and villages of other regions? To use but one town as an example, I shall quote from some accounts relating to Pailin.

Pailin, a quiet little place west of Battambang, had grown up around miners—prisoners at first, then Burmese colonists—who came to seek their fortunes extracting the rubies, zircons, and other precious stones and minerals embedded in the volcanic soil of the region. In spite of a particularly vicious local form of malaria, the town had grown steadily during Prince Sihanouk's reign, and since 1970 large numbers of Khmers of all origins had come to swell the ranks of the gem-seekers, so that by 1975 the population of the town must have exceeded 100,000.

"On April 17," says Phat Saren, a twenty-seven-year-old radio technician,

Radio Phnom Penh broadcast an order to all armed forces to cease fighting, from Mey Si Sichan, the chief of staff. The governor of Pailin, Colonel Hou Tong, mustered the auxiliary troops in front of the prefecture and said to them, "Let us remain united, whatever happens, for life and for death! We must be firmly resolved to defend the city!" But the troops refused: "We don't want to go on fighting against Khmers."

Around three o'clock, the town became strangely agitated; all you could hear was the noise of motorcycles and cars belonging to a large number of civil servants, military people, and wealthy businessmen who were heading for O Lat to try to cross into Thailand. Around 5:00 P.M. another military convoy went through on the way to the border, carrying rice, gasoline, and weapons. Then a long silence followed, interrupted by a convoy of six M-113s, bearing the republican army insignia of the Black Cobra, and two troop trucks, which drove through town and went in the same direction. Then Pailin went deadly quiet; it was enough to make your flesh crawl.

Around eleven that night I was awakened by shouting and the noise of motors. I was very frightened and had no idea what was happening. I went outside and saw oil lamps hung on barriers in front of every house all down the path, lit up just like for the Cambodian New Year. I took out my motorcycle and rode around town; the streets were full of people, motorcycles and cars were bringing people in from the neighboring villages by the hundreds, adults and children alike. They were all walking along, singing and jumping for joy, beating war drums to make noise and shouting, "Long live peace!" Those who had generating units started them up and the villagers sang and danced all night long as though it was the New Year. Others played cards and gambled on the sidewalks. While this was going on, a group of men went to rob the governor's house, the prefecture, and the barracks.

On the morning of the eighteenth, some officials and military personnel formed a "central committee" to organize the town and welcome the victors. They waited all day long but nobody came, only a few loudspeaker cars that drove through town insulting the Lon Nol regime, which everybody hated anyway.

On the nineteenth, several Khmer Rouge arrived and mixed with the local people. The central committee had organized a cortege to welcome them, with white flags flying on cars and cycles. The orchestra from the Chinese community was also there to play for them. But around five o'clock we heard heavy bursts of gunfire, as though the town was being attacked; then one troop of about thirty fighters, mostly *neary* and children, under the orders of Met Bun, entered the town and received an ovation from the cortege, which had been waiting for them for several hours. Soon after that, the Khmer Rouge prohibited all motor traffic.

On the morning of the twentieth they ordered all prices cut. The Chinese merchants looked pretty grim at that, because people were swarming in to buy food. For rice, the Khmer Rouge went from house to house asking for contributions in kind to feed the troops, a large body of whom had arrived under the command of comrades Say, Rom, and Ngev.

On the twenty-second one of the three leaders—for wherever they went and whatever they did there were always three of them—went upstairs in the prefecture and made a speech from the balcony to the defeated officers who were still in Pailin: "Comrades, we ask you to assist the revolutionary Organization! We ask you to go to Battambang to train our soldiers to drive armored tanks, operate radios and cannon, pilot aircraft, and clear minefields, for our soldiers are ignorant and do not know how to do any of these things. We ask you to come forward tomorrow without fail." The Khmer Rouge leader told the subalterns what a disaster the war had been and how it was necessary to rebuild the country at once. He told them they would be taken to the country the very next day and given land to cultivate. All the soldiers went home delighted with the magnanimity of the Angkar, which was being so good as to take them into its ranks.

Around nine o'clock the next morning the Khmer Rouge took away about forty officers who had come forward; among them were Lieutenant Colonel Aem Akkaseri, Lieutenant Lav Song, and Lieutenant Khoun Sabin. Afterward, the drivers told us in confidence that they had all been killed near Treng, on the road to Samlaut, about a hundred meters from the crossroads. Then they took the noncommissioned officers and shot them at Trapeang Ke and near the first bridge on the Battambang-Pailin road. It was the truck drivers who told us this as well. Then they took the ordinary soldiers to some place near Samlaut and made them do extremely heavy work. They founded a village called the War Prisoners' Village, where the food rationing was very strict and the work exhausting and there was no medical care, so that now, October 31, 1975, there are very few survivors.

The group of Black Cobra soldiers who tried to cross into Thailand on April 17, 1975, had come back and surrendered to the Khmer Rouge. They refused to give up their weapons to the Thais: "Our weapons are Khmer and they'll stay Khmer," they said when the Thais tried to take them away. They wanted to join the Khmer Rouge and fight against the Thais. Most of the people who fled on April 17 also came back to

Pailin, for after watching from a distance for a day or two they decided that the new regime wasn't as terrible as they had feared.

From the twenty-fifth to the twenty-eighth, the Khmer Rouge collected all the arms and ammunition in the barracks and in people's homes and stocked them outside Pailin in one of their bases at the foot of Mt. Vai Chap in the Sdau Srok. The truck drivers were not permitted to go that far and those who did never came back.

On the twenty-sixth, loudspeaker cars drove through Pailin and ordered everybody to get out of town within three days. Everyone had to apply for a travel permit and find some means of transport back to his birthplace. The people began leaving town, mostly on foot, taking a few things with them.

Another refugee, Chan Dara, a court clerk in Pailin, adds:

I and my family, that is my wife and five children, left on foot along the Battambang road, walking day and night. When we got as far as Trapeang Ke we could smell the corpses of the people who had been shot by the Khmer Rouge. My wife and the children were afraid to go any farther, because of spirits. We saw many bodies on both sides of the road, but the largest number were near abandoned military posts.

At Bridge 1 and near the intersection with the Samlaut road we saw many bodies scattered everywhere, some were swollen and smelled very bad.

We walked for six nights, then we came to a pagoda near the Snoeung market with many other people from Pailin. There I met Mr. Eng, ex-customs officer from Pailin, who told me he was one of the last to leave town; he had seen all the municipal authorities, eighty people in all, taken away. All of them had been killed at the Samlaut crossroads. After that the Khmer Rouge went out to catch all the officials and military who had not come forward, and killed them down to the last man.

The people of Pailin were sent into the forest, to Treng, Chak Chha, Romus Ngea, Roung, Kompong Kol, and Boeung Trasal, all villages inside the forest parallel to the Pailin-Battambang road. Another group went north of Pailin to the villages of Sala Krau, Sre Anteak, Khay, etcetera. My family and I asked for hospitality from the villagers of Kien Koh, five kilometers from Snoeung. Nobody in that village knew me.

Another witness, Mean Chey, who reached Thailand in May 1976, said that he saw a Frenchman, a M. Bonzon, who had been taken away in a jeep with his driver, killed at a place called Phous Meas, seven kilometers from the crossroads. Bonzon was the director of the Pailin coffee plantation. Another refugee who had been the plantation's bulldozer driver said he dug a communal pit at that place and bulldozed Bonzon's body into it along with a number of dead Cambodians.

Phat Saren had asked to work with the central committee as a radio expert, thinking it might be easier for him to get out of Pailin that way.

On April 29 the Khmer Rouge ordered all the families working on the central committee to assemble; they wanted to know exactly how many people were still living in the town. The next morning, the three leaders again convened the central committee and each spoke in turn, but they all said the same thing. They asked everyone to relate his personal history from March 18, 1970, when Prince Sihanouk was deposed, to the present. I was instructed to tape-record each history. Then everyone had to write out the story of his life; several people openly told everything they had done, their service in the army or administration, hoping that would put them in good with the new regime. When this was done the Khmer Rouge ordered us all to leave the premises, except those who had worked in the administration and army; they were taken away and shot. One of them was a French citizen from Pondicherry.

That evening my family and I left Pailin, pushing a cart in which we had put some supplies. The road was empty and silent. From time to time we heard shots, which were the signal for a change of guard, because the Khmer Rouge don't talk much among themselves, they would rather fire a shot in the air to signal to each other. On the morning of May 1 we continued on our way; it was a desolate scene—empty houses, litter everywhere, rice strewn about under the houses. People weren't allowed to take bags of rice, so they emptied them and used the bags to hold other things they wanted to take. Farther on there was a dreadful stench, as many people died during the exodus. At four o'clock we reached Treng, where a huge crowd was waiting to see what would happen next. We stayed there two days and nights, waiting too. Then on May 3 my family and I set out for the foot of Phnom Chak Chha where we were to found a village, for there was water there. A week later the Khmer Rouge divided up the land among the families and gave us permission to build bamboo huts.

With occasional variations, the seizure of power followed the same course in other provinces and provincial towns, as dissimilar and far-flung as Koh Kong, Kompong Som, Oddar Mean Chey, and Siem Reap. Almost everywhere the people were either eagerly looking forward to the conquerors' arrival or at least meant to behave as though they were, because these were the new masters of the country.

After cutting food prices, the new authorities called together all the officers, noncommissioned officers, ordinary soldiers, and civil servants in separate groups. Each group was then taken away to an unknown destination; for the officers, senior officials, and the wealthy it was immediate death, and for the rest, execution at some later date or slow death in the special camps. Lastly, the entire civilian population was ordered to leave the towns and villages, which remain totally deserted to this day. Some refugees went through Kompong Thom, Pailin, and other towns early in 1976 and found them already invaded by vegetation.

The liquidation of all towns and former authorities was not improvised, nor was it a reprisal or expression of wanton cruelty on the part of local cadres. The scenario for every town and village in the country was the same and followed exact instructions issued by the highest authorities.

One possible explanation is that there weren't enough trained officials in the new regime, so it had to do away with all the old ones, who might have formed an intellectual or armed opposition. But this total purge was, above all, the translation into action of a particular vision of man: a person who has been spoiled by a corrupt regime cannot be reformed, he must be physically eliminated from the brotherhood of the pure. "The regime must be destroyed" (*vai robap*); "the enemy must be utterly crushed" (*kamtech khmang*)[4]; "what is infected must be cut out"; "what is rotten must be removed"; "what is too long must be shortened and made the right length"; "it isn't enough to cut down a bad plant, it must be uprooted": those are among the slogans used, both on the radio and at meetings, to justify the purge. The authorities of the former regime were not fellow creatures who had been misled, they were enemies and as such had no place in the national community. Several accounts state that in many places

---

[4] Slogans frequently heard on Radio Phnom Penh, e.g., April 11, 1976, and April 17, 1976.

the officers' wives and children were killed too: the theme that the family line must be annihilated down to the last survivor is recurrent in such reports.

In other countries, such as China and Vietnam, the revolutionaries tried to reeducate the former cadres, bring them to think and act in conformity with the country's new policies. The Khmer Rouge believed that was impossible. One Khmer Rouge official, in an interview cited in the Thai journal *Prachachat* (June 10, 1976), said that the Vietnamese revolutionary method was "very slow," and that "it took a great deal of time to sort out the good from the counterrevolutionaries." The journal itself concluded:

The Khmer methods do not require a large personnel; there are no heavy charges to bear because everyone is simply thrown out of town. If we may take the liberty of making a comparison, the Khmers have adopted the method which consists in overturning the basket with all the fruit inside; then, choosing only the articles that satisfy them completely, they put them back in the basket. The Vietnamese did not tip over the basket, they picked out the rotten fruit. The latter method involves a much greater loss of time than that employed by the Khmers.

FOUR

The Calvary of a People

On the "glorious seventeenth of April" a new era began in Cambodia: over four million Khmers who had been living in the government-controlled zones went back to their ancestral forest, the cradle of their race.

After leaving the towns many of the deportees walked, for weeks in some cases, without any specific destination, at the whim of orders and counterorders. The luckier ones were transported by truck or oxcart to the village in which they were supposed to settle. Villagers living in the "liberated" zones did not dare give shelter to those on foot; contrary to the tradition of Khmer hospitality, they also had received orders not to give food to the deportees. All they could do was provide a temporary roof overnight between the stilts under their houses. The deportees secretly traded their few belongings for a little rice. One chief physician from the Kompong Chhnang hospital whom we met in the forest during our journey to Thailand had been walking for three weeks with his wife and five children and had traveled more than a hundred kilometers, this way and that, at the foot of the mountains. He had traded everything he owned, down to the clothes on his back; when he had bartered them too there would be nothing left for him, he said, but to die.

Whenever they came to a village in the "liberated" zones the deportees were classified: "The Khmer Rouge called the people together and asked them to state their identity. Those who told the truth would not be punished. Otherwise they would be." Near Chamcar Leu several independent accounts state that the deportees were asked to register in one of three lists: military, civil servants and intellectuals, or ordinary people. The military were separated and then disappeared, in small groups; the civil servants and intellectuals were sent to special villages. The rest of the people were divided in different ways, the luckiest being sent to villages of "old" or "primary" people—that is, those who had been liberated longest.

Rong, a pharmacist who left Cambodia for Vietnam in June 1975 and later came to France, gives the following account of his first months in the village of Svay Teap:

The villagers of Svay Teap were crude but not bad. You had to understand them; they had suffered a lot from the government air force. Several people in every family had been killed in the bombardments. There were still trenches in front of every house, because the planes used to come every day to disrupt the work in the fields. The head of the village was named Ky. He was nice, but very ignorant. One day he had to draw up a list of "new people"; there were thirty-eight of us before and then fourteen more came. The chief scratched his head in perplexity. I whispered, "fifty-two." Then a few more had to be added. I whispered the answer again. Another day he had to share out a hundred and forty-four kilos of tobacco among twelve groups of families. The chief leaned over and started making complicated calculations on the ground. I told him, "Give twelve kilos to each and keep anything left over." It worked out, so after that he called me "the Learned" and treated me like a friend.

Every day we went to work two kilometers from our houses, but we had to cross another village to get to the fields. We had to walk through it in silence because we weren't allowed to talk to people. First, I built a long fence of stakes. My friend Kim Sok, another pharmacist who was also deported, wasn't any more accustomed to working with his hands than I was, and the hatchet was dull, so our hands were soon bleeding, but we weren't allowed to complain. Then we had to plant maize, cassava, and rice. Since we weren't very strong physically, the village chief sent us to work with the women's group, where a man went along in front making holes with a stake and we would put in a few seeds and fill up the hole by scraping our feet over it.

One day the village chief said to me, "Rong, you're very clever, you learn fast. In a year you can have a pair of oxen and a house!" "What about the ones who aren't so clever?" I asked him. "In three years." I was a bachelor but not by choice, because my wife was in France. A girl in the village was chosen for me but I got out of it by telling them I wanted to wait for my team of oxen before I thought about getting married. You had to be awfully careful about that sort of thing, too, because love affairs were punishable by death. So everybody had to watch his step.

For food we had rice mixed with sliced green bananas, maize, cassavas, or *tracuon* [a water plant]. It made a brownish paste that wasn't very good to eat, but since that was all there was we had to be content with it. We husked the rice ourselves with a sort of foot-pump pestle, and we weren't used to doing that either, so we found it hard work. The villagers were allowed to fatten pigs; when a pig was ready the person who fattened it asked the village chief for permission to kill it. Half the meat went to the family who raised the animal, the other half was divided into equal shares among the other families in the group. Since we were "new people" and hadn't been there long, we only got a half-share. We ate meat twice during the month of May 1975.

Above the village chief there was a Khmer Rouge in charge of general supervision. In Phnom Penh he used to drive a cycle rickshaw but now he carried a gun. Political education was pretty rudimentary: few meetings in May, and always the same speech: "The Revolution has conquered, we must work and keep on working to rebuild the country." The Khmer Rouge were decent enough but if anyone resisted them or didn't obey at once, it meant death.

Rong almost lost his life over a few kilos of tobacco which he traded to another villager, for the law only allowed trading among the members of a single ten-family group.

Apart from one or two differences in detail, this seems to have been the life of everyone in the "old" villages in mid-1975. For the "old people" things must have gone on in the same way for another few months. But beginning in May or a little later, depending on the region, the "new people" had to leave the "old" villages and share the fate of the "prisoners of war"—that is, the population of Phnom Penh and the other towns of Cambodia.

As soon as they left the city these deportees were sent into the forest, which they were to clear; they were given a few days in which to build a bamboo cabin or branch hut, then set zealously to work under the nervous supervision of armed Khmer Rouge. The entire population was immediately split into groups of ten to fifteen families, with a chief at the head of each group. A tract of forest land was allotted to each family. At Boeung Trasal (between Pailin and Battambang), to where sixty thousand people had been deported, every family was given three hectares (more than seven acres). The "new people" had to clear the land and plant new crops such as maize, cassava, yams, and sweet potatoes. In most cases, the rice paddies had been taken away from the villagers and nationalized; they were cultivated by Khmer Rouge soldiers using tractors, which were also nationalized.

The life was very hard, for most of these new farmers were not used to working the land, had no proper tools and no oxen to plow with—the livestock in the countryside had been severely depleted during the war. The refugees say that in several places they had to pull the plows themselves because there were no oxen. Sam Suon did this at Bak Prea, east of Battambang, and when he got to France he could show the marks of his yoke. At O Popoul a plowing team was made up of nine men; two teams of four pulled while the ninth held the handle. In other places there were seven men to a team, and in one place only three. Having no tools, people scratched at the earth with sharpened bamboo canes. Others built dikes, lifting the mud with their hands.

Suon Phal describes the work performed by the young men of his group in the region of Koas Krala (south of Battambang) between July and September 1975: "Because of the rains we couldn't hoe and had to work the fields with plows. We didn't have any oxen, so we formed a team of eight men to pull the plow. Several of my comrades, exhausted by this work, began spitting blood and died."

Almost everywhere, the work day was very long: a gong rang to wake people up around 5:00 A.M., then breakfast—rice soup—and by 6:00 everybody left for work, sometimes very far away; there was either a pause or a return to the village around 11:00, to husk rice and eat. Back to work from 2:00 to 5:00 P.M. or in some places 5:30 or 6:00. Often, at Koh Thom (south of Phnom Penh) and west of Krakor; at Kauk Thlok (in Kompong Thom), near Takhau; at Varin (west of Siem Reap); and in other places, the refugees say that work went on at night until 8:00 or even 11:00 P.M.; when there was a moon they worked by moonlight and when there wasn't huge torches were lit.

All the refugees complain of the relentless, goading nature of the work. "We were made to work like slaves, like beasts of burden, with no thought for the human losses!" The human organism was used to the extreme limit of its physical endurance; no effort was made to spare it and it was never given a day of rest.

In some areas, work could be more immediately dangerous, because of the unexploded bombs and shells lurking in the grass or brush. In the region of Phnom Baset, northwest of Phnom Penh, a day never went by without several villagers being injured or killed by explosions.

During the month of May people were apparently not compelled to work, but food was distributed in proportion to work accomplished, so the result was the same.

At Bak Prea, on the other hand, workers who did not meet their day's quota were reprimanded, and if they did not improve they were sent to the Angkar Leu (Higher Organization) from which none ever returns.

Around Thmar Puok, during the harvest season at the end of 1975, the quota for harvesters was twenty "heaps" a day. "If we didn't make it," one of them relates, "we got only half a bowl of rice that day and had to make up the short heaps the next day. Failing to make the quota meant being sent up to the Angkar Leu."

Between September and December the authorities began relocating large numbers of people, either to meet the requirements of the central work program or for some other, unknown reason. Hundreds of thousands of the original inhabitants of Phnom Penh, initially deported south to Koh Thom Province or to provinces in the southwest (Takeo, Kompong Speu), were moved again to the Pursat, Sisophon, or Oddar Mean Chey regions. This time they were transported by truck or boat to Pursat, then to Sisophon by train.

A single account is enough to show what this second migration was like. Im Sok reached Thailand early in July 1976; he had left Phnom Penh on April 17, 1975, with his father, mother, wife, and a three-year-old daughter, to go to a village named Phum Krang in Takeo province.

In September 1975 the Khmer Rouge told the "new people" and the "old people" in some areas to assemble at Prey No in preparation for their return to Phnom Penh. "You don't need to take anything with you," they told us, "because everything has been made ready to welcome you in Phnom Penh: you will all have identical houses, equipped with everything you need." More than thirty large trucks were waiting for us; we traveled more than a hundred to a truck. As we were getting in, the soldiers took away everything we had brought with us; all we could keep was a kettle, four tins of rice, and a bit of food for two days on the road.

During the trip we were crushed together like a load of pigs. The trucks stopped every five or six hours to let people relieve themselves. We took Highway 2 and then Highway 3 to Phnom Penh, but then we bypassed the city center through Tuol Kauk district and the trucks turned north down Highway 5. We were all surprised at this, and everybody fell silent. It was already dark and we were still going. The children were crying and the babies screaming because they were hungry. Around eight o'clock the trucks stopped north of Longvek to let us cook some rice. At midnight we drove on again, as far as Pursat. There we were given enough rice and salt for three days. There were no camps or shelters, so we had to sleep alongside the railroad. Several thousand people had been brought there, from all over. The sun was hardly up the next morning when the Khmer Rouge soldiers ordered us to get ready to continue the journey by train; they removed anything we had managed to keep hidden until then, and after that we had nothing but a mat, a kettle, and one plate. The train came in; we were shoved into the cars like a herd of cattle, more than a hundred and fifty to a car. After a day of traveling we reached Sisophon. From there tractors hauling trailers took some of the people to Phnom Srok; others went by oxcart. Many old people and children died on that trip, certainly not less than ten percent.

It was growing dark. Around four o'clock the carts transporting us reached the edge of the forest near the village of Pongro in Phum Srok sector. I climbed down quickly to find shelter under a tree for my wife and child bcause the sky was full of threatening clouds. The Khmer Rouge handed out enough rice and salt for one day. Then the sky favored us with several downpours. We were shivering with cold, having nothing to cover ourselves with, and we looked and felt like the objects of divine malediction.

The next day each family was assigned to a particular plot of land. We had to clear the ground and build cabins, each ten meters away from the next and all identical. It was the group of ten families that took charge of building the houses; we built them with the trunks of trees we felled in the forest and covered them with straw. There was no [water] jar, no mosquito netting, no blanket. As the Khmer saying goes, we had the ladle by the handle and the kettle by the spout, but there was nothing inside. The chief would tell us, "The revolutionaries suffered ten times worse than you during the war; they had no rice and no medicine and nothing to eat but the leaves on the trees."

According to many of the refugees this second deportation was even more deadly than the first, for people's systems were weaker and could not take the journey. A doctor, redeported from Phnom Baset to Sisophon, says that the Khmer Rouge stood, with stretchers, waiting for every train that came in to remove the dead and sick. People were gaunt as skeletons, their legs full of abscesses. Another witness says that some people fell under the train on purpose to commit suicide. He speaks of 250 such suicides near Mongkol Borei. Yet another says, "On the road to Phnom Srok there were tens of thousands of people from Phnom Penh, all gaunt and lifeless, marching in columns several kilometers long. They were going to the rice paddies for the harvest. Some were laughing and dancing, shouting and eating raw rice— many had gone crazy from fatigue, privation, and fear."

Apart from the fiercely compulsory aspect of the work, what the deportees felt most keenly was the lack of food and inhuman discipline.

Cambodia had never known a famine; the plains around Battambang, Kompong Cham, Takeo, and Svay Rieng were, with Cochin China, the granary of all Indochina. The banks of the Mekong and smaller streams were covered with flourishing stands of bananas, mangoes, breadfruit trees, and food crops of all sorts. After the beginning of the war in 1970, however, the food shortage gradually became increasingly acute for both revolutionaries and government, since so many peasants had fled the combat areas and were huddled unproductively in and around the towns. Also, because of the bombardments—first the government planes and later the American B-52s—the rice paddies could not be properly cultivated. By 1974 the food crisis was creating serious problems for both sides. Even then, large numbers of people were being driven out of the "liberated" zones by hunger. The government was feeding most of the population under its control with Korean rice flown in by American planes.

After April 17 the food situation fluctuated considerably, depending on the region and time of year. Throughout most of the country the ration was one tin of rice (about 180 grams) per person every two days. The normal ration for a manual worker under ordinary conditions is between 500 and 800 grams a day. In June the ration at the Phnom Koulen work sites was three tins a week; at Lahat Teuk near Mongkol Borei it was one tin of paddy a day.[1]

At Koh Kong a half-tin of rice was the daily ration; at Koh Thom the ration was cut to two tins of rice per week, as it was in the area around Pailin. Between June and August 1975 in the region of Kompong Cham, food allowances were as follows: able-bodied working people were given sixteen kilos of paddy a month; youths fourteen and fifteen years old got twelve, old people who were unfit for work got eight. Distributions took place every two weeks. One account gave further details:

There were six persons in our family: one old woman, an orphan of fifteen, and four people working. According to the rations then in force we were allowed forty-two kilos of paddy for twenty-five days. At each handout we were also given six hundred grams of salt per family. Apart from that we got nothing, not even the slightest bit of equipment we could use to catch fish with, such as the native village people had. We often ground up peppers, salt, and bitter fruit to season the rice. Sometimes Cham fishermen came to us to trade fish for rice, but we had to be very careful, because we were closely watched.

I could quote many more examples, and could even name villages in which the population was given virtually nothing to eat

---

[1] Paddy is unhusked rice. It is inedible and must be husked before being cooked. One hundred kilos of paddy generally yield sixty kilos of rice. Paddy has no relation to brown or whole rice, which is husked but has a little of the bran left in.

and had to live on what they could forage for themselves. "The Khmer Rouge explained that we had to get used to eating little and working a lot, so that we could follow the path of revolution and defeat American imperialism as well as the old regime. Then we would be able to build a rich nation."

To offset the shortage of rice, which is the basis of the Asian diet, the Khmer Rouge followed the Vietnamese revolutionaries' example by growing more yams and sweet potatoes. They taught the "liberated" people how to make a black gruel out of rice, green bananas, and red or white maize. Sometimes they also mixed in the stems of bananas cut into thin strips, which used to be food for swine. "They called us 'the pigs' because we ate it." At work in the fields, the laborers walked around with a sack over one shoulder and picked up snails or paddy crabs to eat. "But their flesh has no blood and it gave us boils," one refugee bitterly observes. Others tell how, during the break between 11:00 A.M. and 1:00 P.M., people would scatter through the forest to look for bamboo shoots, leaves, and roots to vary their diet. After a few months they were so worn out that they stopped doing this.

"We weren't allowed to complain about the food, because the Khmer Rouge said, 'If you're not happy we'll take you to a place where there is more than enough to eat.' They meant the rice paddy where they executed people who were dissatisfied."

In the last months of 1975 the people had nothing but rice bran to eat. "We had no more paddy, so the Khmer Rouge distributed bran and told us not to waste it." Even in the villages close to Battambang they were giving out bran. Some villagers had kept some paddy in their homes, but the Khmer Rouge ordered them to produce it. The villagers thought it would be used to feed the village, but the Khmer Rouge stored it in the storehouses of the Angkar. The rice-husking factories of Battambang were working day and night, but there was no rice for the people! Sometimes the bran they distributed was poisonous; many villagers died of food poisoning.

There is nothing surprising in the fact that food should be poor and scarce after so devastating a war. But what hurt the people even more than famine was the flagrant injustice. While the workers were literally dying of hunger, the Khmer Rouge soldiers who were supervising them had more than enough to eat and refused themselves nothing; they had rice, meat, and fish in plenty. Their reasoning was simple enough: "You are prisoners of war. We went hungry for five years. Now it's your turn!"

There was only one way for the deportees to obtain food—by barter—and the system flourished according to fluctuations in supply and demand. "During the first few months, the rate at Phnom Thippadey was seventy tins for one gold damleung.[2] A month later, twenty tins for a damleung. But this kind of barter was more and more strictly prohibited, and anyone caught at it was sentenced to death. Yet it was the Khmer Rouge themselves who organized the barter, in order to get our gold away from us."

At Sdau the rates were different: "For one gold damleung we could get thirty-five kilos of rice or twenty kilos of salt or one kilo of powdered soup or five kilos of white sugar or five kilos of prahoc.[3] But it was very hard to find any prahoc. Two and a half kilos of tobacco or one liter of serum were worth one and a half to two damleungs. People who had no gold, like my family, had to dig in the earth for sweet potatoes, day after day."

At the end of 1975 a collective system was introduced. Meals began to be eaten in large groups; a team was put in charge of cooking rice for the community, but each family had to find something to eat with it. The first harvest in 1976 was excellent, and for a time the workers no longer went hungry. After August 1976, however, all rice was stocked in the state storehouses before being transported to Phnom Penh en route to some unknown destination. The Angkar stopped rice distributions and called upon the villagers to make a renewed effort to achieve self-sufficiency. Once again, there was famine until the end of the year. The peasants have lost faith in the Angkar because it has lied to them too often, and they have no desire to make this renewed effort, at the end of which they feel they will be despoiled yet again. The

---

2 One damleung = 37.5 grams of gold.
3 Prahoc is fermented fish paste, a staple of the Cambodian diet.

first crop in 1977 was mediocre, and the rice went to Phnom Penh as before, leaving the peasants with empty stomachs.

In addition to the toll taken by extreme hard labor and chronic malnutrition, there is virtually a total lack of sanitary equipment and medical care. The city-dwellers were used to minimum standards of modern sanitation, which protected them from many tropical diseases—the water they drank was filtered by municipal water departments and the Chinese merchants drank nothing but sterilized water, so that malaria was almost unknown in the towns, and the relatively numerous hospitals and dispensaries enabled even the poorest to obtain some form of treatment. But now the city people are living in heavily malaria-infested forests, sleeping without mosquito netting most of the time, drinking stagnant pond water, and eating a primitive fare to which they are not accustomed. So it is not surprising that their defenseless systems should fall prey to dysentery, malaria (the fatal *falciparum*), beriberi, and all sorts of other fevers, which every individual must either overcome with his own resources or succumb to.

After leaving Phnom Penh we crossed the Tonle Sap near Prek Kdam, then went on to Banteay. A child of seven had been walking with his parents through the hottest part of the day. He was very thirsty and drank from a pond by the side of the road. An hour later he was taken with dreadful stomach pains, which nobody could relieve. He died during the night.

Incidents as cruel as this are legion. Several refugees state that there were cholera epidemics in April and May 1975 in the area of Neak Luong and Skoun. The Khmer Rouge themselves avoided the area and forbade anyone else to enter it. This is perfectly plausible, for it is at this time of year that cholera always breaks out, and there was no vaccine available in 1975.

What the deportees feared most was falling ill, because that was virtually equivalent to a death sentence. Every refugee family lost one or more members through illness; one couple lost all three of its children; in the family of Phat Saren, which originally had eleven members, three died in three months.

Eight days after we moved to Chak Chha a fifty-year-old man who had joined us died of malaria. On June 6, my mother died after an illness of five days. On July 19 one of my nephews died after being sick for three days. Afterward my brother fell ill too and we had to work very hard in his place so that he could rest a little. There was good reason to be afraid, because several people in our village died every day. All the members of some families had died of a very virulent form of malaria. Those who came down with it did not linger long, three or four days at most, and then came their final release.

Sometimes the ailing had to work alongside the able-bodied, or at least go out to the work site. Their food ration was half the normal amount, and sometimes it was cut completely, so many would rather do whatever work they could in order to get a little food. "Only the person who works has a right to receive food," the cadres used to say at ideological training meetings. "We were never allowed to complain," reports Ros En, a twenty-eight-year-old electrician. "When we said we were ill the cadres told us we were sick in our minds or imagination. Only when we dropped down exhausted would they consent to take care of us. It happened to me once." True, there were hospitals in the countryside, but they were more like death houses than real centers for treatment. The only medicines prescribed were those of the traditional pharmacopoeia: tree bark, roots, ground or boiled tubercles swallowed in liquid form or injected. But they could do very little to cure disease.

So the deportees made desperate efforts to obtain "French" drugs. Since money was still prohibited, they traded rice for medicine. To give one example, in the northern part of Kompong Cham, between June and August 1975, the rates of barter were as follows:

1 aspirin tablet = 1 kilo of rice
1 nivaquine tablet = 1 kilo of rice
1 vitamin B-12 ampul = 7 kilos of rice
1 vial of streptomycin = 15 kilos of rice

The many doctors and nurses working under the Lon Nol regime were also sent out to the rice paddies but were not allowed to practice, even though some were perfectly willing to work under the new authorities—such as the doctor from the Preah Ket Mealea Hospital who had insisted on remaining in Phnom Penh until the end to take care of his fellow Khmers, regardless of their political affiliations. He was sent to the country, where he was appalled by the state of the people's health and his absolute inability to do anything for them. It became known that he was a doctor. After a lengthy term in prison, he was sent back to the rice paddies.

Malnutrition and disease killed many, but some were the victims of mind-crippling terror. "Their regime is too severe! I'm not against work, or the goals of the revolution either, because that is how Cambodia can develop its agriculture and become a great country. But the regime is too tense." This is how Lao Bun Thai summarizes the views of many refugees; the regime ruthlessly exterminated any who did not walk the straight and narrow path laid out by the Angkar. "In Kampuchea there are no camps or prisons. For every crime, the only punishment is death. Anyone who protests shows that he doesn't want to be part of their society. Anyone who doesn't want to be part of their society should be shot. There is no pardon." These are not the words of just one refugee. All the witnesses I have recorded show a disturbing unanimity on this point. Another young man quotes what he was taught during his daily political education sessions: "The law of Kampuchea is at the end of a gun barrel" (*canon*, in French in the original). Someone from Phnom Thippadey adds, "We didn't dare suggest any changes that could lighten the work, for they killed people who asked questions. The only punishment and the only law was shooting and killing."

The early months were those of blackest terror: "We have beaten the enemies outside, the Americans and their lackeys. Now we must defeat the enemies within, for there are still some left," was one announcement made over the radio and at evening propaganda meetings. Everyone was suspected of being an "enemy" or of "maintaining relations with the enemy." The new authorities had done their best to annihilate the cadres of the old regime but they were convinced that some were still in hiding. Units of "spies" (*kang chhlop*), composed mainly of children, were instructed to listen to what the "new people" said and report back to the Angkar.

The children mingled with us; we thought they were the villagers' boys, but when one or another member of our group was summoned and then disappeared, we realized that they were reporting what we said to the Angkar.

We gradually learned who had been told to spy on us, and we took refuge in silence. The Angkar told us, "If you want to live, surround your house with a wall of ceiba trees [kapok]." Everybody understood that that meant a wall of silence, because the word *kor* means both "ceiba tree" and "silence." "See nothing, hear nothing, know nothing, understand nothing," was the advice of the cadres at evening meetings. The deportees' survival depended on their following it.

To speak at work was to incur suspicion of conspiracy. Even at night children hid under the houses on stilts, with orders to report any words spoken by the people inside.

"We know that there are still officers, soldiers, officials, students, and engineers hiding among you. But we shall find them out and kill them all," one cadre said during the evening meetings at Staung (Kompong Thom).

"The Khmer Rouge were very well informed about us all," adds a former officer. "Nobody could hide his true identity for long. everyone had to tell who was living near him. In this way the Khmer Rouge knew all about the peasants under their authority. 'Hiding something,' they said, 'is punishable by death. Everything must be clear between us; everyone must know everyone else as well as the image of his own face reflected in a mirror.'"

When a man was suspected of having been in the army of the former regime, a civil servant, a "commando" (in the territorial militia), or the head of ten, fifty, or a hundred houses, he was killed on the spot or disappeared.

"One day," a teacher relates, "the work-site chief, who was called Hanh, discovered someone who had been a soldier. He questioned him and then killed him. Then he cut out his liver."

Captain Mam Sarun explains why he ran away:

One day we were working in the rice paddy. A Chinese, also a de-
portee, pointed at us and shouted, "That man is an officer, his brother
is a lousy policeman!" It was during the harvest. The Khmer Rouge
threw themselves at my brother. I managed to get away, because the
guards didn't have guns.

All the refugees say that people would disappear almost every
evening, summoned to the Angkar Leu. One evening one would
go, another day two more, and so on, regularly. "Everything is
secret in that Angkar Leu, but the secrecy doesn't last forever
because two or three weeks after someone's disappearance the
Khmer Rouge would say, 'We killed so-and-so at such-and-such a
place.' It was true because we saw the bodies afterward and we
saw the people's clothes being worn by the Khmer Rouge, so that
way we were sure that some of the people we knew had been
executed."

The family of a person who disappeared should not try to find
out what had happened to him, or they would risk the same fate.
One woman who was weeping over her husband's death was told,
"Why are you crying about the execution of an enemy? That
shows you don't love the Revolution." Sometimes the cadres
themselves admitted to killing a man without good reason. "Better to kill an innocent person than leave an enemy alive," they
said to justify their action. In any event, the Khmer revolutionaries attach very little value to the lives of any of their compatriots who have not been won over to their cause: "Nothing to
gain by keeping them alive, nothing to lose by doing away with
them." All the refugees were familiar with this grim sentence.

The Khmer Rouge seldom give much publicity to their killings.
As a rule, a villager receives a paper ordering him to report to the
Angkar Leu. He is taken there at night, by soldiers. From there he
goes to his place of death. To save bullets, the necks of the condemned are usually broken with the handle of a pick. "One
shouldn't waste cartridges on those people," they say. The young
soldiers have been nicknamed *A-ksae nylon* (nylon rope) or *A-
ksae teo* (telephone wire) because that is what they use to bind
the condemned person before killing him. Moreover, they make
no secret of the fact that they enjoy killing. In 1974 I met a young

acquaintance in Phnom Penh whom I had not seen for some time; once he had been shy and timid, but the Khmer Rouge had turned him into a killer who made no effort to hide the pleasure it gave him to see the blood of the republican soldiers flow, first, and, second, that of the Khmer Rouge themselves.

A few refugees had belonged to or been in contact with groups of the condemned.

"At the beginning of January 1976," one primary schoolteacher relates,

twenty of us were sentenced to death for traveling without permission. We were taken away in a truck with our hands tied behind our backs. One Khmer Rouge sat behind with a gun and two more sat in front with the driver. One of us managed to free himself and secretly untied eleven others. Then one of us tried to kill the Khmer Rouge sitting in the back of the truck, but the guards in front saw him and turned around and started shooting. The twelve who had their hands free jumped down from the truck and dived into the Mongkol Borei River by the side of the road, then disappeared into the forest. The other eight were killed on the spot.

Among other and equally shocking cases, the Pailin court clerk gives an account of one execution:

In October 1975, the Angkar chose us to cut bamboo at O Ta Tam, near Phnom Rodaong, for eighteen days. One afternoon we were in a group of thirty wagons carting bamboo to the national highway. We had loaded and were about to turn around when we saw a military truck enter the forest, carrying about ten young men and girls. A moment later we heard shots, then the truck came back empty. We were very frightened, and harnessed up to go home. Then we heard moaning and somebody calling for help. One of our group, named Sambath, went over and saw a young man with bullet wounds in both arms and one thigh, and his arms still tied behind his back. Sambath untied him, gave him a little rice, and told him how to get to the road to the west. On the way home Sambath told us, "That young man told me that the people who had been shot hadn't done anything wrong, they had simply gone to look for food in the forest, so they weren't working with their group. That's why they were killed."

It would be very easy to blacken the picture by stringing out a long list of similar incidents. Hang In of Pailin even drew a map of the main execution sites along the Pailin-Battambang road. And although we cannot verify them in person, many of the indications on his map have been confirmed by the large number of refugees from that region.

Sometimes the Khmer Rouge resorted to cunning, to detect "anti-Communists." Several refugees tell how, in December 1975, "they circulated a false report that In Tam and his troops had attacked several villages and were twenty kilometers from Battambang. The Khmer Rouge watched the expressions on people's faces in order to find out anybody who didn't like the new regime. They massacred several families."

Discipline was not always so summary, however. Many refugees speak of being subjected to "construction," or reeducation.

At Prek Sangkar, from June to August 1975, they watched every sign of behavior at work, both speech and acts: if we were slow at work they reprimanded us; a sad face attracted their attention; anyone grumbling was followed; lateness at work meant reproaches. During the evening meetings after work they recited all these failings in order to "construct" the guilty person. Anyone who had been the subject of several "constructions" without mending his ways was sent to the mountain for a week. We each had to take rice, mosquito netting, and a mat. When we got there, there was one shelter: a forty-bed hut for men and another, similar one for women. The rice was pooled and one person was responsible for cooking it. The morning gong rang around 4:30 and then people had to clean up around the buildings. At five we shouldered our picks and went into the forest, where we worked hard all day. At eleven we came back to eat: men and women ate separately, and always in silence. If one week wasn't enough to change the guilty person's attitude, then he stayed two or three weeks without coming down.

There are several other accounts of similar punishments: as a rule the cadres began by giving criticism and inviting the person to improve; a repeated offense was followed by punishment of the type described above or, more often, by being left without food or water for twenty-four hours, exposed to the sun and the night chill. If he or she remained unconverted, the Angkar "shared two meters of rice paddy" with him, where he was sent to "make fertilizer"—both being ways of saying that he was killed. Not an entirely useless death, however, since it enriched the earth. The object of this type of reeducation was to "forge" (*lot dam*) the character of the "new people," *lot dam* being the term for both tempering and hammering iron.

The executions continued after the early months of the massive purge of the former regime's civilian and military cadres and the many recalcitrant elements, but they became less frequent and less summary. After September 1975, it seems certain that organized reeducation camps were set up. The doctor deported from Phnom Baset to Sisophon in September 1975 spent three months in such a camp.

When we got out of the train at the station in Sisophon a reception committee was waiting for us. Loudspeakers welcomed us and asked all "specialists" to step forward: doctors, architects, schoolteachers, students, technicians, and skilled workers of all kinds. The Angkar was going to need them. I didn't move, but a man who had been a nurse under me and was now a Khmer Rouge cadre recognized me and strongly advised me to tell them my true identity or risk punishment. Then all the "specialists" were taken to Preah Neth Preah, where we had to work the land as before. One day we were taken to Chup, a village on the road between Siem Reap and Sisophon. There the Khmer Rouge received us with open arms and gave us three meals a day! That was a real treat! At one big meeting, attended by 397 "specialists," a Khmer Rouge asked us to write our biographies and set down our desiderata. He even invited us to come up to the platform and offer our suggestions as to how the country could be better run. Teachers and students went up and began criticizing the Angkar for not giving people anything to eat, and for treating the sick with medicine that was more like rabbit dung than real pills; they asked for the bonzes to be reinstated and the pagodas reopened, and the high schools and universities, and for everyone to be allowed to visit his family, et cetera.

The Khmer Rouge said nothing, but we could see plainly enough that they didn't like it. After we had written our autobiographies they called out the names of twenty young people who had been most outspoken in their criticism, tied their hands behind their backs the way you tie a parrot's wings, and took them to Sisophon, where they were put in prison.

The rest of us went back to the village of Preah Neth Preah. A month later, on January 6, the Khmer Rouge came to get some of us and took us to the Battambang prison. There were forty-five of us, and we were the first "guests" of the prison since the new regime began. We had to write out our autobiographies several more times. Each time the cadres became more insistent: "You've made good progress since the last time but we know that some of you are still not telling the whole truth! We know what that truth is, why hide it? The Angkar doesn't want to kill you, don't be afraid! By acting the way you are, you show that you have not been converted." After three sessions, one of my friends revealed that he had been an army doctor. A week later he disappeared.

We had been there two weeks when the group of twenty young people interned at Sisophon were brought in; their arms were still tied at all times, even during meals, and the ropes had cut deep furrows. We also saw a former lieutenant colonel of the government army brought in, and about twenty [republican] MPs. After a few days they were taken away one at a time and we didn't see them again.

Now and then one of us was summoned for a "meeting," and sometimes the person did not come back. At the end of two and one-half months in prison fifteen of us were taken to the Van Kandal pagoda, which had also been made into a prison. There were three buildings in the pagoda: The doors and windows of one were kept permanently shut—that was where the prisoners were beaten, and some people had been in it for seven months. The windows of the second building were opened from time to time. The third building, where I was put, was for prisoners who stayed only a short time, usually two or three weeks. Its doors and windows were always open until 6:00 P.M. We had reeducation sessions, study meetings, we were subjected to constant interrogations. Those of us who were European-trained doctors and engineers were questioned even more than the others, because we were suspected of having worked with the imperialists or been engaged in secret activities.

In the evening, when we were taking our bath in the Stung Sangker, we saw other prisoners bathing, for although the houses on the other bank were always shut up, there were prisoners in them too. After ten days we were given a black garment and a gray and red *krama* [scarf] and put in a truck. Half the group was let out at Poy Saman and the other half at Kauk Khmwn, to go on working in the fields. That was April 6, 1976.

Unending labor, too little food, wretched sanitary conditions, terror, and summary executions: from these, the hair-raising human cost of the Khmer revolution can be imagined without much difficulty. In 1970 the population of Cambodia was usually estimated at eight million, 400,000 of whom were Vietnamese and a slightly larger number Chinese, both of which groups had been living in the country for a number of years. In 1975 Prince

Sihanouk—in agreement with the Americans on this point—reckoned the number of war-dead at 600,000, to which should be added 600,000 injured. On the first anniversary of the liberation, April 17, 1976, the authorities of Kampuchea declared 800,000 dead and 240,000 disabled as a result of the war.

As to the number who have died during the "peace," nobody can suggest a reliable figure but it certainly exceeds one million. At the end of 1975 French diplomatic sources unofficially estimated 800,000 dead; American embassy sources thought 1.2 million, and the American charities working in Bangkok said 1.4 million. No one will ever know the exact number of victims, but judging by the refugee accounts of those who died in their own families it must be substantial.

A large part of the deported population appears to have been sacrificed. Its role in the history of Democratic Kampuchea will thus have been to build up the country's economic infrastructure with its own flesh and blood.

FIVE

Independence-Sovereignty

Nothing in Democratic Kampuchea seems to happen by chance; on the contrary, everything appears to be planned in advance and executed methodically and with relentless consistency. In order to arrive at a correct interpretation of the numerous refugee accounts, we must try to reconstruct the vision of the world, society, and man, which they reflect. "The Voice of Democratic Kampuchea"[1] and the official publications of the new regime outline the contours of the ideology underlying all the activities of the Khmer people in the course of their revolution.

The preamble to the Constitution of Democratic Kampuchea repeats the objectives of the Khmer revolution as first proclaimed several years ago and often reiterated over the radio since: "On

---

[1] Radio Phnom Penh broadcasts every day between 6:00 and 7:00 A.M., 11:00 A.M. and noon, and 8:00 and 10:00 P.M. local time, over 61 and 327 meters; all three broadcasts present the same text, read in Khmer. Translations of extracts from the broadcasts may be consulted in the BBC *World Broadcasting Summary*.

the basis of the sacred and fundamental aspirations of the people, workers, peasants, and other laborers, as well as those of the fighters and cadres of the Kampuchean Revolutionary Army," the Revolution seeks to achieve "an independent, unified, peaceful, neutral, nonaligned, sovereign and democratic state enjoying territorial integrity, a national society informed by genuine happiness, equality, justice, and democracy, without rich or poor and without exploiters or exploited, a society in which all live harmoniously in great national solidarity and join forces to do manual work together and increase production for the construction and defense of the country."

Three or four main forces (*kaul chomhor*) or guiding principles are essential to the achievement of this ideal society: to "attain independence-sovereignty," "rely on our own strength," "defend and construct the country," and "take our own destiny in our hands." These fundamental aims are the slogans governing all revolutionary action and teaching in Kampuchea.

"Independence-sovereignty" (*aekareach-mochaskar*): this is the term most often used over the radio, in propaganda in the countryside, and in official texts intended for foreign consumption. The two formerly separate terms, "independence" and "sovereignty," have now been welded into one.

All the slogans designed to mobilize the working people entail either being or becoming

> master of the country
> master of the earth and water
> master of the rice paddies and fields, the forests, and all plant life
> master of the water problem, the annual floods
> master of nature
> master of the future, of our destiny
> master of the revolution
> master of the factories, of production

or achieving "total mastery over water at all times, mastery during the dry season and the rainy season," et cetera.

The new leaders are convinced that economic independence is

the only way for the country to attain the desired independence-sovereignty.

"To achieve our independence-sovereignty we must ensure domestic peace and unity, mobilize the people's forces to build an egalitarian society without rich or poor, and increase production according to the just and enlightened policy of the Angkar." "If the economy grows, society grows too," and ensures true independence-sovereignty. "Looking back to the glorious past of the struggle against the imperialists, we are impelled to continue the fight to build a new Kampuchea with a radiant future, overflowing with happiness, and to build a modern economy by transforming our traditional agriculture and industry into a modern agriculture and industry." "We have to build the nation, to build our history."

In accordance with these principles, the radio gives greatest attention to problems of economic construction: it is to "the heavy task of economic revival that the entire population was immediately harnessed."[2]

Cambodia derives most of its resources from agriculture, so the nation's forces were initially mobilized on this front, and mainly for the cultivation of rice.

"With rice we can have everything: steel, factories, energy, tractors." "We defeated the Americans because of the rice we produced." "By exporting rice we shall obtain currency." The conclusion is that the cultivation of rice must be intensified "to the utmost" by putting more land under cultivation, gaining control of the water system throughout the year, and increasing yields by using fertilizers and selected seed.

People are reminded that "the land must not be allowed to remain unproductive" and that the forest must be cleared to increase the amount of arable land. The number of hectares of new farmland in this place or that is loudly proclaimed.

"The one great problem" with rice, however, "is water." As the

---

[2] Ieng Sary, speech at the Conference of Non-Aligned Countries at Lima, Peru, August 25–29, 1975. *Bulletin du GRUNK*, no. 220b/75 (September 4, 1975), p. 9.

old saying goes, "The rice paddy is made with water, and war is made with rice." "We have the Mekong, the Tonle Sap, many streams and springs, but their water must be used scientifically by gaining control of the floods and building up water reserves, which will be needed in the dry season. That way, we can harvest three crops of rice each year and ensure complete independence-sovereignty." "We used to rely on the sun or on nature alone to grow rice, but now we must try to control the water all year long, in dry and rainy seasons alike; we must ensure our victory over nature in order to become masters of our fate."

The annual monsoon rains begin in mid-April and fall abundantly in September and October; while they last, the paddies can be cultivated and the rice sown, transplanted, and allowed to ripen. Between December and April, on the other hand, there is total drought and nothing can be grown throughout most of the country. The Mekong, one of the largest rivers in Asia, begins to rise in June, after the snow melts in the Himalayas, and reaches its high point in September, when it floods the lowlands and covers them with a layer of fertile silt. The Tonle Sap, or Great Lake, in the lowlands of central Cambodia, regulates the Mekong system to some extent, for the river empties part of its floodwaters into the lake, which gradually releases them as the water table falls. The Mekong is an exceptional source of energy, but it has still to be tamed.

The rains and ensuing floods, sometimes insufficient and sometimes overabundant, subject the peasantry to the "whims of nature," to "undisciplined powers," and so the country people have become relatively "fatalistic," trusting to the goodwill of the gods. And they are likely to remain that way "so long as liberating technology has not enabled them to command nature."[3]

Enormous efforts have therefore been undertaken all over the country, to "master" the water system; the population of Kampuchea is constructing a vast network of dams, canals, and dikes intended to ensure the nation's prosperity. One sort of dam, the

---

[3] Hou Youn, "La Paysannerie cambodgienne et ses problèmes de modernisation" (Ph.D. diss., Sorbonne, 1955), pp. 7–17.

tomnop teuk, prevents chaotic flooding of the lowlands and stores excess water. By building these, floodlands such as the Boeung Snao, south of Phnom Penh, and the Chruoy Chang War peninsula have been protected against flooding and transformed into paddies. Another sort of dam forms huge *baray,* or reservoirs, which store irrigation water for use during the dry season. The country is crisscrossed by several types of canals. The radio seldom speaks of *prek,* or canals connecting the river with the hinterland; it more often mentions the digging of *pralay,* canals that link one pond to another to convey the water needed for irrigation.

To galvanize the people and stimulate their zeal for work, the radio issued detailed daily reports, until December 1975, of the projects being carried out in different regions. Broadcasts carefully specified the length, width at base and summit, and height of the dikes built; they mentioned the length and depth of canals and their width at top and bottom. Sometimes details were given of the number of cubic meters of earth that had been displaced, or the number of hectares irrigated or rendered arable by these schemes. The list of tasks completed is endless. To give one example among a myriad, on September 30, 1975, in the area of Ba Phnom (Prey Veng province):

> The people have built two very large dams and two canals. The dams are 372 meters and 1,100 meters long respectively; width at the top, 8 to 12 meters; width at the base, 20 to 30 meters; height, 2 to 8 meters. The canals are 24.5 and 26.6 kilometers long; surface width, 4 meters; width at the bottom, 2 meters; depth, 2 meters. To sum up, our production development solidarity group has labored to build 58 dams, 79 canals, 6 reservoirs, 70 ponds, and 26 wells.

Despite this impressive list, the radio hastens to add: "These achievements are already considerable, but much remains to be done." In one district mastery of the water was "only fifty percent, it must become one hundred percent," and in another place the radio said two hundred percent. "Now the rainy season is ending, we must think about saving water for the dry season and we must set to work without delay." Several times the radio announced that "we have altered the geography" of some canton, or "such and so region has a new face."

In 1976, the emphasis seems to have shifted to the construction of a dense network of smaller dikes and canals designed to blanket Cambodia with a checkerboard of rice paddies. The squares of the board measure between 500 and 1,000 meters on a side, and are separated by 10-meter irrigation canals. Each square is outlined by a small dike measuring 2 to 3.5 meters at the base, 1 to 2 meters at the top, and .8 to 1.2 meters high. Two intersecting pairs of parallel dikes 3 to 5 meters apart divide each square into 4 parts, and the space between the parallel dikes is filled by an irrigation canal. Each of the 4 squares formed by the parallel dikes is again subdivided by smaller mini-dikes into 16 squares measuring up to 100 meters on a side. Dikes and mini-dikes are "works of art" which should be "loved and cared for."

It is easy to see that the entire working population must be mobilized to take on a project of this scale. Building dikes and digging canals appear to be the main concerns at this time. Whether in a speech at a meeting to celebrate the adoption of the new constitution or during elections or in a harangue to the army or factory workers, the conclusion is always and obsessively the same: "We must hasten to build dikes and dig canals." During the harvest season in December 1975 and January 1976, the radio was urging the peasants to "hurry, get the rice in quickly, in good time, fast, so that we can continue building dikes and digging canals and thus move another step forward toward mastery of the water when the next rainy season begins."[4] From this we can see how Cambodia has become "one vast work site, where day and night have become one, and work continues without pause and without fear of fatigue, in joy and enthusiasm."

Slightly dampening this enthusiasm, Pol Pot, the premier of Kampuchea, told a group of Vietnamese journalists:

We have drawn up a plan to build a network of canals in the delta, which should irrigate about one and one-half million hectares. At present we have completed one-third of the program. However, in the

---

[4] Radio Phnom Penh (January 4, 1976).

area covered by that thirty percent we have still not mastered the problem of the water supply and we are still dependent on the rains. We
cannot pretend to forecast the results of our labor but we have made
every effort in this direction. We have not yet obtained any quantitative
results but we have launched a powerful agricultural movement and we
still have many difficulties to overcome.[5]

In the far-off days of Fou-Nan, at the beginning of the Christian era, the ancestors of the Khmers began draining the lower
Mekong swamps, which were later to become the fruitful Cochin
China. The sixth-century kings undertook to irrigate the higher,
dryer land in the Cambodian northeast; and between the tenth
and eleventh centuries the Angkor kings fulfilled their predeces-
sors' dreams by constructing a complete and highly efficient
irrigation system composed of huge *baray* eight kilometers long
and two kilometers wide. In those days it was possible to harvest
three rice crops a year to ensure the country's prosperity, but
foreign invasions destroyed the system and, in the end, the
Khmers almost forgot it ever existed. Prince Sihanouk tried to
encourage his people to rebuild the old hydraulic infrastructure.
He had part of the *baray* dug out again, along with a few canals,
and he launched the construction, subsidized by foreign capital,
of dams at Prek Phnaot and Bavel. He also created a voluntary
service organization for "work of national utility," i.e., dikes and
canals. He periodically embarked on new irrigation projects, but
the corruption and incompetence of the people responsible for
carrying them out often postponed their completion indefinitely.
Thanks to the efficiency of a Marxist power control, the people of Kampuchea are now making a thousand-year-old dream
come true.

The lessons of experience, however, seem to have brought
about a change of objectives toward the end of 1975. Until then
the ideal, according to the radio, was to produce two or three
harvests a year; but perhaps someone realized that at that rate
even irrigated soil would soon be exhausted. In any event the
emphasis has now shifted to improved yields per hectare and

---

[5] Vietnam News Agency (July 29, 1976).

higher quality rice. The goal now is to produce three tons per hectare. Abundant advice is given on how to "transform the soil quality" by using such natural fertilizers as the manure of buffalo, oxen, and pigs; guano; the dirt from termite hills; alluvial soil; human excrement; et cetera. Much advice is also given on the choice of seed: "Do not select seed like a rich man who wants only the best rice even if he gets little of it, but select it like the poor who care more about quantity than taste," the radio said on January 15, 1976. However, the different sorts of rice and their respective characteristics have been carefully described since the beginning of 1976. When a Chinese delegation came to Cambodia in December of that year, they congratulated the leaders in Phnom Penh for obtaining yields of two, five, and seven tons per hectare.

In addition to rice, which is held to be as primordial, people are also encouraged to grow many other plant crops, which are curiously called "military crops": bananas, soya, sweet potatoes, sugarcane, yams, sesame, sweet corn, et cetera. Daily accounts tell the number of hectares planted in different types of crops and the number of banana trees and sweet-potato plants, coconut palms, and so on, which have been set out. Industrial crops are also mentioned—although the word "industrial" is not used—such as jute, cotton, rubber trees, and mulberries (with hints on the breeding of silkworms). Banteay Srei may be given as a typical example:

In the canton of Banteay Srei the people have planted 225,545 yam plants, 1,689 sweet-potato plants, 32,196 banana trees, 1,217 coconut palms, 92,496 mulberry trees, and 8,892 cotton seedlings.[6]

Stock-breeding also receives its share of attention in editorials and reports:

The breeding of oxen and buffalo is very important:
(1)   as an aid to agriculture, to produce strong animals that can pull the plow and harrow. There may be a petroleum crisis in the rest

---

[6] Radio P.P. (October 24, 1975).

of the world, but we shall have nothing to fear. Oxen and buffalo can always transport our produce, with or without roads, on dry ground and in mud. With them, there are never any problems of batteries or gasoline;

(2) because every stable is a miniature manure-factory with which we can improve soil quality and increase the size of crops;

(3) because livestock produces meat which gives the people strength and enables them to raise their standard of living;

(4) because if there are many cows, there will be milk for the sick and children and girls;

(5) because if there are many oxen and buffalo we can export meat abroad, for every country needs meat.[7]

Complete instructions have been issued on the feeding and cleanliness of pigs and hygiene for their breeders.

"They need no rice, only balls of bran soaked in water and mixed with chopped banana stems." In raising pigs, people are exhorted to revert to traditional practices, but these are not specified.

Further advice has been given on raising chickens, ducks, and fish near houses and in canals and ponds. There has even been talk of using elephants to carry wood and as a means of transport in the forest. On December 29, 1975, the village of Teuk Chrey was raising "3,102 buffalo, 4,342 oxen, 2,093 pigs, 23,221 chickens, 2,417 ducks, 37 horses, and many other animals."[8]

In short, "Cambodia has everything necessary to raise animals. This will make possible our national independence-sovereignty and transform the lives of the people."[9]

While the achievement of independence-sovereignty accordingly depends chiefly on agriculture, which occupies the majority of the workers of Kampuchea, the authorities have not forgotten industry. "In the economic policy of Kampuchea, agriculture is the foundation and industry the dominant factor," Ieng Sary, deputy premier in charge of foreign affairs, told the seventh extraordinary session of the U.N. General Assembly in 1975.[10]

---

[7] Radio P.P. (October 13, 1975).

[8] Radio P.P. (December 29, 1975).

[9] Radio P.P. (October 13, 1975).

[10] *Bulletin du GRUNK*, p. 19.

Even though less stress is laid on industry than on agriculture, the rehabilitation of industry has definitely been launched. From the Thursday workers' broadcasts we can learn something of the factories now operating in Cambodia. Mention is made of textile factories in Phnom Penh that are making sampots (the long black gown that is the traditional dress of Cambodian women), blankets, mosquito netting, fishing nets, sewing thread, and clothing; and of the manufacture of soft rubber, bicycle tires, and automobile tires; of tire repairs, bicycles, electric batteries, paint, glass, soap, paper, orangeade, milk, soya oil, fish brine, bran oil, cigarettes, a sawmill, and so on.[11] At Battambang the radio mentions a jute factory and a textile mill.[12] In several districts there are semi-industrial textile works, for instance at Prey Chhor. Elsewhere, there are silk-weaving factories,[13] a fish-pickling factory at Kompong Ampel,[14] a saltworks at Kampot,[15] a small blast-furnace at Phnom Dek,[16] another on Mt. Aural, and a cement-works at Chakreytin;[17] but nothing more has been said of the petroleum refinery that was to have been repaired by the beginning of 1976. The reason for this may be a disagreement between the Cambodian authorities and the Chinese experts who allegedly agreed to repair the refinery on condition that Kampuchea would import crude oil from no country other than China and would supply a certain amount of refined fuel in exchange. For the sake of their fierce sense of independence, the present authorities would rather do without the refinery.[18]

The fighting men and women and the workers have had to clean up all these factories that were partially or entirely destroyed by the gang of the traitor Lon Nol. At present they are working to their utmost

---

[11] Radio P.P. (January 15, 1976).

[12] Radio P.P. (February 25, 1976).

[13] Radio P.P. (March 23, 1976).

[14] Radio P.P. (April 6, 1976).

[15] Radio P.P. (February 5, 1976).

[16] Radio P.P. (February 23, 1976).

[17] Radio P.P. (March 8, 1976).

[18] It is said to have been repaired anyway, then totally destroyed again in a raid by anti-Communist resistance forces in September 1976.

limits to serve the people in the achievement of independence-sovereignty and to help the country to become self-sufficient.[19]

According to refugees, many of the factories in Phnom Penh are being run by experts from mainland China. Others say that the people who formerly worked in the factories were understudied by soldiers from the revolutionary army for several months and then, around mid-December 1975, were ordered to leave and help with the harvest in the northeastern part of the country, after the young revolutionaries had become proficient enough to take over and run the factories themselves.

The Kampot saltworks are run by women soldiers, presumably because of the importance of salt in the Khmer diet.

Special mention is made on the radio of those employed in transport, whether road, river, rail, or coastal. As though to call attention to the fact that the communications network is of vital importance to the country, these workers are given particularly plentiful advice: they must take good care of the motors, pay attention to their cargo or load and to warehouse storing, avoid accidents so as not to jeopardize the good of the people, et cetera. We are even told that women, like men, drive trucks and are highly honored to do so. Most of the main routes are back in working order: beginning in June 1975, trucks and trains could bring material from the seaport at Kompong Som up to Phnom Penh, and the Poipet-Pursat railroad has been operating since December 1975, although the line is still unrepaired between Pursat and Phnom Penh.

"Since 1975," Pol Pot told Vietnamese journalists,

we have been busy with repair work and restoration to the exclusion of all else. We have not yet built any new factories. Under the old regime factories were dependent upon foreign countries for raw materials. We are trying to solve this problem. Our first consideration is for the factories whose products will serve the people and the agricultural establishments. As yet we have no intention of enlarging them.

---

[19] Radio P.P. (January 15, 1976).

Democratic Kampuchea is a long way from achieving its goal of self-sufficiency. It still has to have help from friendly countries. At the time of Prince Sihanouk's return to Cambodia in September 1975, the press announced a five-to-six-year billion-dollar interest-free loan from China in addition to a nonrepayable subsidy of $20 million to cover Cambodia's foreign-trade deficit.[20] The press agency's figure for Chinese aid is apparently high. It is generally thought that the loan was more likely to have been for $150 million, repayable in five years. We have learned from the radio that several commercial and economic delegations from China and North Korea spent lengthy periods in Cambodia in the early months of 1976.

The refugees confirm Chinese aid; one eyewitness who left Kompong Som on October 2, 1975, reports that beginning on April 27 of that year, the port was filled with Chinese ships unloading rice, cloth, drugs, gasoline, and machines. Many refugees have seen Chinese experts directing airplane repairs, irrigation projects, and railroad repairs. Korean experts have allegedly been sent as electrical technicians.

There is very little foreign trade as yet: in 1976, China delivered a large number of trucks, and Albania sent tractors, in exchange for rubber, coconuts, and wood. In December 1975, Kampuchea imported twenty-five thousand tons of salt from Thailand and sent wood, dried fish, and gemstones in return. The frontier smuggling which had replaced ordinary trade was curbed, and on August 30, 1976, the Khmero-Thai frontier was officially opened; at that time Kampuchea imported petroleum products, fabric, medicine, and spare parts for vehicles and pumps. Trade was interrupted following incidents on January 28, 1977, which caused bloodshed in some Thai border villages, and several Thai smugglers have been executed by the authorities in Bangkok.

Apart from 3,000 tons of rice exported to Laos in 1975 for political reasons, the export of rice has not been resumed on any substantial scale. In good years and bad, Cambodia used to export around 500,000 tons of rice; but in April 1977, Ieng Sary

---

[20] Agence France-Presse (September 11, 1976).

could offer only 100,000 tons to the governments of Malaysia and Singapore. And it was poor quality rice, thirty percent broken.

As for rubber, Pol Pot said in July 1976, that "our 1976 production plan includes the production, for export, of twenty thousand tons of crepe." And thirteen thousand tons actually were exported, to China and North Korea, during the first half of that year. In April 1977, on a trip to Kuala Lumpur, Ieng Sary asked the Malaysian government to help Kampuchea locate European outlets for its rubber; but its quality was too poor to find any buyers.[21]

During the second half of 1976 Cambodian diplomats sought to resume relations with some foreign countries, chiefly for economic reasons. In September 1976, Ieng Sary set out on a long international jaunt that took him, first, to Japan—a former colonialist country that had previously been damned on every side for flooding all the underdeveloped countries of Asia with its industrial products. Contracts were signed in the course of this visit, and in February 1977, Kampuchea was understood to be importing ten thousand tons of finished iron and steel products from Japan. At the end of 1976 North Korea gave further assistance to Kampuchea, in addition to the technicians already working in the country. On December 25, 1976 new trade agreements were signed with a Chinese delegation. In January 1977 the Yugoslav freighter *Hrvaska* left the port of Rijeka carrying 1,300 tons of goods, worth $3 million, bound for Kampuchea. This cargo, consisting mainly of tractors and mechanical equipment, was part of the economic aid promised to Ieng Sary when he visited Belgrade the year before.

In October 1976 Kampuchea opened a trading company in Hong Kong, called the Ren Fung Company, for dealings with non-

---

[21] The Cambodia of old exported forty-five thousand tons of rubber per year, representing over forty percent of its total exports; seven thousand tons went through Thailand in 1976, en route to Singapore. This would seem to indicate that Highway 4, which links Phnom Penh to its port at Kompong Som, is not safe for traffic. The importation of twenty-five thousand tons of salt from Thailand might indicate the same thing. Why have the Kampot saltworks failed to meet domestic demand as they used to do? Lack of skilled personnel? No fuel to transport the salt? Unsafe roads? All these are possible reasons, but hard to verify.

Socialist countries. Its purchases are made through a Chinese bank, the China Resources Company. In the last three months of 1976 it purchased $1 million worth of assorted goods: spare automobile parts, motor pumps, gunny sacks, electric generators, telephone equipment, pharmaceutical products, et cetera. Through the Ren Fung Company Kampuchea has also obtained four hundred tons of DDT, purchased from the Montrose Chemical Corporation of California and worth $450,000. The United States government granted a special authorization for the sale. In the first three months of 1977 the Ren Fung Company bought $3.5 million worth of goods, mainly from France, England, and the United States.

Despite this timid opening toward the outside world Kampuchea will not accept help from everybody: in 1976 OPEC was prepared to make the country a loan of 3.5 million petrodollars, repayable in twenty-five years, but found nobody to talk to on the Khmer side.

The economy inherited by Democratic Kampuchea had been totally devastated by the war. In proportion to its size, it was more badly damaged than any other country in Southeast Asia: in 1970 the South Vietnamese were so determined to drive out the Vietcong and North Vietnamese that they unhesitatingly demolished a large part of the economic infrastructure of the Cambodian territory. When it came the turn of the Americans, their flying fortresses heavily bombed the rubber plantations, last vestiges of the French colonial interests. The republic's soldiers were ill trained and oversupplied with ammunition, and, following their instructors' example, buried their own country under their bombs and shells. And the Khmer Rouge, with the zeal of the neophyte and their hard, pure flame, razed everything in their path that could in any way be connected with the West. The rage to destroy, on both sides, left an exhausted, bloodless country.

Under the vigorous drive of the Revolutionary Organization, Democratic Kampuchea hopes gradually to emerge from its poverty through efforts no less Promethean than those of the Angkor Wat period. Unlike Vietnam, which has skillfully contrived to take advantage of the widest possible range of international assistance, Kampuchea has preferred to curl up in its lair and lick its

own wounds. "You must rely on nothing but your own strength"
shows a sense of pride and dignity; but is it a viable precept for a
small country emerging half-annihilated from a disastrous war?

The Chinese revolutionaries also shunned help from the outside world; but China is a vast and overpopulated continent in
itself, with virtually limitless resources. Can this philosophy be
adopted wholesale by Kampuchea, which is barely one-third the
size of France and has a population of a few million, relatively
poor soil, and no mineral or industrial wealth?

An Army at Work

"The methodical organization of the dormant energy in the peasant mass will increase its efficiency a hundredfold and enable new land to be cleared, irrigated, and protected from flooding."

This was one of the prospects envisaged by Khieu Samphan in 1959, at the end of his study of his country's agriculture.[1] Long ago, the kings of Angkor had succeeded in mobilizing their people and by doing so brought their empire to the summit of its glory and power. Since April 17, 1975, the Khmer have again been mobilized, "under the just and enlightened leadership of the Angkar"; "they are conscious of entering upon a new period even more prodigious than the age of Angkor Wat."

The Angkar is the true prime mover of the Khmer revolution. Some refugees think the word for "organization" was chosen in preference to "party" because the people, reacting to negative propaganda which had presented the Communist party as a

---

[1] Khieu Samphan, "L'Économie du Cambodge et ses problèmes d'industrialisation" (Ph.D. diss., Sorbonne, 1959).

monster, might be frightened of the latter term. It would seem, however, that the revolutionaries chose "organization" because the word corresponds to their true objective. Insofar as the organization of the people has typified all Marxist regimes, which are essentially regimes of order, then "organization" is particularly appropriate to the regime in Kampuchea.

Like the kings of Angkor Wat, who were divinities incarnate, the anonymous Angkar is a new divinity to which the people are to devote themselves body and soul. Listening to the radio, one is struck by the expressions of almost religious respect for the Angkar, and by the use of terms more commonly employed in the language of Christian religions: the Angkar is "believed in"; it is "loved"; its "blessings" are "remembered"; it is "thanked for the good it has done us, for freeing us from slavery," for "resurrecting the national soul," for "freeing us from the scorn of the imperialists," for "making us masters of the factories and land"; "I respect and I love it"; "thanks to the Angkar, every day is a holiday"; "thanks to the Angkar, rice is beautiful"; "I sing thanks to it with all my voice"; et cetera. In one edifying tale a hero who is dying on a battlefield expresses the following parting sentiment: "I thank the Angkar, which taught me how to fight with ardor and to keep my anger ever keen against my enemies." Everything in Kampuchea is done "under the very intelligent, very enlightened, and very just leadership of the revolutionary Angkar." Everything is organized: water, earth, rivers, animals, and men. All must be incorporated into the harmonious plan of the Angkar, and all must contribute to the good of the people.

The new social categories can be learned from the radio broadcasts: there are "workers," "peasants," "fighting men and women," and "cadres." In the Chinese fashion, the new language distinguishes between "poor peasants" and "poor peasants of the lower middle class," but there is no means of discerning the basis for this distinction. Official texts often speak of "people," "fighting men and women," and "cadres" as though the last two did not belong to the "people." This is apparently the real line of demarcation in the new Khmer society, or at least the boundary among the new classes of an egalitarian society.

First, the people (*pracheachon*) are factory workers and peasants. Workers are always named first, though there are far fewer
of them than peasants; but this is presumably in conformity with
an international cliché. Everything must promote the good of the
people. Those whose behavior is detrimental to the people, and
even Khmer Rouge who make mistakes, are called "subpeople"
(*anoupracheachon*). This helps explain why the townspeople
were treated so harshly: they weren't really part of the people,
just as the cadres of the former regime could never become part
of it even if they were converted.

The basic cell of the people is the "group" (*krom*) of ten to
fifteen families, depending on the locality. It is run by a "group
chairman" assisted by a "vice-chairman" and a "member." The
chairman is usually appointed by the Angkar, but sometimes he is
elected by the group by show of hands. The refugees all agree
that these chairmen are ignorant men who seldom know how to
read or write and usually come from the ranks of the "old people."
Their role is to act as go-betweens, transmitting orders from
above to those beneath them and communicating their observa-
tions on the work and attitudes of the members in their groups to
their superior, the "village chairman." Their deputies draw up
lists of families, specifying the number of old, disabled, and
married people, young men, girls, and children. For this reason
the vice-chairman and member are chosen from among those who
can read and write.

A number of groups form a "village" (*phum*), the number vary-
ing widely from one place to another. The village is administered
on the tripartite model, run by the village chairman, who is usually appointed by the Angkar but occasionally by the villagers.
The refugees have observed that the village chairman is in many
cases an ex-drinker or former cardplayer transformed into a brute
by the Angkar, which has exploited his bad habits for its own
ends. The village chairman, or chief, collects information from
those under him, especially about people who have "ties with the
enemy" or are potential traitors to the revolution, and passes it on
to those above. This enables the Angkar to eliminate any soldiers
or officials of the former regime who may still be lurking unde-

tected. It is also the duty of the village chairman to transmit
orders to group chairmen and arrange political meetings involving the entire village and meetings of group chairmen, who then
convene the families in their groups. He issues written authoriza-
tions to leave the village and travel in the canton. He has two
deputies: a "village vice-chairman," whose job is to allocate the
tasks to be performed by the village and specify how they are to
be performed, and a "member," who is responsible for social
matters.

As before the Revolution, several villages are combined into a
"canton" (*khum*), again with tripartite administration, each of
whose members has similar duties. The *kana khum* or "canton
chief" has powers of life and death over the villagers under his
authority. Appointed by the Angkar, he metes out punishment to
wrongdoers brought in by village chiefs or denounced by the
chhlop, or "spies." He runs the Angkar Leu, of which villagers are
so terrified because the summons to appear before it usually
means death. In theory, he should consult his own superiors before
executing anyone, but he often does so only after the sentence has
been carried out. The atmosphere of tranquillity or terror reign-
ing among the villagers depends to a large extent on him. In
addition to his deputies for economic and social affairs, he has
another for military matters and numerous cadres performing
various functions.

Cantons are combined into "sectors" (*srok*), which seem to
coincide with the traditional administrative divisions. The radio
continues to call them by their former names, but the refugees
say they are also designated by numbers. Their authorities, also
tripartite, are said to be former officers of the revolutionary army.

Since the Revolution a new administrative unit has appeared,
the *damban*, or "district." This has replaced the traditional
"province" (*khet*) but the boundaries are not the same. Each is
called by number, in military fashion. Damban 5, for example,
includes the sectors of Sisophon, Thmar Puok, Preah Neth Preah,
and Phnom Srok, and its capital is Sisophon. The radio does mention provinces as well, but now this means a geographical region
and not an administrative entity.

The whole of Kampuchea is divided into six "areas" (*phumpheak*), designated by terms for the main directions of the compass—Oddar (north), Bophea (east), Bachim (west), Eysan (northeast), Nirdey (southwest), and Peayap (northwest). They are administered by "regional chiefs," who are veterans of the revolution. In addition to these areas, there are five "autonomous districts" (*svayat*): Kratie, Preah Vihear, Siem Reap, Oddar Mean Chey, and Kompong Som. The capitals of the areas and autonomous districts are not the same as those of the former provincial regions, all of which have been evacuated. For instance, the capital of the northwest area is not Battambang but Thmar Kaul. This change has been confirmed by the radio broadcasts announcing the results of the elections on March 20, 1976: the large towns no longer exist. The areas and autonomous districts receive their orders from the "central committee" (*kanak machim*) of the revolutionary Angkar.

In addition to this administrative reorganization, the country has also been restructured in terms of production. The population is organized into "forces," which consist of "cooperatives" (*sahakar*) or "unions" (*sahachip*) on "work sites" (*karathan*) or "state farms" (*kasethan*). Each category of producer has a specific mission, depending on age and capacities.

Leaving out children under fourteen, who are still at school, the Khmer people are divided into three forces:

The "first force" (*kamlang ti mouey*) is composed of every unmarried person over the age of fourteen. These are the "elite labor troops" or "most streamlined force."[2] In every village they are divided into a "young men's group" and "young women's group" headed by a chairman or chairwoman, vice-chairman or -chairwoman, and member. These groups nominally work for the village, but sometimes as separate units. They often work on community projects or on the state farms; in the latter case they may travel far from their families and villages and stay away as long as several months. They are also called "mobile troops"

---

2 Radio Phnom Penh (February 11, 1976).

(*kang chalat*), for they are officially attached to nothing but the Angkar, which can use them according to its needs.

The "second force" (*kamlang ti pir*) consists of married people with children, or "people of middle age," as the radio calls them. "They perform everything the Angkar asks of them with great energy, men and women alike; whatever the men do the women can do too."[3] Women beyond the seventh month of pregnancy or those with infant children work special hours. In many areas the men of the second force are also said to be sent away from their families and villages for three months of hard work, cultivating or harvesting. They return home for a day or two and then leave again for some other task.

The "third force" (*kamlang ti bey*) is composed of "elderly men and women"; it is also known, oddly enough, as the "young-old" (*youveachas*). Like every other unit, it is divided into men's and women's groups with a tripartite authority structure. While the young and adults are working in the rice paddy, digging canals or building dikes, the old folks "sit in the shade under the trees or near the shelters [*ktom*] and plait ropes and weave hampers and winnowing baskets with joy and skill and a high degree of enlightenment."

The old women "devote all their efforts to tending the small children, preparing rice and water for them and seeing that they sleep properly." To educate the youngsters, they tell "short heroic tales, to develop the children's revolutionary spirit."

The old folks like to say that "it is a great honor to live in revolutionary Cambodia."[4]

Each group of families, or village, is or forms part of a cooperative. "The cooperatives made a powerful contribution toward winning the war. Since the victory they have played an important part in building up the economy and it is thanks to them that we had such fine rice at the last rainy season. After the harvest, the task of our cooperatives during the dry season is to launch an offensive to build new mini-dikes."[5] These cooperatives have

---

[3] Radio P.P. (February 11, 1976).
[4] Radio P.P. (October 17, 1975).
[5] Radio P.P. (January 23, 1976).

recently been transformed and it is difficult to know exactly what is meant by the term now. In their Ph.D. dissertations in economic science Hou Youn[6] and Khieu Samphan[7] advocated the creation of "mutual assistance groups" which would later be superseded by "high-level [i.e., semi-Socialist] cooperatives" and "cooperatives for the provision of supplies and for selling."

Until 1973, mutual assistance groups (*krom pravas day*) were functioning in the "liberated" zones; their object was to rationalize mutual aid among the peasants in working the fields, especially during cultivating and harvesting. In these groups, only labor was pooled. Then it was decided that work would be communal always, not just at certain times.

Around 1973 "low-level cooperatives" appeared, in which the peasants began to pool their means of production as well—land, oxen, tools. "The peasants contribute their plot of land and organize the work in a system of united leadership. The land and means of production remain the peasants' property but are placed at the disposal of the cooperative for use by all."[8] This form of organization was intended to achieve a more rational use of land and higher productivity. Each cooperative was also required, as directed by the Angkar, to take part in the war effort and the country's reconstruction, in accordance with planned needs.

Around 1974, in part of the "liberated" zones, and in October 1975 in the "new people's" villages, these cooperatives were transformed into high-level cooperatives in which all means of production were pooled and the harvest belonged to the cooperative, which distributed it according to the deserts and needs of every individual. In these there was no longer any private property, but families still preserved some measure of freedom in the arrangement of their meals. This relative autonomy was also abolished in January 1976, when "communities" (*sahakum*) were set up: food is no longer distributed, meals are eaten communally,

---

6 "La Paysannerie cambodgienne . . ." (Sorbonne, 1955), pp. 248–54.
7 "L'Économie du Cambodge . . ." (Sorbonne, 1959), p. 274.
8 "La Paysannerie cambodgienne . . ." (Sorbonne, 1955), pp. 251–52.

and the only thing that belongs to anybody outright is his physical strength, which he contributes to the cooperative.

Until January 1976, cooperatives were called "production solidarity groups" or "solidarity groups for the construction of dikes and digging of canals." Thereafter the official name became "production cooperatives." It is hard to estimate the size of individual cooperatives, however; some refugees say that *cooperative* is only another word for the ten-family group mentioned earlier as the basic village unit, in which case the village would be the "group of cooperatives" mentioned by the radio. Three cooperatives would thus form a "small group"; four small groups form a "large group" of 120 families. Other refugees say that a cooperative contains 100 families, all of whom eat together. Still others think that the cooperative is composed of a thousand families. Whatever their numerical dimensions, however, cooperatives are all run by the same tripartite authority of chairman, vice-chairman, and member.

Since the high-level cooperatives came into being, agricultural activities have been rationalized and specialized. Some teams do nothing but plow, others harrow, others build fences, others make tools, others set out plants, and so forth. Each cooperative also has a depot where rice, material, tools, and all other things needed by the people are stored.

The chairman is often chosen among those from the most modest backgrounds; sometimes, if the cooperative is a big one, he is a Khmer Rouge. It is his duty to supervise the members of the cooperative, make certain that everything is scrupulously fair, and investigate the members' activities. In this task he is helped by the *chhlop*, whom he chooses himself in great secrecy. It is also his job to make arrangements for the rice, food, seeds, and plants which the Angkar orders to be grown, and to encourage the members of the cooperative to raise pigs, chickens, ducks, cows, and oxen, which are all common property. He also directs the censuses of livestock, fowl, and plantations in the different districts, whose results are so often and so proudly proclaimed over the radio.

Since the end of 1975 another sort of agricultural enterprise has begun to develop, the state farm. These are collective farms placed directly under the authority of the "district committee" (*kanak damban*), and their entire production goes to the state. On these farms tractors are used to work the fields; one refugee was a cadre in charge of all the vehicles on his *kasethan*. When mechanized resources give out, however, they are replaced by human tractors, as reported by one refugee among many: "In 1975, in Damban 5 [Sisophon], there were not enough tractors to finish the work on time, so all the buffalo and oxen in the region were called to speed up the plowing on the Sala Krau state farm ten kilometers from Sisophon on the Siem Reap road. At Chruy Sdao, in Damban 3, men had to replace oxen to plow and harrow." The district's Khmer Rouge soldiers work on these state farms, but so also do the mobile troops of young men and women who come to work for fixed periods.

In addition to the cooperatives and state farms, which appear to be the stable production units, the radio and the refugees give many details of work sites on which the majority of the population is now engaged in constructing communal works. On March 11, 1976, the radio gave a report on them:

Democratic Kampuchea is one huge work site; wherever one may be, something is being built. The people, children, men and women, and the old people of all cooperatives are enthusiastically building mini-dikes. At Chikreng, in Siem Reap province, almost twenty thousand people are united in an offensive struggle to build dikes with a positive and combative attitude and unflagging revolutionary dynamism. Today the dike-building sites are the front lines of the battlefield on which the struggle is being zealously waged, and the peasants of our cooperatives are striving to fight vigorously and without pause, day or night, to achieve the great leap forward and to solve the water problem for the coming rainy season.

The radio lists various other work sites along the main national highways: "work sites occupying four thousand to five thousand persons or up to several thousand workers." At Prey Chhor in Kompong Cham one site employs twenty-five thousand;[9] near

---

[9] Radio P.P. (March 4, 1976).

Pursat almost twenty thousand workers are digging a canal more than twenty kilometers long.[10] The list is very long.

Before daybreak, the radio says, the neighborhood of the work site resounds with the joyful cries of the peasants on their way to work. Their places of origin are mentioned; sometimes they come from scores of kilometers away, which explains the existence of camps. At 5:00 A.M. they start work in the place marked out for each group. And they work with joy, the blood-red revolutionary flag whipping in the wind and urging them forward "with extraordinary revolutionary courage of a very high level." They work from dawn to dark without a moment's thought of fatigue. "The earth may be hard as stone and the sun may burn, but nothing can stop the ardent war of production which consumes like a flame."[11] While they work, the children and young people sing revolutionary songs to encourage them. "Every day goes by in a holiday atmosphere"; "songs and shouts of joy ring out on every side."[12]

Working hours are no longer the same as they were at the end of 1975. From 5:00 to 10:00 A.M., during the cool of the day, the hard work is done; then from ten to three the workers weave baskets, plait ropes, and repair their tools in the shade under the trees. Regular work resumes at three and continues until after 6:00 P.M.[13] In some places generators have been installed so that work can go on at night.[14] Meals are eaten at the work site "to avoid wasting time." Never a day of rest; election days and the anniversary of the capture of Phnom Penh are the only brief moments of respite in this forcing process.

The work sites are all organized on a military model. In a radio interview one man described the setup at his work site as follows: "A committee of cadres is formed at district level, and it is responsible for the work site as a whole; then another committee of cadres is set up in each sector; then a third at the work site for the

---

10 Radio P.P. (February 19, 1976).
11 Radio P.P. (March 11, 1976).
12 Radio P.P. (March 24, 1976).
13 Radio P.P. (April 8, 1976).
14 Radio P.P. (April 30, 1976).

teams, groups, sections, companies, battalions, regiments, and even divisions. There are also chairmen of teams and groups who look after the workers' morale. For example, they see to their welfare and health, and supply whatever they may need."[15] Sometimes the young men and women work in independent groups of one hundred to two hundred, as at Kompong Chhnang[16] and elsewhere.[17] These are presumably the mobile troops mentioned by refugees. At the Angkor Borey work site in Takeo province, details of the "scientific allocation of workers" are given: "eighty percent are building dams, ten percent canals and mini-dikes, and ten percent manufacture tools, prepare food, and provide medical care."[18]

Every evening the workers meet in groups "to reflect upon their lives" (*prachum cheavapheap*) and "learn from their experience at work" (*prachum dak pisaot*); "each person expresses his ideas." Every ten days the workers assemble for a joint meeting,[19] the size of which is not known. At these meetings such decisions are taken as "to build dikes which are neither too high nor too low, but just the right size."[20] Building them too high would mean a waste of time, loss of land, and lowering of soil quality. The object "is to make as many mini-dikes as possible and as quickly as possible before the rainy season, so as to advance one step further toward the mastery of the water problem. Next year we shall embellish and fortify the dikes."[21] The workers at each site hasten to complete their work in order to begin at a site somewhere else.

The regular meetings are supplemented by special occasions designed to galvanize the workers. In 1976, the elections on March 20 were the occasion for a fresh outburst of zeal, and, even more so, the preparations for the first anniversary of the liberation

[15] Radio P.P. (March 24, 1976).
[16] Radio P.P. (March 26, 1976).
[17] Radio P.P. (March 24, 1976).
[18] Radio P.P. (March 23, 1976).
[19] Radio P.P. (March 10, 1976).
[20] Radio P.P. (March 9, 1976).
[21] Radio P.P. (March 10, 1976).

on April 17, so that programs in progress could be completed in time for the celebration. This is in keeping with the peasant motto "Do as much work as you can, as well and as quickly and as economically as you can."[22]

Apart from the agricultural activities, which occupy the majority of the workers in Democratic Kampuchea, the radio divides the laboring population into "factory workers," "ministries," "revolutionary constructions," and "unions," but it is difficult to make out exactly what is meant by the last three.

The radio mentions various ministries—"industry," "agriculture," "commerce," "public works," "foreign affairs," "social affairs and health," "propaganda"—but it would appear that these terms simply designate the laborers and office workers who are employed in the corresponding fields but are not organized into any distinct units.

As far as the revolutionary construction projects are concerned, the radio uses the word *monti* (edifice) to designate hospitals, disabled veterans' homes and, occasionally, schools, and nothing else. There does not seem to be any special unit of labor here either.

About the unions the radio says absolutely nothing. The term is an old one, but was seldom heard on the air before March 1976. It probably refers to the groups of industrial workers mentioned in the list of social categories to be represented in the People's Assembly before the elections of March 20: "factory workers, workers in river and road transport, on railways, docks, rubber plantations, in mines and saltworks and fisheries." On the radio, the word has been specifically applied only to the "workers on rubber plantations"[23] but nothing more has been said about the internal organization, role, objectives, or leaders of these unions. Like the cooperatives, their purpose is undoubtedly to achieve a higher degree of rationalization of labor and control over workers.

We know from the radio that the aim of all factory activity

---

[22] Radio P.P. (March 24, 1976).
[23] Radio P.P. (May 25, 1976).

should be to help the peasants grow rice; by providing them with the equipment, tools, and clothing they require, factory workers "are raising the standard of living of the people." Most workers in all branches of industry also perform some type of agricultural labor. Those in the Battambang textile mills "cultivate 195 hectares of rice paddy, plant vegetables on all available land near the factory, and spend part of their time building dikes."[24] Is this a first step toward Chinese-style people's communes? Some, on the other hand, do nothing but their own special type of work; this is the case of the "weavers of sarongs, who labor to meet the needs of the union and produce goods for barter with other cooperatives."[25]

A radio broadcast on June 2, 1976, gave information about the intensity of "political, cultural, and technical education" in a textile mill in Phnom Penh:

> Every evening the workers meet in teams to learn from the day's experience and look for weaknesss in their working methods, so that they may do better in future. Every four days they meet in groups and every ten days in branches [*phnaek*: units performing particular types of work in a factory], to awaken the workers' political consciousness and thus give them the strength to perform their tasks. One day a month, all the workers in the factory meet for a full day of political thought and discussion.[26]

The same broadcast mentioned that "a school has been built in the factory to teach children and fellow workers who had not been able to learn about politics, culture, and techniques before."

Health-care facilities are beginning to exist for the working population. A hospital and maternity clinics have been set up in every canton, with "a team of men and women fighters in the

[24] Radio P.P. (February 26, 1976).
[25] Radio P.P. (March 10, 1976).
[26] Radio P.P. (June 2, 1976).

social field." "The social work and health services of the old imperialist regime and those of today are as different as sky and
earth." It used to be that only the rich could obtain treatment, by
bribing doctors and nurses; but today "the men and women fighters in the social field, all sons and daughters of the poor, want to
serve the peasant people and give them ever more strength so
they can work and build dikes." The Angkar has trained nurses in
the field, "educating them in politics, mental attitudes, obedience,
the study of culture and literature, and science, as well as in
medical matters."[27]

"They are trying to invent new medicines, searching out raw
materials locally, and performing experiments." "Using plants,
roots, and the bark of trees, they are applying our ancestral customs to the manufacture of new medicines," and have already
discovered and manufactured "seventeen sorts of injections and
twenty-two sorts of pills to treat dysentery, malaria, and various
fevers." In June the radio even announced the manufacture of an
anticholera vaccine. "Medicines are becoming increasingly scientific."

Hospital teams work in constant rotation. "One team is in
charge of the kitchen, another gives injections, another makes up
prescriptions, another gathers wood, another draws water; and
others are engaged in production work so that the hospital may
be self-sufficient. The people are the point of departure in all
their work and research, and they devote themselves night and
day to the service of the people." "They do not simply wait until
patients come to them, as did the doctors in the old regime, but
go out themselves to the work sites assigned to them, where they
work just like everybody else while treating people in need."

The refugees confirm some of these assertions: there are indeed
a fair number of hospitals in the countryside, but they are of two
kinds. One is for the army, and these are relatively well stocked
with European medicines collected from the shelves of the drug-
stores of Phnom Penh when the city fell. But the trouble is that

---

[27] Radio P.P. (April 4, 1976).

few nurses can read either Russian or any European language, so they have to ask the few schoolteachers around for help in translating dosages. The hospital at Mongkol Borei, one of this type, is very well run and has a European-trained doctor.

The other kind is for workers only. It is true that there is one in every canton. They are shacks with thatched roofs and not enough room for their patients. The sick are cared for by a few nurses chosen from among the deportees. A recent refugee, one such nurse gives the following account:

> In the hospital where I worked there were about three hundred patients. It was a hospital in name only, because sick people were brought there so that their families wouldn't waste time looking after them instead of working. The only medicines came from the traditional pharmacopoeia. Large numbers of patients died every day. The twenty or thirty people running the hospital both cooked the rice and carried away the corpses to bury them.

This witness relates that the inexperienced nurses often broke off hypodermic needles in the patients' flesh. Moreover, injections often caused abscesses.

Keum Chaom, a doctor from Pailin, worked the land as a peasant for months. Once his true identity became known the Angkar instructed him to manufacture medicines from roots, bark, and sweet potatoes. He had to gather the potatoes himself, grind them up, dry them, and mix them with bark to make little pills. He found this even more exhausting than working in the rice paddies. This is not an isolated case. Many others mention coconut milk being used for glucose serum; and two liquids, which were used for injections—one brown and the other white—were kept in fruit-juice jars and served as remedies for every ailment.

Some refugees also speak of medical or surgical experiments being performed on a few deportees, but this has not been confirmed. Others mention the use of human bile removed from executed persons, for bile is a component of many medicines in the Khmer pharmacopoeia.

The Khmero-Soviet Friendship Hospital in Phnom Penh has become the April Seventeenth Hospital. Doctors Di Phon and

Thiounn Mum treat soldiers there, with the help of Chinese physicians. The Calmette Hospital has been turned into a pediatric hospital, but other hospitals and clinics have now been closed.

In the interview mentioned before, Pol Pot gave the following account of the health situation to the Vietnamese press:

> Malaria is our primary source of concern. To our knowledge over eighty percent of our working force is infected. During cultivation, and even more at harvest-time, many country people suffering from malaria became totally unfit for work. We have founded hospitals and quite a few health stations, both during and since the war. The level of health personnel, however, is still low. We do not have enough medicine. We have manufactured traditional remedies but they are not very effective. The importation of pharmaceutical products, on the other hand, is limited.

Ieng Sary painted a similar picture on a visit to Tokyo in September 1976; at that time also, more than eighty percent of the peasants were suffering from malaria. "We hope," he said at the end of his talk, "that by the end of the three-year plan now about to begin we shall have succeeded in eliminating this scourge."

In 1976, this imperative need drove the authorities of Kampuchea to accept twelve thousand dollars worth of aid in the form of antimalaria drugs from the American Friends Service Committee, and it was this body that compelled the country to negotiate with the United States and France for four hundred tons of DDT and the ingredients for manufacturing antimalaria medicines. The refugees who left the country in 1977 report that the "old people," at least, were being given Chinese-made quinine tablets.

If the workers and peasants of Kampuchea, thus organized, form the "flesh and blood" of the people, the army, with its men and women fighters and its cadres, is the backbone. The army, moreover, is the model on which the whole of Khmer society is gradually being fashioned.

The three categories of the Kampuchean Revolutionary Army—regular, regional, and guerrilla—form an army of the people made up of men and women fighters and cadres who are the children of the laborers, peasants, and other working people. They defend the power of the people of independent, unified, peaceful, neutral, nonaligned, sovereign, and democratic Kampuchea, which enjoys territorial integrity, and at the same time they help to build a country growing more prosperous every day and to improve and develop the people's standard of living.[28]

The regular army of "elite troops" are also called "regional" or "central" troops by the refugees. Their orders are to take action whenever and wherever needed: to put down local uprisings, protect frontiers, et cetera. They wear olive green, are the best equipped and best fed of the three groups, and do not perform agricultural work.

The second tier, or regional troops, ordinarily stay within their district or sector, under the authority of local chiefs. Every district has at least two battalions commanded by a "chairman," "vice-chairman," and "councillor," or political representative—and it is he who actually wields the power. These troops are dressed in black and are usually less well armed than the regular troops. They are responsible for security within their assigned territory, and for the protection of local authorities. They also work the land; these are the troops who cultivate the "Angkar's land," or nationalized farms.

The guerrillas, or "spy troops" (*kang chhlop*), are villagers, young and old, male and female, and have neither arms nor uniforms. Their duties are to observe the behavior of the other villagers and report to the Angkar. Little by little the villagers learn who is a *chhlop*—often some highly virtuous person who sets a good example for a few hours and then withdraws, leaving the rest to continue. The *chhlop* are responsible to the village political or military authorities, but they do not meet openly. It is through them that the Angkar manages to be so well informed, rather than the autobiographies which people had to write several times over during the first few months after the liberation. In the colorful words of one old revolutionary soldier, the *chhlop* are

---

[28] *Constitution of Democratic Kampuchea*, Article 19.

the means by which "the Angkar has eyes like a pineapple and sees everything."

The organization of regular and regional troops varies little from region to region. At the 'bottom is the "group" of ten or twelve commanded by a "group chairman" who has two "team chairmen" and a "group vice-chairman" under his orders. The group chairman administers the unit and gives instructions to his three subalterns, who pass them on to their teammates. These three are usually "old people" whose role is to "follow tracks," or supervise, their teammates. There are no markings by which one can distinguish among the military; the only way to know someone's rank is by his weapon.

Three groups form a "section" containing from thirty to thirty-six men commanded by a "section chairman" who has political responsibility, a vice-chairman in charge of military matters, and a second vice-chairman in charge of supplies. The first plays the main part and is sometimes known as a "commissar"; the triumvirate may also be called a "commissariat."

Three sections make a "company," with the same authority system as in the section. Three companies form a "battalion." The battalion leader has a radio transmitter and is assisted by an "economic committee" of fifty persons and a command unit of from ten to twenty. Three battalions form a "regiment," three regiments a "brigade," and three brigades a "division." The refugees had little opportunity to frequent the upper echelons of the army, and can supply few details; it would seem, however, that the tripartite collegial command is the rule for all bodies directing any form of operations, and all the chiefs are recruited from the ranks of veteran revolutionaries.

The army is divided into a great number of scattered units, linked by "emissaries," whose role is often praised by the radio. During the war their perilous missions were performed by mere children, crossing back and forth through the enemy lines barefoot. Nowadays these liaison agents travel on bikes or motorcycles.

Army recruitment conditions vary with the region and moment. In some places no member of the "new people" is allowed to join the revolutionary army, and this appears to be a general rule as far as the regular troop units are concerned. In one district, only volunteers are taken; they must promise to devote themselves wholly to the service of the Angkar, relinquishing all family ties. In other places the Angkar selects: at Ta Pho, north of Sisophon, 88 out of 200 young people in the village were chosen, and at Tuol Ampel, near Maung, 110 out of 250. A refugee from Tuol Ampel claims that the Angkar was intending to recruit 100,000 young people in Battambang province alone. Their consent is a foregone conclusion: "If we don't accept, it is proof that we don't love the Angkar, therefore . . ." Another says he volunteered because that way he was sure of having enough to eat, and otherwise he might starve to death. Those chosen are from the poorest families, "the ones that can't make ends meet."

Military training is primarily ideological and moral but more intensive than that administered to the ordinary people.

The army's mission is "to defend and construct the country." "The soldiers carry a weapon in one hand and a shovel in the other," or sometimes a sickle; they carry a gun and they "fight on the dikes." "The army joins the people in transforming the country into a checkerboard of rice paddies and in harvesting the crops."[29] "The soldiers set an example at the worksites"; "to protect the revolution and the country, they keep their vigilance razor-sharp, as though they were sharpening a knife";[30] "they are loved by the people, who are their flesh and their blood, their father and their mother; they learn from the people."[31] "The highly courageous and extraordinary army" never has time to rest, its heroic battle continues unendingly for the construction of the new economy.

"The disabled veterans show their combative courage by devoting themselves to production work according to their abilities, inspired by a highly patriotic and revolutionary spirit." There are special establishments for them, such as the veterans' home near the state glassworks at Phnom Penh, which houses about a hundred persons. Each one works according to his capacities:

---

[29] Radio P.P. (January 1, 1976).
[30] Radio P.P. (April 17, 1976).
[31] Radio P.P. (February 22, 1976).

Those who are only slightly disabled work almost as much as other citizens, but remain close to the home. Those with only one arm or leg herd cattle and buffalo or weed the rice paddies. Those who cannot move about much joyfully perform small tasks within their ability, such as sweeping the courtyard, weaving bamboo baskets, planting vegetables near the home, feeding the pigs, chickens, and ducks with energy and diligence and a fighting spirit. Those who have been to school teach the children their alphabet, as well as adults and fellow soldiers who have not yet learned how to read or write.

In Democratic Kampuchea "the people are sovereign," "firmly grasping their own destiny"; the state administers and the Angkar directs.

On January 5, 1976, the *Constitution of Democratic Kampuchea* was approved, embodying the basic and sacred aspirations of the laborers, peasants, and other workers, and the fighting men and women and cadres of the revolutionary army. It is the fruit of the proceedings at the third National Congress held in Phnom Penh from December 15 to 19, 1975.

In pursuance of Articles 5 to 7 of the constitution, the people elected, on March 20, 1976, the 250 members of the "Representative Assembly of the People," allocated according to a novel system—not by geographical sector but by social category: there are 150 peasants' representatives, 50 for laborers and other workers, and 50 for the revolutionary army. Members are elected for five years, and they are "responsible for legislation and for defining the various domestic and foreign policies of Democratic Kampuchea."

To be eligible, candidates have to be at least twenty-five years old, have fought for the revolution without flagging or faltering, set an example of high morality, and have the support and approval of the people. Every candidate also has to be approved by the elections committee set up at the second congress (April 25–27, 1975).

In fact, all the candidates have to be military cadres or former soldiers. At the first Representative Assembly of the People, which was held on April 11, 1976, a warning was addressed to the newly elected members: "You are the people's representatives, but you do not belong to the class of leaders of the people forever, and you must live among the people."[32] As for the electorate: "Every man and woman over twenty-eight years of age who has committed no crime since April 17, 1975, whatever his or her previous social class, political or religious ideas, is entitled to vote, whether his or her liberation occurred before or after April 17."[33]

Refugees who left the country after March 20, 1976, have supplied a few details about the elections: in many villages only the fighters cast votes because "new people," still regarded as prisoners of war, had forfeited their civic rights. In other villages only part of the population was released from work to place in the ballot box a slip of paper bearing the name of a single candidate of whom they had never heard.

All the forces of the new Khmer nation are "organized" into a military society engaged in a continuing struggle, and in this way they are to overcome Cambodia's economic underdevelopment and bring about lasting happiness. As in the days when the king was the incarnation of Brahma on earth, the anonymous Angkar is the incarnation of the people's will. Since it has been transformed into a deity, it too can decide which is the path to true happiness. But does happiness imposed from without have any meaning?

---

[32] Radio P.P. (April 14, 1976).
[33] Radio P.P. (March 10, 1976).

SEVEN

"The Angkar Gave Me a Second Life"

"Man is the determining factor in the victory, and his political conscience is the decisive weapon." These are the words with which Ieng Sary explained the rapid military advances made by the Cambodian resistance movement since 1972.[1] This attitude applies to the construction of the new society as well: "We have not achieved any great results," observed Pol Pot in July 1976, "we have only launched a revolutionary movement within the people."

Revolution is primarily a matter of education. "In the present period our Revolutionary Organization sees it as its duty to give the people a firm foundation of mental attitudes, politics, and order."[2] During the first months of the revolution it may have seemed as though the ideological education of the newly "liberated" people was virtually nonexistent. The radio was almost

---

[1] Ieng Sary, *Cambodge 1972* (distributed by RGNUK), p. 7.
[2] Radio Phnom Penh (April 17, 1976).

never used as a means of propaganda; political meetings were not held regularly; and those who were unenthusiastic about the new order were offered no chance to mend their ways, but were physically eliminated. "Enemies have no right to education," some cadres told the urban deportees, who were beginning to fear for their lives.

The refugees themselves, however, have proved that the educational effort went deeper than appeared on the surface. Many of them speak the new revolutionary language, which closely resembles that used by the radio. And ideological training was very thorough for those in the army.

Above all, the "revolutionary spirit" requires a conversion. It is symptomatic that the Angkar's educational program aims primarily at building a new mentality, and is only secondarily concerned with politics. The radio often defines what is involved in this new mentality: "a spirit of combative struggle, economy, inventiveness, and a very high level of renunciation."[3] At the beginning of 1976, emphasis was placed most heavily on community-mindedness, service, responsibility, and vigilance. All these were components of the "revolutionary spirit" by which every initiative must be inspired, whether individual or collective, economic or military.

Priority has been given to the "spirit of combative struggle": life in Democratic Cambodia is an unending battle. "As we struggled to drive out the French and Japanese colonialists and, only recently, the American imperialists, we are now continuing the struggle to build and defend the country with the same revolutionary heroism."[4]

Workers, peasants, and revolutionary troops, firmly determined to achieve a very high level of independence-sovereignty, are launching an offensive to develop the economy and to build and protect the country. Just as they struck down the enemy and his lackeys in the time of the revolutionary war waged by our nation and our people . . . they are now resolved to launch another violent and relentless offensive. Our

---

[3] Radio P.P. (April 17, 1976).
[4] Radio P.P. (April 8, 1976).

workers are engaged in an unceasing offensive aimed at a very spectacular great leap forward. Our peasants are waging a continuous offensive to
achieve a very spectacular great leap forward. Our revolutionary troops
are also waging a permanent offensive aimed at achieving a very
spectacular great leap forward. The factories are waging an offensive
too; the rubber plantations are waging an offensive; all our cooperatives
are waging an offensive, struggling on the network of dikes and canals
so that there may be many of them in a very short time. . . . The people
in every district and every establishment all over the country are waging
an offensive, doing their duty for the sake of a very spectacular great
leap forward. All are waging the offensive and thereby achieving the
very spectacular victory of the great leap forward.[5]

This text, which is not an isolated example, shows the extent to
which the efforts of the Khmer people are being treated as a form
of warfare. Numerous other expressions are employed in this context of struggle. Now there are two battlefields: "the advanced
battlefield," which used to be the front lines where people fought
against human foes and has now been transferred to the work
sites, where the major community projects are being carried out;
and the "rear battlefield," which refers to all other kinds of work.
On these battlefields the words "struggle" (*prayot*) and "launch
an offensive" (*vay samrok*) are found in some rather unexpected
contexts:

"struggle to plant strategic crops"
"struggle to plow and rake"
"struggle to produce courageously"
"struggle vigorously to clear the forest"
"struggle to cultivate the rice paddy"
"struggle to defeat the water problem"
"struggle to build dikes and dig canals with great courage"
"struggle to catch fish"
"struggle against flooding"
"struggle to dredge out the alluvial deposits"
"struggle to solve the fertilizer problem"
"struggle to invent and manufacture medicines"
"struggle actively with a combative spirit."

[5] Radio P.P. (April 11, 1976).

The best form of struggle is the offensive: "launch an offensive for stock-breeding," "launch an offensive to develop production," "launch a rice-growing offensive," "launch a harvest offensive," "launch an offensive to make networks of dikes and canals," "launch an offensive to perform one's duty," et cetera. And, of course, "launch an offensive" means "work with combative zeal." A whole new vocabulary formed from the root *youth*, which means "war," has come into everyday use: "fighters," "comrade-fighters," "young-man-fighters," "fighting solidarity," "fighting activity," "strategic crops," et cetera. To listen to the radio, and even to the refugees, one would think that only fighters were working, or that everybody who works is a fighter.

The old words for "work" meant "perform an action" (*thveu kar*) or "seek food" (*rok si*). These venerable terms have now been replaced by "struggle" or "launch an offensive," used without objects.

Economic achievements are proclaimed as so many victories: "victory over flooding," "victory over the elements," "victory over nature," "new victory in the construction of the country," et cetera. In a routine account of the achievements of the "production movement of Banteay Srei canton," lasting five minutes and twenty seconds, the term "struggle" was employed in six phrases, "attack" in two, "victory" in one, "strategy" in three, and there were seven adverbial phrases expressing determination and military courage.[6]

This struggle is communal; it is waged as a "service," a concept that regulates relationships among members of the new society: youth, laborers, peasants, and military "serve the people, the revolution and the Angkar. . . . They serve the people by improving the standard of living, . . . they serve agriculture, commerce, industry." "They serve the movement of the great leap forward." The women working in the Kampot saltworks are conscious of "serving the Angkar, the people, the revolution, and their brothers and, in this way, of taking part in the building of the country."[7] The themes of service and community-mindedness

---

6 Radio P.P. (October 24, 1975).

7 Radio P.P. (March 17, 1976).

are played over and over in every key: "solidarity," "union," "participation." "The entire people, united in great solidarity, is participating in the construction of the country."

The spirit of responsibility, a corollary of community-mindedness, is also energetically encouraged. On the work sites where dikes and canals are being built the workers "have a highly responsible attitude"; in the factory, driving a truck, watching the frontier—everyone everywhere has the same responsible attitude because he knows that the country's future depends on each individual. "Take your destiny firmly in hand" is one of the slogans designed to mobilize the worker.

The spirit of responsibility in all things encourages a spirit of inventiveness in the worker. "Help yourself" is another of the guiding principles of the revolution. Examples of this ingenuity are legion: near Chhlong "the peasants are searching for new techniques to obtain a steady increase in rice production. They have converted a forty-horsepower gasoline motor to work with coal. Now it consumes one hundred kg of coal every ten hours and produces energy equivalent to fourteen horsepower, with which it pumps water from the river and propels it one thousand meters to irrigate one hundred hectares."[8]

In other places the peasants are irrigating by means of a train of buckets activated by bicycle chains, wooden pedals, or traction.[9] The peasants in Battambang have invented a threshing machine,[10] and elsewhere a machine for setting out rice plants and planting beans, maize, and soya.[11] They have made insecticides out of plants.[12] "Thanks to their inventive spirit the peasants are rapidly achieving mastery over wheat, the rice paddies, and water."[13] Nothing has any value unless it is invented or reinvented by the people. "There is no need to import machines built

---

[8] Radio P.P. (March 10, 1976).
[9] Radio P.P. (March 23, 1976).
[10] Radio P.P. (March 25, 1976).
[11] Radio P.P. (February 25, 1976).
[12] Radio P.P. (February 27, 1976).
[13] Radio P.P. (March 8, 1976).

in foreign countries; the only worthwhile ones are those invented by the peasants."[14]

Laborers in other fields are also inventing machines and production processes. Those in the Battambang textile mills have devised a small blast furnace so they can manufacture their own tools. They have transformed motors to make them cheaper to operate.[15] "With shrapnel from American 105-mm shells they are smelting very good plowshares."

This spirit of inventiveness represents a revolution in the traditional mentality. In the past, Cambodians were content to let Chinese and Vietnamese residents take all the initiative for technical innovations; but now the workers have become as ingenious as "the men and women fighting in the social field" who are running the hospitals: "they fight against what they do not know until they know it."[16]

Refugees relate the jeering boasts of the Khmer Rouge: "Soon we will be able to manufacture automobiles as beautiful as the American cars! Everybody will have one! We shall even invent a rice-eating machine!"

Experience is the basis for this inventiveness; all research is guided by it, agricultural, industrial, and medical—whence the importance of the daily meetings at which different groups pool their experience. "The people are the brain of the Angkar," as one young refugee puts it.

To contribute to community growth, everyone must also have a spirit of economy. Again, there are many examples. At the Battambang textile mills, paddy-ball is used as fuel to cook rice, thus saving firewood.[17] In the same factory, "old nails, which used to be thrown away in the days of the archtraitor Lon Nol, are now saved by the workers. They do not waste so much as a drop of oil: when the oil is changed in the machines, the old oil is filtered so it can be used again. Then the residue in the filter is

---

14 Radio P.P. (February 25, 1976).
15 Radio P.P. (February 25, 1976).
16 Radio P.P. (April 4, 1976).
17 Radio P.P. (February 20, 1976).

poured over old rags, which can be used to light fires. They wring out the rags used to clean machines, to recover every drop of oil left in them."[18]

This collective struggle, demanding a spirit of economy and ingenuity, further implies total renunciation. The radio makes frequent use of the word, but it is the refugees who explain what it means. It has three aspects: "renunciation of personal attitudes," "renunciation of material goods," and "renunciation of personal behavior." Renunciation of personal attitudes primarily means applying one's whole mind to one's mission or job without thinking of oneself, and finding joy in being a docile tool in the hands of the Angkar. "Out of a sense of renunciation you pay no attention to whether it is day or night, you take no account of your fatigue or the difficulty of your work." Renunciation of material goods means no longer being attached to anything—house, wife, or children. Renunciation of personal behavior means extirpating pride, contempt for others, and the tortuous thoughts of old. Making an individual decision can be severely punished, even by death.

A conversion like this obviously does not take place overnight, so "there must be revolutionary vigilance." Not only must the military who protect the country be vigilant, but so must the workers, peasants, and especially the cadres.

The future lies with the young: "the young people are building [i.e., educating] themselves more and more radically and solidly according to revolutionary ideals. As they learn, they reject the spirit of ownership and follow the ideal of the community. This ideal incites them to give up everything for the revolution, to respect the moral code, and show a high degree of economy and inventiveness."[19]

Political education becomes important only after this transformation of mentality has been completed. At one meeting, a young woman praised the generosity of the Angkar, which had at last given her an opportunity to receive a political education.

---

[18] Radio P.P. (February 25, 1976).
[19] Radio P.P. (February 2, 1976).

Workers and peasants labor "with a high degree of political enlightenment." "During the last thirty years this political enlightenment has enabled us to recognize our friends and identify our
enemies."[20]

The first step in a political education is to become aware of the
oppression during the time of the French and Japanese colonists,
followed by the American imperialists and their lackeys. The
structure of a large proportion of radio broadcasts is extremely
simple: In the past, under the regime of Lon Nol the archtraitor,
arch-corrupt one, arch-Fascist, and archdestroyer, you were oppressed, unhappy and never knew any joy; you were dispossessed
of your land by the military. Now you are masters of your
country, your land, your water, your destiny, and your factories.
Now you can achieve true independence-sovereignty!

This quality is a source of revolutionary pride for all workers,
both in field and factory: "For thousands of years the colonialists,
imperialists, and reactionary feudalists have dragged us through
the mud. Now we have regained our honor, our dignity; now we
smell good again!"[21] "By driving out the imperialists we have
liberated our country, we have retrieved the glory of our people,
recovered the unique quality of our nation, and acquired revolutionary pride."[22] "The imperialists, the capitalists, and feudalists
utterly destroyed our national soul for hundreds of years. Now
our soul has risen again, thanks to our revolutionary Angkar!"
"Workers, peasants, and soldiers know very well that they must
build up the personality of our country, and enhance its honor; that
they must exalt its glory and defend its pride and its soul by
defending and building up the country to gain true independence
and the happiness of the people."[23]

The workers' revolutionary pride gives them "unspeakable joy";
"they are as happy as if they had just been reborn."[24] All feel the
pride and joy of living in a historic time: "Long live April 17, the

---

20 Radio P.P. (March 23, 1976).
21 Khieu Samphan, Radio P.P. (April 15, 1976).
22 Radio P.P. (March 1, 1976).
23 Radio P.P. (April 17, 1976).
24 Radio P.P. (March 10, 1976).

day of the very spectacular victory, whose great consequences will be more far-reaching than the age of Angkor Wat." This line from the national anthem is reiterated in various forms in almost all revolutionary songs. On the occasion of the approval of the new constitution, speakers took turns celebrating the historic day: "Never, since we were born, have we had the honor to speak out, to express our ideas, to be the masters of our fate. This truly is a historic day and fills us with great pride."[25] "This is the first time in history that there has been such a surge of production";[26] "this is the first time in history that the people have been masters of the factories and the land";[27] "this is the first time in history that the people have had the right to vote";[28] "this is the first time in history that property has belonged to the community."[29] Therefore, the people can look forward to the future "with very great revolutionary optimism."

Until September 1976, the radio and cadres often referred to the "international revolutionary movement" and the "construction of socialism," but they never, contrary to the usage in eastern Cambodia between 1970 and 1975, claimed kinship with Marxism or communism. Local cadres did sometimes mention the "Khmer Communist party"; and "party celebrations" were held in Battambang and Angkor in 1975. But no official declaration has ever qualified the new regime in Kampuchea as "Communist." There was talk of "breaking down the class system" and "breaking the regime," but the words "dictatorship of the proletariat" and "class struggle" were never heard. Nevertheless, the radio lavished praise on the Chinese Communist party and its achievements, and on the leaders of Communist parties in other countries.

At the death of Mao Tse-tung the Khmer leaders sent sympathy telegrams to their Chinese counterparts. They exalted the pure line of Chinese communism, as exemplified in the class struggle and dictatorship of the proletariat, inherited from "Marx, Engels,

---

[25] Radio P.P. (January 5, 1976).
[26] Radio P.P. (February 21, 1976).
[27] Radio P.P. (March 16, 1976).
[28] Radio P.P. (March 17, 1976).
[29] Radio P.P. (March 26, 1976).

Lenin, and Stalin."[30] At a meeting in Phnom Penh on September 18, 1976, Pol Pot paid tribute to the memory of Mao Tse-tung as the "foremost master after Marx, Engels, Lenin, and Stalin."[31]

To be made effective, the new revolutionary mentality and new political enlightenment must be accompanied by a third element, which is training in "order." It is hard to know exactly what this third component entails, for the radio gives few particulars. According to the refugees it means blind obedience to the will of the Angkar: "Rain or wind, in sickness and in health, day and night, you must do, correctly and without complaining, what the Angkar orders you to do." That is what one revolutionary soldier learned during his training. The radio often repeats this instruction.

The different social categories—young, laborers, peasants—frequently express their determination "to perform all the tasks laid down by the Angkar." At the end of every meeting, whatever its purpose, the people proclaim their determination to work, out of loyalty and gratitude to the Angkar. "To thank the Angkar for the honor of being able to elect our representatives, we are all determined to push production growth to the utmost."[32]

The foundation for this unanimous loyalty and faith is the observance of the Angkar's commandments. The radio quotes the twelve revolutionary principles, and refugees fleeing the "liberated" zones in 1973 had already learned them. After the liberation of Phnom Penh, the Khmer Rouge soldiers guarding the French embassy would recite them every morning.

1. Thou shalt love, honor, and serve the people of the laborers and peasants.
2. Thou shalt serve the people wherever thou goest, with all thy heart and with all thy mind.
3. Thou shalt respect the people without injury to their interests, without touching their goods or plantations, forbidding thyself to steal so much as one pepper, and taking care never to utter a single offensive word against them.

---

[30] Radio P.P. (October 1, 1976).

[31] Radio P.P. (October 4, 1976).

[32] Radio P.P. (July 2, 1976).

4. Thou shalt beg the people's pardon if thou hast committed some error respecting them. If thou hast injured the interests of the people, to the people shalt thou make reparation.
5. Thou shalt observe the rules of the people, when speaking, sleeping, walking, standing, or seated, in amusement or in laughter.
6. Thou shalt do nothing improper respecting women.
7. In food and drink thou shalt take nothing but revolutionary products.
8. Thou shalt never gamble in any way.
9. Thou shalt not touch the people's money. Thou shalt never put out thy hand to touch so much as one tin of rice or pill of medicine belonging to the collective goods of the state or the ministry.
10. Thou shalt behave with great meekness toward the laboring people and peasants, and the entire population. Toward the enemy, however, the American imperialists and their lackeys, thou shalt feed thy hatred with force and vigilance.
11. Thou shalt continually join in the people's production and love thy work.
12. Against any foe and against every obstacle thou shalt struggle with determination and courage, ready to make every sacrifice including thy life for the people, the laborers and peasants, for the revolution and for the Angkar, without hesitation and without respite.[33]

To be master of the country and master of the revolution is to be engaged in a determined struggle for self-sufficiency and to show a spirit of creativity; it is to endure all hardships, to be conscientious, thrifty, and upright. This also means to show respect for freely accepted discipline and democratic centralism, and to love, defend, and respect the people. Finally, it means turning humbly to the people to learn, and sacrificing all to the interests of the nation and the revolution.[34]

In a program like this, people are subjected to unrelenting pressure. Life is an all-out battle against nature, the enemy, and the self. From it a new race of men should be born. But only by killing an old art of living compounded of freedom, tolerance, and respect for life.

---

[33] Radio P.P. (January 31, 1976).
[34] *Bulletin du GRUNK*, no. 207/75, p. 1.

EIGHT

"Uproot the Three Mountains"

On April 18, 1975, as I was on my way to the French embassy in Phnom Penh, I overheard an altercation between an older woman and a young Khmer Rouge. The woman was imploring the soldier, her hands joined together in the highly elegant gesture of Khmer courtesy. "Why are you putting your hands together like that, like the imperialists do? From now on nobody raises his hands to anybody anymore, because we are no longer slaves!" The poor woman lowered her hands and continued to implore. "*Dekkun*, give me permission to return home and get my child." This time the soldier became angry and refused point-blank, with a wave of his gun: "There aren't any more '*Dekkuns*'! We're all equal now, thanks to the Angkar!" *Dekkun* is a taboo word, because it means "power and favor": it was a courtesy title used by people in the lower classes when respectfully asking some boon of the powers of this world—administration, police, doctors, or bonzes. The poor woman hadn't yet learned that nobody had any more favors either to ask or to grant, and all Khmers were equal.

So the gracious Khmer greeting has been replaced by the ordinary European handshake, as a symbol of liberation. In the past no woman of modest status, whatever her age, would have dared to shake a man's hand; it would have shown a want of feminine modesty. Women in a certain class, who had contacts with Westerners, were beginning to shake hands with men, but always somewhat uneasily. But now women were "liberated" and had become the equals of men.

It is not just this simple gesture of courtesy that has disappeared; human relations themselves have been completely transformed by the revolution. The exquisite traditional forms of courtesy were accompanied by a highly complex linguistic code. There are no personal pronouns in Khmer; everyone designated himself and the people he was addressing by some appelative: "child," "father," "mother," "uncle younger than parents," "uncle older than parents," "sage," "potency-blessing," and so forth. These appelatives emphasized the ties of blood, the age, social rank, and quality of the person speaking and the person spoken to. They signified respect. For Europeans it was almost impossible to grasp all the finer points and not make mistakes when using these terms. But Europeans had the advantage of the indulgence with which the Khmers treated anyone they regarded as not belonging to their extended family. Any mistakes made among themselves, however, could lead to a serious quarrel. Now, ties of blood and levels in the social hierarchy have disappeared. The entire Khmer population consists exclusively of *met*, or "comrades."

This elimination of appelatives made journalists believe refugees' statements that all Khmer names had been arbitrarily changed. This was partly untrue. When a man enters the revolutionary army it is true that he must change his name, as though he were being born again. Henceforth, no one must recognize him, not even his parents. The leaders of the present government themselves use diminutives. A good many civil servants and soldiers in the old regime also changed their names to hide their identity, like one former minister who made his children recite their parents' new name, every night. And Khmers never minded changing their names anyway, even long ago. An ailing child took the name *"Chea,"* which means "cured," to foil the influence of evil spirits. Often parents did not even know their children's official names as printed on their birth certificates—which were only issued when needed, moreover, usually when the child first went to school.

It would therefore be wrong to draw too many conclusions about alleged changes of names;[1] but the abolition of appelatives, on the other hand, is of far deeper consequence: it represents a genuine egalitarian revolution, expressed in the new terms employed. Everyone is now known by the last syllable of his given name, preceded in popular usage by the term *met*. A man named So Sophin, for example, is now called Met Phin.

The radio, confirmed by refugees, calls the present period the "mom-dad period" (*samay poukme*), because all adults are called "Mom" and "Dad" by cadres and young, although it is not clear exactly why. People of the same age call each other "Junior Comrade" or "Senior Comrade" and adults call both their own children and those of others "Comrade Child," for all children are regarded as the infants of the Angkar.

This compulsory transformation of human relations shows a determination to bring about a radical metamorphosis of a whole culture.

> The culture of Democratic Kampuchea is of a national, popular, forward-looking, and healthful character such as will serve the tasks of defending and building Kampuchea into an ever more prosperous country.
>
> This new culture is absolutely opposed to the corrupt, reactionary culture of the different oppressive classes of colonialism and imperialism in Kampuchea.[2]

The desire to purify the culture has been expressed repeatedly:

> The young people of the towns are furious with the imperialists for leading them so far astray . . . that they had completely lost their national identity. The imperialists had misled them in order to turn them into good-for-nothings, a process typical of the *dépravée* and *fasciste*

---

[1] Cf. Jacques Ellul, "Un pas de plus," *Le Monde* (November 8, 1975).

[2] *Constitution of Democratic Kampuchea*, Article 3.

culture of the Americans and the traitors of Lon Nol's clique. In matters of fashion, a number of young men had even changed sex and wore their hair falling on their shoulders. Now they have woken up. They were slaves. Now there is no more prostitution, no more gambling, no more evil habits. The young are learning their knowledge from the workers and peasants, who are the sources of all knowledge. Besides, no knowledge can be higher, more worthwhile, or more useful than that which has to do with production, agriculture, industry, and the experiments and techniques of production. And this knowledge is possessed by the peasants and laborers alone.[3]

The passion for diplomas, which formerly drove young people to study, even when they had no purpose in view, has now given way to a more prosaic form of education: "It is the people alone who confer true diplomas." The cadres express their contempt for the old-style intellectual by saying, "Intellectuals are nothing but lazy good-for-nothings" and "Diplomas can't get you anything to eat!" They make a distinction between "paper diplomas," those of the old educational system, and "visual diplomas," the certificates of good conduct awarded by the Angkar after visually approving work accomplished. "The fountain pen of today is the hoe!"

Former school pupils and university students are actively engaged in building the country: "They are happy to live in the community of the people . . . to work, dig, and plant. They are proud to live with the workers and peasants, and take part in the construction of the country with their hands." "Nothing is more honorable or more dignified than to work building dikes. Nothing is more honorable or more dignified than to build and defend the country."[4]

Children's education begins early, with the revolutionary tales told by the old women who rock them to sleep.

In the cooperatives, factories, and revolutionary establishments children follow a cultural and literary program. Beginning at the age of six, all attend the special children's establishments to learn how to read and count. After they reach the age of twelve, they are gradually introduced to politics. They learn to love their country, to hate the Americans,

---

[3] Radio Phnom Penh (February 21, 1976).
[4] Radio P.P. (March 26, 1976).

and to love the workers and peasants who are their moms and dads. The children of the cooperatives are revolutionary artists; they sing songs and perform communal revolutionary dances, with purity and in the traditional manner, aimed at furthering the expansion of the country. They are filled with fighting energy, as befits the dignified civilization of our people.[5]

Other broadcasts announce that the entire population learns to read and write in the evenings after work. The refugees who left the country before the beginning of 1976 saw very few schools in the areas through which they passed, but those who have come more recently say that children between the ages of six and twelve form "children's groups" with a tripartite authority-structure like those of their elders. They meet every day to study somewhere in the village, and return home in the evening. If the school is very far from their home they only see their families once a week and sometimes less. Their parents no longer have any authority over them; they can never offer any criticism, much less strike them. On the contrary, they are to honor their children, whose spirit is pure and unsullied by the corrupt past of the adults.

When they come home from school, the children talk very little to their parents, and then only in monosyllables, as though they feel no need to communicate with them. Most of their studies revolve around revolutionary songs and dances, for reading and writing are not "necessary for the proper cultivation of the earth."

The Angkar calls upon the children, who are the "hope of the nation," to assume responsibility and make their contribution on the "rear battlefield." Their share in building the country may take a thousand forms: feeding chickens, ducks, and pigs, taking the buffalo and cows to pasture, weeding the rice paddies and plants, watering newly sown patches, destroying pests among the seedlings, taking care of the mini-dikes, carrying earth to build dikes or wood and cow dung for fuel, making cages for pigs and chickens, removing the pig manure to make fertilizer.

During the war some of them bore arms like their elders, and

---

[5] Radio P.P. (April 9, 1976).

transported ammunition on bikes or in rowboats; now they are engaged in a different battle, their country's reconstruction. "They never quarrel, they love working with their hands more and more every day." "Under the enlightened guidance of the Angkar the children are acquiring political awareness and marking a new phase in the revolution. It is a great honor for them to live in the new Cambodia." In some cantons the children study in the morning and work in the afternoon; on the plantations they spend the first part of the day picking up rubber-seed to make soap or weeding new plantations; then, "after three o'clock they study their letters and numbers."[6]

Despite this nonintellectual and almost exclusively peasant-oriented education, there is a distinct and striking tendency in the new Khmer language to make increasing use of abstractions or "noble" expressions of scholarly origin. Some of the new words come from the Marxist ideological panoply: "cadres," "sovereignty," "collectivism." Others have been adapted to serve the needs of abstract propaganda: "awareness," "pride," "community," "government." Scholarly words previously found only in the writings of the literati have also come into common use and are found alongside folk expressions and the redundancies so dear to the Khmer tongue. A whole vocabulary from remote country districts has replaced the more refined phrases of urban *savoir-vivre*: the word *hop*, for example, has supplanted a host of terms designating the act of eating, with all their shades of meaning determined by the age and social condition of the persons concerned and the respect felt for the person addressed.

Out of consideration for the people, several of the former terms describing persons have been replaced by loftier expressions: *pracheachon* (a people of citizens) has supplanted *reastr*, which meant "a subjugated people"; *srey* (girl) has yielded to *neary* (young lady). *Khmeng* (child) and *pros* (boy) have disappeared and their places been taken by high-sounding words such as *komara* and *komarey* (children) and *boras* (man). Also, the people no longer sleep, they "rest" (*samrak*).

---

[6] Radio P.P. (October 1, 1975, and October 10, 1975).

The use of foreign languages, of course, is strictly prohibited, but for "meeting" and *fasciste*, oddly enough, no equivalent in Khmer has yet been found.

The transformation of the language has been astonishingly rapid, and many refugees continue to use the new expressions even after their arrival in France. This new vocabulary will undoubtedly help to bring about a deeper transformation in the Khmer mentality.

Similarly, the traditional arts of dancing and theater have been radically altered. The dance has adopted warlike Chinese rhythms, and songs broadcast over the radio leave no room for either poetry or repose.

Marriage customs are a reflection of a people's culture. Official writings do not mention them, and refugees' accounts differ widely on this point, presumably because of variations in regional practice. It would also seem that customs of the army differ from those of the people in this respect. Some refugees say that the age of marriage is fixed at twenty or twenty-five for girls and at twenty-five or thirty for men, but these do not seem to be general rules. The restrictions undoubtedly apply to fighting troops, however, as many military leaders are unmarried.

Marriage ceremonies are said to have been held for military heroes and disabled veterans who had arbitrarily chosen wives from among the girls deported from towns. If this did occur, it was not a usual thing. Accounts more often refer to individual soldiers who exert pressure on the parents of the girl they want to marry (by offering small gifts); and it is hard to refuse anything to a man holding a gun. Sometimes girls move in with a man and claim to be married in order to avoid being paired with a soldier they don't like. Some have committed suicide.

Among the people, on the other hand, young men and women are equal and free to choose their mates. If a boy wants to marry a girl he applies to the chairwoman of the village girls' group, who transmits his request to the girl and brings back her reply. If the initiative is taken by the girl, she submits her request to the chairwoman of her group, who passes it on to the chairman of the boys' group of which her chosen one is a member, with instructions to give her his answer. Parents are no longer consulted, as they used to be, because every individual is "master of his body; no one is superior to anyone else." When at least ten couples have gone through these formalities, the canton chief sets the date and place for a communal wedding. On that day the canton chief and chairmen and chairwomen of the various girls' and boys' groups offer their good wishes to the newlyweds, who are then bound by an indissoluble tie. A refugee bonze relates what he can recall of the speech pronounced on one such occasion: "Comrades being married today: you consent to be responsible each for the other, as husband and wife, as long as you live. Help each other to serve and walk in the path laid out by the Angkar, without faltering, until the end of your days."

Then the couples eat a rice soup together and everybody goes back to work.

The religious aspect is not the least significant part of the cultural transformation being brought about by this revolution.

Although most Buddhist temples have been destroyed, the temples at Angkor Wat are still being kept up. Sometimes visiting dignitaries are taken to see the great ruins.

In its innermost recesses, the Khmer soul is populated by the gods of Hinduism and animism, but since the fourteenth century Theravada Buddhism (the Little Vehicle) has left deep marks on Khmer society and sculpted the soul of the people. Until April 1975, the word for "race" and "religion" was the same, and in everyday language "Khmer" implied "Buddhist." In his search for some common denominator into which he could assimilate people of different tendencies, Prince Sihanouk actually thought of founding a "Buddhist socialism." Among the educated, however, religion had lost much of its influence. When the constitution of the 1972 republic was being drafted, many intellectuals and parliamentarians objected to Buddhism being maintained as the state religion, but in vain.

Article 20 of the *Constitution of Democratic Kampuchea* stipulates that:

Every citizen of Kampuchea has the right to worship according to any religion and the right not to worship according to any religion.

All reactionary religions which are detrimental to Democratic Kampuchea and the Kampuchean people are strictly forbidden.

In the eyes of the revolutionaries, Buddhism is apparently a reactionary religion: with its goal of inner purification through detachment from all worldly passions, the Buddhist Way might easily lead to passivity and a lack of enthusiasm for the collective construction of the country. And the Buddha's teaching that the world is only an ephemeral appearance could incite people to seek harmony with the cosmos rather than mastery over it. Also, Buddhism in Cambodia carried the heavy weight of a sacred tradition.

Following the example set by the succession of authorities which have governed Cambodia, the revolutionaries began by borrowing Buddhist precepts to justify their own ideology: "The Buddhist religion teaches us to rely on our own strength without waiting for saviors from without." " 'Help yourself by yourself' is one of the teachings of Buddha!" "All men are equal; princes and the powerful must purify themselves no less than the rest of the people." This sort of propaganda was directed toward the government zones at the beginning of the war.

But after the victory of April 17 the mood quickly changed. On the day Phnom Penh fell, the bonzes in the capital left for the countryside, each carrying his own suitcase or pack. Never before would a Khmer have consented to let one of the "venerable" carry his burden himself; it was the duty of the faithful to earn a few credits by assisting the man of God. But since April 17 the man of God has become just another man.

In the ensuing weeks, a number of bonzes were killed. Among the most noted were Samdech Sangh Huot That, leader of the Buddhist community of the Mohanikai sect, who was executed at Phnom Penh, and the venerable Krou Thomabal Khieu Choum, who was killed at Kompong Chhnang. He was noted for his opposition to Lon Nol, and famous for his plans to modernize Khmer Buddhism. Samdech Preah Vannarat, leader of his region's bonzes, and his assistant Preah Krou Siri Settakaev Sangh were executed at Battambang: "On April 24," says Bandet, a twenty-four-year-old former bonze who subsequently became a Khmer Rouge cadre and then a refugee, "the soldiers came and asked the two dignitaries to go to Phnom Penh to welcome Prince Sihanouk. They were killed at the city airport. At Maung the soldiers also executed two bonzes, one of whom was chief of the pagoda, because they had too much influence over the people." Although several other instances have been reported, killing of the bonzes does not seem to have been a general practice. But just as the revolutionary authorities decapitated the republic's administrative and military structure, so they crippled the clergy by eliminating its leaders and the most influential bonzes. The rest were collected together, separated from the general population, and put to work on collective projects. By June 1975, three hundred bonzes were building a dam west of Krakor. At Seung, near Maung, all the local bonzes were grouped together in one unsanitary location far from Highway 5.

The groups of bonzes are placed under the authority of a *kanak sang*, or "cadre in charge of clergy." In the northwest region, Comrade Tri is the cadre in charge of bonzes for District 4. The bonzes work as hard as everybody else. During the rainy season, the time of their annual retreat, they worked as usual even though the rule forbids all bonzes to leave their pagodas: "It doesn't make any real difference if you break your retreat, and performing the *vossa* [retreat] won't make the rice grow," explained Comrade Tri.

They suffered even more from hunger than the rest of the population, because their rule forbade them to kill crabs and snails. Comrade Tri lectured the priests in his group, telling them, "If you love your country you must develop your muscles and not complain, even if you don't have enough to eat; otherwise you are unworthy of the revolutionary troops. You oppress the workers by waiting for people to come along and fill your begging bowls. Let no bonze take it into his head to impede the march of the revolution, for if he does the Angkar will not answer for the consequences."

In the months following the liberation there were still a few bonzes living in the pagodas, but since December 1975, the Angkar has forced them to leave their monasteries and even to quit wearing their robes. One bonze who fled to Thailand on January 15, 1976, gives the following account:

I was husking rice, as I did every day. Suddenly a letter came from the cadre in charge of clergy for District 3, ordering all bonzes to go to Ta Ngo. I went to ask the chief if I could leave a little later in order to have time to finish my work. I had hardly submitted my request when another order came in: "All bonzes must cease wearing robes by the ninth of the new moon in *mekaser* [toward the end of December]. The Angkar will take no responsibility if this order is not carried out." I didn't want to give up my robe, so a group of *chhlop* came to arrest me. Some people warned me ahead of time, so I hid in the forest, where I stayed for two weeks. As it was becoming difficult to stay there any longer I fled to Thailand, and I was very sad to leave my country and my friends.

Another bonze, from the White Elephant pagoda in Battambang, says that there were more than two hundred bonzes in the temple in September 1975. By December, after repeated harassments, only a few dozen remained. In January 1976, the Khmer Rouge forced them to give up their robes. But in other places, on the contrary, the bonzes have been compelled to continue wearing them; if they do not they must stay where they are and are not allowed to return to their village or family.

The radio never speaks of either Buddhism or the bonzes, with the single exception of the religious act performed by Prince Sihanouk when he returned to Phnom Penh bringing the ashes of his mother, who had died in Peking. According to one eyewitness, a few bonzes who had converted to the new regime in 1970 were brought to Phnom Penh from the country, to officiate at the occasion.

In the revolutionaries' plan to overhaul Khmer society completely and on a rigorously egalitarian basis, there is no place for bonzes or pagodas. The temple used to be the cultural and social center of the village, gathering place for festivities, school for the children, and wellspring of traditional wisdom for the elders. A European passing through Cambodia may have found surprising or even scandalous that there should be sixty thousand bonzes in a total population of seven million, but to Khmer peasants it was natural, for under the monks' religious robes were their own sons or brothers, who were receiving a sort of education obtainable in no other way. The clergy also fulfilled a social function by piling up merits for the villagers who fed them. They gave a sense to life, death, and work. In their attitude toward Buddhism the Khmer Rouge have reacted like Westerners, seeing only the sur- face, the seemingly parasitic existence of this clergy, and that is why they have been in such a hurry to get rid of it. And if the bonzes are driven out, Buddhism itself and its spiritual values will disappear along with them, for there can be no Buddhism with- out bonzes.

In the country the propaganda endlessly repeats the same themes: "The bonzes are bloodsuckers, they oppress the people, they are imperialists." "Better give any extra rice to the nation, not the bonzes." "It is forbidden to give anything to those shaven- asses, it would be pure waste." "Begging for charity like the bonzes do is an offense to the eye and it also maintains the work- ers in a downtrodden condition." On the feast of the dead in 1975, the following instruction was issued in the Battambang area: "If any worker secretly takes rice to the bonzes, we shall set him to planting cabbages. If the cabbages are not full grown in three days, he will dig his own grave." "The bonzes aren't any wiser than you: the only wise man is the man who knows how to grow rice." "Only the man who eats is full."

The propaganda statement "Only those who work deserve to eat" transposes the Buddhist principle that actions lead to merits.

Despite the gradual disappearance of the clergy, some of the older believers were continuing to recite their prayers. The authorities have taken steps to forbid this as well. So to uproot the traditional Buddhist faith, the Angkar must strike at the very heart of religion.

One refugee bonze reports:

While the transformation of everyday life was going on, a cadre named So Chim, called Chet, who was in charge of a group of bonzes, told the workers under his orders, "Buddha wasn't born in Cambodia, so why should Khmers follow a religion that came from India? This is why our revolutionary party categorically refuses to honor the Buddhist religion. All of you brothers who are following the revolutionary Angkar must give up this religion, for it is the enemy of the Angkar, it is an ideology developed by imperialists, and can bring nothing but confusion and distraction to people's minds." In a political education speech, Khen Pen, called So, harangued the Buddhist clergy in the following terms, "The Angkar must uproot the three mountains of imperialism, feudality, and reactionary capitalism." By "feudality" he meant the officials, religion, and folk traditions.

Propaganda campaigns are plentifully seasoned with anti-religious slogans: "Pray to Buddha and wait for him to give you something to eat!" "The Buddhist religion is good for nothing, it won't lead the country forward. Whether or not you say your prayers makes no difference to how the rice grows." "The Buddhist religion came from Siam and it deceived the people's minds and put them to sleep." "The Buddhist religion is the cause of our country's weakness."

In the northwest, all the sacred places and objects of the Buddhist faith have been systematically destroyed or profaned— the temples, statues of Buddha, and places where the peasants were secretly continuing to worship. Most of the temples that were not destroyed by the war are being used as storehouses or camps for soldiers. The grounds outside them are often used for pigsties. Many refugees have been shocked by the attitudes of the soldiers, who profane statues of the Buddha by using them as clothes racks. Many have been smashed. At Otaki (in Battambang province), for example, some soldiers climbed astride the statue of the Blessed, broke off his feet and hands, and then shattered his body, saying, "It's been more than two thousand years since this hideous thing came to make us bow down and prevent us from standing up again." Some have taken statues to use as wheel blocks to keep their trucks from rolling away, observing that "they're only worthless bricks." Bandet, the former bonze, adds: "They break the statues, overturn them to use them as jars, and urinate on their heads. At Prek Tauch they turned the temple into a storehouse for rice and used the sanctuary as a dormitory. That's where I slept. They took the statues from Po Veal temple, where I was a bonze, and sold them." Indeed, there is a lively trade in cut-rate Buddhas on the Khmero-Thai border.

Another bonze, forty-two years old and originally from Battambang, tells a similar tale:

> They destroyed all the ancient and precious objects in the museum of the Po Veal temple, as well as the relics and ornaments of the White Elephant temple in Battambang. They did the same thing at the Sangkar and Kandeung temples. At Kompong Seung they threatened the bonzes who were still on the premises, took the key to the sanctuary, and carried away all the antique works of art. They loaded them into a truck to sell or trade for salt at the frontier.

According to the same observer, Comrade Mul Sambath, nicknamed Kav Nhung, formerly a bonze and chief of the northwest region, summed up the policy of the Angkar during a speech to the peasants at Sisophon on the evening of December 14, 1975: "Buddha is just a statue made by human hands. We are not to honor it, because it is an imperialist ideology. The bonzes invented this doctrine for the sole purpose of deceiving the people and getting free food. Our Angkar has now awakened you. You must drive this religion out of you. Otherwise you are enemies of the Angkar!"

If the anti-Buddhist campaign continues at this rate the religion, or at least its outward manifestations, will soon vanish. But can a spiritual current that has shaped the Khmer soul so profoundly and for so many centuries ever be torn from the hearts of men?

Other religions in Cambodia are no better off. There are about 250,000 Mohammedan Chams and Malays. Prince Sihanouk tried to integrate them into the national community by giving them the name "Islam-Khmers." The descendants of a conquered people with whom the Khmers often came to blows in the Angkor Wat period, they were regarded with suspicion by Cambodians because of their cultural and religious separatism. In 1970 many Chams enlisted in the revolutionary movement in the hope of evening up the score with their oppressors, the Khmers, and in many cases they proved to be cruel and bloodthirsty fighters.

Islam was the cement that held this marginal community together. At present the community is being harassed by the Khmer Rouge: its sacred books are torn apart, its members are forced to raise swine near the mosques, and to dress like Khmers. In November 1975 the Chams in the village of Trea (north of Kompong Cham) rebelled. "Then the Khmer Rouge tore the village apart with B-40s and smashed the heads of any survivors with pick handles. The corpses were thrown aside and left. They even stuck heads on pikes and exposed them along the banks of the Mekong." Mat Sleman, a forty-year-old Cham born in the northern part of Kompong Cham, who escaped to Thailand in June 1976, tells a story worthy of the Horatii:

> At Kroch Chhmar there was a Cham who had two sons. Both joined the army of liberation. One night the sons came home to visit their father and told him all their exploits—how they had killed Khmers, eaten pork, and liberated the country. "Come with us," they told him, "and follow the revolution." The old man didn't say a word but went out of the house; he came back armed with a cleaver and killed both his sons. He covered their bodies with a big cloth and then went to tell his neighbors: "Come and see the two enemies I've killed!" When he pulled back the cover his friends said, "But those are your sons!" "No, they're not," he retorted, "they are enemies of our people and our religion and so I killed them." He told his story and everybody said he had done right, and they decided to kill all the Khmer Rouge in the village. They did it that night. The next morning the village was surrounded by troops who killed everybody in it, with mortars, machine guns, and bayonets.

There were not many Christians in Cambodia—about five thousand Roman Catholics and three thousand Protestants in 1975. There had been Catholics in the country since the sixteenth century, but after 1880 the majority were immigrant Vietnamese, and, because of this, the Khmers often entertained unfriendly feelings toward a religion that was regarded as alien and suspected of foreign allegiance. Such racial misunderstandings account in part for the horrible massacre in Chruoy Chang War by General Lon Nol's troops in April 1970: During the night of the first day of the Khmer New Year, all the men in the district of Phnom Penh where the Vietnamese Catholics lived were arrested, loaded onto barges, and massacred on the banks of the Mekong. There were 515 victims. Also, the five priests working in zones "liberated" by the Khmer Rouge were systematically eliminated long before the fall of Phnom Penh.

After the massive departure of the Vietnamese, who were evicted in 1970, the remaining five thousand Khmer Roman Catholics became noted for their loyalty to the Khmer culture and their service to the poor. A few were supporters of the revolutionaries, even in the higher ranks of the Angkar, but most were town-dwellers and therefore on the side of the government. They had been to mission schools and knew French, and several were civil servants or officers.

The Protestants were relative newcomers, having arrived only at the beginning of this century. The Buddhist clergy took a dim view of their proselytism and suspected them of wanting to destroy Buddhism and import a new culture.

As there were so few Christians the new authorities have not bothered them much, and the refugees' accounts seldom mention them. One, however, says that "if the Khmer Rouge know that a person is a Christian they take him away and kill him, accusing him of belonging to the CIA."

The new revolutionary culture aims to be absolutely, exclusively national, purged of all foreign impurities—even ones that are centuries old. How far back are the Khmers supposed to go, one wonders, to recover their true identity? On what criterion is the "Khmer-ness" of the new culture based? Does the new society owe nothing at all to foreign influence? Perhaps, when Prince Sihanouk said the revolutionaries were "de-Khmerified," he was not so far wrong!

NINE

The Revolution
of the Ultras

"A radical revolution, more radical and destined to go further than that of China or the USSR": That was the conclusion of the Swedish ambassador to China Kaj Bork on his return from a visit to Democratic Kampuchea, February 20 to March 6, 1976. I can ony agree: abolition of the towns, total liquidation of the former administration, total restructuring of the society and economy, recasting of the culture, and prohibition of all religion—in all likelihood no revolution has ever traveled so far or so fast toward the achievement of its goals.

The world was shocked by the violence of the Cambodian revolution—how did those mild and peaceable Khmers come to transform the land of soft and gentle living into one enormous *gulag*? Even the Khmers in foreign countries don't understand: "They used to call us the champions of corruption; now we've become the champions of barbarity! Let the journalists into Cambodia so they can prove that the things people are saying about our country are not true!" was the anguished plea of Son Sann, former premier and director of the National Bank, during a broadcast televised in Paris in June 1976. For even if the refugees' affirmations are assumed to be exaggerated, the terrible truth remains: the Khmer revolution is one of the bloodiest of the twentieth century.

Many Khmers blame foreign influences for the extremes to which this revolution has gone: "The revolutionaries' behavior is not Khmer. It is inspired by the Vietnamese, who want to annihilate our people and weaken the country so they can take it over." And appearances were so much on their side that I was almost ready to believe them. In 1970 we often saw Vietcong and North Vietnamese soldiers fighting the republican army. In the northern part of Kompong Cham, I myself was arrested by Vietcong patrolling Khmer territory forty kilometers within the Cambodian border. On October 8, 1972, we saw the corpses of eighty-five Vietnamese commandos abandoned at Phnom Penh after an attack on the capital's main bridge. Those same Vietnamese were still there on the banks of the Mekong in April 1975, for many refugees saw their remains.

As time went by, however, there was no denying that the Vietnamese revolutionaries had truly gone home. Proof of this comes from several refugees.

Beginning in June 1975, the Cambodian Vietnamese were allowed to return to their own country. At Chamcar Leu, for example, on June 3, a *giai phong* (South Vietnamese National Liberation Front) officer came to tell the population that "the three peoples of Vietnam, Cambodia, and Laos are brothers. If the Vietnamese want to return to their homeland they can." A number of residents of Phnom Penh passed themselves off as Vietnamese and left for Vietnam on June 6. On the way, they met many *giai phong* cadres who had been in Cambodia for several years, all returning to Vietnam with goods and family. The cadres were repatriated in trucks hired from the Khmer revolutionaries, but Vietnamese civilians living in Cambodia went on foot.

At the same time a Vietnamese doctor from Battambang was permitted to return to Saigon. Around July a Vietnamese delegation came to fetch Vietnamese nationals in the Takmau region. They left by boat, between five hundred and one thousand on each trip. Toward the end of October several thousand Vietnamese in the Battambang area were repatriated by river. On November 8 the Vietnamese in the Kroch Chhmar region were ordered out.

Did the same thing happen in all the provinces near Vietnam? We have no confirmation.

Some refugees mention large numbers of troops being sent to the northeast to protect the area against the Vietnamese, but this is also unconfirmed. On several occasions the press has referred to armed fighting between Khmer and Vietnamese, chiefly for possession of the Poulo Wai islands[1] and control of the Ratanakiri mountain zones.

The fighting must have been violent, because it necessitated a lightning trip to Phnom Penh by Le Duan, secretary of the Vietnamese Communist party, to clear up the situation. After this visit the Hanoi newspaper *Nhan Dan* spoke of a "complete identity of views with Phnom Penh."[2] This visit coincided with the official appointment of Ieng Sary and Son Sen as deputy premiers, for foreign affairs and defense, respectively. Several commentators jumped to the conclusion that Vietnamese influence was increasing. However, as Prince Sihanouk stated in October 1975, the Khmer Rouge leaders are "ultra-nationalists" and have been very careful to keep their distance from their socialist big brother.

At the diplomatic level, Kampuchea has dissociated itself from Vietnam on several occasions. In 1975, when Hanoi was calling the Bangkok government a bunch of foul reactionaries and slaves of the Americans, Phnom Penh was maneuvering to begin political and economic negotiations with Thailand. This may have been a defensive reaction of "brown" Asia, populated by Khmers and Thais, against the dynamic imperialism of the sons of Uncle Ho. Also, unlike their neighbors, Kampuchean leaders condemn the Soviet "hegemonism" and have also refused to form the Indochinese federation which was Ho Chi Minh's dying wish.

In March 1977 Ieng Sary went to Rangoon and his Burmese counterpart made an official return trip in August. Perhaps

---

[1] *Le Monde* (June 21, 1975).

[2] *Le Monde* (August 9, 1975).

Kampuchea and Burma, with the help of China, mean to form a third group, unaligned either with the United States–supported ASEAN countries or Soviet-aided Vietnam and its protectorate, Laos.

At a meeting held in Paris on April 22, 1976, to celebrate the New Year and first anniversary of the liberation, the representative of the NUFK mission repeated a statement made by Khieu Samphan a few days earlier in Phnom Penh: "Kampuchea will never allow any imperialist, small or large, near or far, to invade its territory." The Vietnamese representative at the ceremony made himself conspicuous by his failure to applaud these words.

Around the middle of 1976 there seemed to be an attempt to renew relations with Vietnam: a Khmer ambassador was appointed to replace the *chargé d'affaires* in Hanoi. And in June 1976 the first delegation of Vietnamese journalists were allowed into Kampuchea. At the end of the year, however, skirmishes broke out along the Vietnamese border, and there was fierce fighting in May 1977, involving the air force and heavy artillery of both countries and necessitating a trip to the scene of the conflict by General Giap himself.

Other foreign observers have blamed China for the evils besetting Kampuchea since April 17, 1975. They argue that the Khmer revolution is a model experiment being performed by China on a small nonindustrialized people. Appearances don't contradict them. Prince Sihanouk and a few of the revolutionary leaders had been living in Peking since the beginning of the war; Chinese experts were assisting the revolutionary troops from 1970; a few days after the capture of Phnom Penh the only planes landing at the Phnom Penh airfield bore the crest of the People's Republic of China; a large number of refugees saw Chinese experts working in Cambodia until the time of their departure; and Chinese equipment of all kinds is being used in the countryside.

It would be wrong to exaggerate Chinese influence on the present leadership of Kampuchea, however. True, China "regards the victories of the Cambodian people as its own." And Chairman Mao Tse-tung said: "The Chinese people have given no assistance to the people of Cambodia. On the contrary, it is the Cambodians who have helped the Chinese," for "the victory of the Cambodian people offers a striking example to oppressed nations and peoples everywhere, showing that a small country can defeat a large one and a weak country can get the upper hand over a strong one."[3] Also, Ieng Sary told the Chinese ambassador to Cambodia that "our victory is yours."[4] So Kampuchea might well seem an excellent test of a revolution in the Chinese manner. In many respects, its leaders have followed the Chinese model, as in their return to the land, their will to self-sufficiency, their use of traditional medicine, rigorously egalitarian society, identical positions on questions of foreign policy, and elsewhere.

But the Khmer revolution is too unlike the Chinese to have been administered directly by the latter country. "China is our best friend but she is not our boss," Prince Sihanouk said on a visit to Paris. Besides, the lengths to which the Khmers have gone have tarnished any image China may have wanted to present of a revolution inspired by her own principles. In August 1975, Chou En-lai is said to have recommended moderation to Khieu Samphan, who was then in Peking, and strongly urged Prince Sihanouk's return to temper the revolutionary ardor. Also, according to a refugee who lived with them, Chinese experts in Phnom Penh were beginning to voice private reservations, although their official enthusiasm never flagged. Furthermore, one Chinese diplomat formerly posted to Kampuchea is outspoken in his disparagement of the new regime, which he also regards as having gone too far. Prince Sihanouk's resignation was not announced in China until a week after it occurred, which may indicate how reluctant China was to express an opinion about an event which did not please her.

No: The Khmer revolution is being run by Khmers. The underlying ideology may come from somewhere else, but the methods employed show every mark of the Cambodian character.

A widespread cliché portrays the Khmers as a mild and peaceful people. And mild and peaceful they are; but their race is also one of redoubtable warriors. For proof, there is the extraordinary

---

[3] *Peking Information* (an organ of the Chinese press for foreigners), no. 34, p. 20.
[4] Radio Phnom Penh (March 12, 1976).

geographical expansion of Cambodia during the Angkor period toward the end of the thirteenth century, when the Khmer kingdom stretched from Point Camau to Luang Prabang, from the Isthmus of Kra to the plains of the Irrawaddy. Since the fourteenth century Cambodia has suffered defeat after defeat at the hands of its expansionist Thai and Vietnamese neighbors, but this is more the result of palace intrigues and the mismanagement of military leaders than of any decline in the warlike ardor of the people. In Southeast Asia the Khmers are still known as valiant fighters. During the first Indochinese war French officers preferred Khmer troops to Vietnamese: the former were said to be tougher, the latter more prone to use cunning. In June 1970, even the North Vietnamese had to retreat from the Khmers at Kompong Thom, leaving thousands of dead behind. In man-to-man fighting the Khmers are considered to have no masters.

During the reign of Sihanouk and then under Lon Nol, methods used by the government forces in dealing with their Khmer Rouge enemies were no less savage than those subsequently employed by Democratic Kampuchea: between 1968 and 1970 prisoners from Samlaut or Dambar, the cradles of the Khmer revolution, were bound to trees with their stomachs cut open and left to die; others, hurled off the cliffs of Bokor, agonized for days; enemy villages were razed and the villagers clubbed to death by local peasants who had been set against them.

Yet the Cambodian shows sincere and immediate friendship for anyone who has done him a favor or helped him out of a difficulty, and the attachment will be lifelong. But a harsh tone of voice, an attitude felt to be condescending, a cross look or a brusque gesture will drive him away no less definitively.

Buddhism preaches mildness, serenity, and pity for the unfortunate. The Khmer concept of forgiveness, however, is more complicated: in a pinch, forgiving someone is almost an expression of weakness, or admission of a sort of guilt—it is "losing face." So it is better not to take too much notice of an adversary's good points. As for the enemy, he is seen as unqualifiedly evil. Recognizing any virtue in him is tantamount to becoming his accomplice.

Such attitudes, incorporated into ideologies and exacerbated by war, can easily be imagined to lead to the wildest extremes. The conquerors can never *forgive* the conquered who had caused them so much suffering in the past. In practice, the nationalist myth that says "we can always come to an understanding among Khmers" turned out to be untrue. The lust for revenge—the timid man's form of violence—has run its course implacably, even at the risk of the country's annihilation.

The Khmers cannot easily accept public criticism, for "words kill just as surely as weapons." To be judged, "to be conquered by someone else's words," incites him to take up the challenge even if it means certain ruin or self-destruction. In this respect, the international condemnation of the horrors being perpetrated in Kampuchea may not have helped to soften the avenging fury of the Khmer Rouge.

The Khmer peasant was a man of the land, influenced by Buddhism, which promised him a personal salvation, and as such he was a profound individualist and did not take to the idea that another man of his own rank should be able to boss him around. Khmer villages were open to all travelers and strangers, and their hospitality was liberal. However, every house, surrounded by a grove of fruit trees, was the inviolable domain of its family. Rejecting all outside interference in his own affairs, the Khmer was equally loath to meddle in those of others. Naturally, people made an effort to live in peace with their neighbors and took an interest in their lives, but concern for the common good could never outweigh their determination to preserve their own individual tranquility and peace.

This fundamentally individualistic attitude may help to account for the failure of the parliamentary regimes of the Sihanouk and republican governments. Ministers and officers wholly devoted to the common weal were few. In February 1975, when defeat was imminent, one general in the Khmer republican army refused to send reinforcements to a besieged company because its colonel belonged to a different party. This is not an isolated case. The few high officials who have escaped abroad since April 1975 began quarreling almost the moment they got over the border, each claiming to be more qualified than the other to lead the resistance against the present regime, and deaf to all argument.

In the time of Sihanouk and Lon Nol opposition was confined to
isolated and disunited pockets, but the revolutionaries now seem
to have learned their lesson—as witness, for instance, the creation
of the collegial system of authority. Kampuchea is not run by a
single leader but by the anonymous Angkar, in which all men are
theoretically equal and no one can justify his actions on the basis
of personal power. We are a long way from the Chinese personality cult.

The old Hindu core, which regarded authority as a divine incarnation, was still strong in the Khmers. *Khmer men chaol
kbouon*—"the Cambodian sticks to the rule"; the Khmer people
still respect authority with a respect that to us is tinged with
fatalism, even passivity, but that emanates from an underlying
confidence in the abilities of those in power. Prince Sihanouk and
Lon Nol and his men abused the confidence invested in them.
They took advantage of the conformism of the crowd, knowing
that for every Khmer the first law of moral and social life was to
refrain from attracting attention, "not to be different from the
rest." Even if many people objected to the corruption of a
former regime, no one openly dared to initiate a complaint for fear
of being left exposed to the eye and possibly the opprobrium of the
public, or to failure. It was presumably Marxism that gave the
revolutionaries the energy they needed to overcome their own
reticence and rise in open rebellion. And after coming to power
they managed to seize on the instinctive capacity of every Khmer
to obey whatever authority happens to be in control and turn it to
their own uses. This makes it easier to understand how four million people could walk out of their homes in the cities almost
without a murmur when ordered to do so by the Khmer Rouge;
and how the republican soldiers and officials could so readily
have let themselves be duped into losing their lives. They could
no more imagine their own countrymen would trick them to that
extent—ostensibly dispatching them to welcome their prince—
than could the Khmer Rouge emissaries who had been sent to
parley in Phnom Penh earlier in the war imagine they would be
assassinated by republican troops! And how a tiny number of
Khmer Rouge soldiers could control such hordes of refugees: one

does not stand up against order; one avoids being singled out in opposition to the crowd; one is too frightened of finding oneself alone.

But even the strongest camel's back can be broken. The Angkar is now ruling the countryside with terror and lies. Under Marxist influence, perhaps the Khmer will suddenly open a critical eye. Having now become aware of his strength, will he demand his rights which are still being confiscated?

Another cause of the radicality of the Khmer revolution lies in the Khmer way of reasoning, which is bewildering to Cartesian minds. The Khmer thinks by accretions or juxtapositions, but adheres strictly to the rules of his own internal logic. In the past, before beginning to act, every committee or council spent long hours and sometimes days drawing up statutes from which nothing was omitted, and constructing schemes, each more impracticable than the last. A simple idea, intuitively perceived, was pushed to the limits of its internal logic and often to the point of absurdity, without any regard for realities or any forethought for practical consequences. In fact, good intentions were enough, and when the scheme or statute was finally produced the difficulties that had led to its formulation were themselves resolved or no longer relevant.

The present regime, showing in this respect its pure Marxist pedigree, is a past master of the art. The Chinese revolutionary principles embodied in the writings of Mao Tse-tung have been taken over and pushed as far as they will logically go, and Marxist praxis undertakes to apply them. "The revolution draws its strength from the peasant masses." "Wars are won by encircling the towns by the countryside." Carried to extremes, this theory leads to the abolition of towns. "Rely on nothing but your own strength" is a golden rule which China can follow with no trouble at all, for China is a continent in herself. But little Kampuchea, with its meager economic resources, is inviting total asphyxiation by trying to apply the same principle all at once and without any qualification. "Capitalism is bad"—therefore, the Khmer revolutionaries conclude, they must do away with money and return to a barter economy. In this respect, they even boast that they are the most advanced Communists in the world. The Khmer revolution is forcing its way to its goal implacably, with no extraneous subtleties or delays.

   Nevertheless, the components of the Khmer personality cannot fully account for this extraordinary revolution. Other causes must have been at work, for on the face of it there seemed so little reason for the Khmers to have a revolution at all: to any Western visitor Cambodia was a land of smiles. The countryside was calm, the peasants "adored" their venerated leader, the neat and well-run little towns presented an image of harmonious human growth in contrast to Vietnam, which had been at war for thirty years, and Laos, which was still sunk in lethargy. There did not seem to be any major social or agrarian problems. Unlike China or Vietnam, Cambodia had few vast estates. The land was ultimately owned by the crown, but belonged to whoever cleared and farmed it. True, the peasants were poor, but seldom destitute, and they lived in harmony with the nature around them. "What does it matter if the house is a little cramped, as long as a person can be at ease in his heart."
   However, this art of living carried within it the seeds of its own destruction. After the grandeur of the thirteenth century, the Khmer kingdom went through a long period of decay. Angkor Wat was first captured by the Thais in 1394 and abandoned by its population in 1432. Aided by palace intrigues, Thais and Vietnamese skirmished in Cambodia for nearly four centuries, each of the two expanding powers acting in response to a call from some pretender to the Khmer throne. Between 1841 and 1845 Vietnam simply annexed the country. Thus the Khmer people had been humiliated and crushed for centuries, had endured devastating invasions, conscription, and taxation levied by the various belligerents. In 1863, at the request of King Ang Duong, seconded by King Norodom, France established a protectorate over Cambodia.
   From 1863 to 1953 French colonization brought order and peace. The French seldom made the Khmers feel the weight of

their authority, as they did their neighbors in Vietnam, and until recently the general tone of relations between Khmers and French was one of mutual friendship. With one exception: the measures adopted by Charles Thomson in 1884, during the Jules Ferry government, which made the Khmers very angry. The effect of the measures was to deprive the sovereign of all but symbolic power, and this led to a full-scale rebellion. However, throughout the entire history of the French colonization in Cambodia, only one French official was ever killed on active duty: in 1925, Felix-Louis Bardez, an administrator, made the unpardonable error of going to collect taxes in Kompong Chhnang during the Khmer New Year religious holiday. And during the Franco-Japanese war many French lives were saved by the Khmers who hid and fed them.

Nevertheless, colonization did help to intensify and ultimately exacerbate Khmer nationalism. The people appreciated peace and order, true, but France was still a foreign country, conscious of its greatness, and it pretended with serene self-assurance to possess the sole and universal standard of *savoir-vivre* and culture. Many intellectuals, and Prince Sihanouk himself, were grateful to France for having saved Cambodia from total annihilation in 1863, but many others resented the French for maintaining their country in a state of economic and cultural underdevelopment. France was also criticized for employing Vietnamese officials as channels for the transmission of her authority; this fed the ancestral antagonism which had placed the two races in opposition for more than seven centuries. And, as a result, when Cambodia became independent it found itself totally unequipped, both economically and administratively. France was also accused of endorsing the separation of Cochin China, cradle of Cambodia, to the advantage of the greedy Vietnamese.

The policy of the colonial administration of republican France with its democratic ideals was to rely on the local regime—in this case a feudal monarchy nearly ten centuries old. The kings had earned a large share of the blame for their country's decadence, but few people were aware of this, for king, race, and religion were the three pillars upholding the nation. The king "ate up the kingdom"—the expressive Khmer image for this form of government—with the aid of feudal mandarins who in turn "ate up the provinces." Power was regarded essentially as a promotion and a personal reward rather than a means of serving the people; but those on whom power was conferred were seldom objects of hatred or resentment: the man who had power was simply lucky, he had a good karma, or in other words he possessed a "credit balance" resulting from the good conduct he had been wise enough to follow in a previous existence. To be sure of gaining such a prominent position in a life to come all an individual had to do was accumulate credits in his present time on earth.

There was some antimonarchist and antifeudal feeling in Cambodia, however. As early as 1336, a "sweet-pickle gardener" had dethroned the gods by assassinating the king and supplanting him. Long afterward, in the 1930s, Son Ngoc Thanh and a group of Cochin Chinese intellectuals influenced by their French education began to make violent attacks upon the monarchy and its shield, France. But when independence came in 1953, the royal power showed few signs of modernization and remained as absolute as ever, regardless of the parliamentary elections.

The official propaganda of the present revolutionary regime is continuing in the same strain of democratic opposition, heaping opprobrium on the monarchy and its feudal system which "reduced the people to slavery and kept them there for two thousand years, and brought the country to ruin."

Economically, France took little interest in Cambodia, which was a minor market with relatively insignificant resources in raw materials. It preferred to invest in Yunnan, Tonkin, and Cochin China, and simply assimilated the Khmer kingdom into its own economic system. If we are to believe the economic analysis of Khieu Samphan, the growth of underdeveloped Cambodia was prevented by its integration into the French economic system. France imported a few raw materials from Cambodia at very low prices and in return sold the country its own manufactured goods at very high prices. Cambodian savings went almost exclusively to buy French products rather than invest in the country. "The only periods of significant industrialization of the underdeveloped countries were during the First World War; that is, at a time when an imposed autarchy reduced foreign competition and foreign capital was no longer coming into the country."[5]

After 1921 the rubber plantations aroused renewed interest among French capitalists, who began investing more substantially. But there again, even though the labor of Khmer and Vietnamese workers brought in the major share of foreign currency in Cambodia's budget, the money aided the growth of the French economy rather than that of Cambodia. On the social level, plantation workers were financially better off than other Cambodian laborers, yet their living conditions were still very much like those of French workers in the darkest years of the nineteenth century. So it is not surprising that the rubber plantations have always been a breeding ground for Marxist ideas, among Khmers no less than Vietnamese.

The rapid growth of French commerce and the rubber trade led to increased land registration and regulation of the system of ownership. Without taking at face value all the arguments put forward by Hou Youn in his dissertation[6]—for it appears to be based more on anticolonialist ideological premises than on any recent documented analysis of land holdings in Cambodia—it is nevertheless clear that the situation was becoming unstable. To acquire consumer goods imported from abroad, the peasant, who had lived by barter until the end of the nineteenth century, was beginning to need money. His only salable asset was his crop. If that was not enough, then his land became currency with which to acquire bank notes. Chinese residents, who were forbidden to farm by 1929 legislation, became the intermediaries or compradores, who sold foreign merchandise to the peasants and bought their products from them. With steadily growing profits, they could lend the peasants the money they needed at usurious rates of interest—sometimes two hundred or three hundred percent per annum! Some peasants' entire earnings went to finance their debt, and sometimes they had to give up their title to the land. So although there was no system of large estates as such, the

---

[5] "L'Économie du Cambodge . . ." (Sorbonne, 1959), p. 128.
[6] "La Paysannerie cambodgienne . . ." (Sorbonne, 1955).

land was beginning to come together in the hands of local capitalists.

In 1956 Prince Sihanouk tried to lower interest rates by founding an agricultural lending bank and a sort of cooperative for the collection of agricultural produce. But the directors of the bank and cooperatives exploited the peasants even more shamelessly than the Chinese merchants. The feudal system, in which any charge must mean profit for somebody, could not be abolished by a law or new type of organization: what was needed was a complete change of mentality.

In the administration, the situation was the same: independence left the feudal power structure virtually unaltered. The provincial governors simply became the new vassals, who skimmed off the people's wealth to offer a tribute to the royal family and, especially, it is said, to the queen mother. The police, customs officers, and information agents were paid absurdly low wages, which they supplemented with contributions from the locals so that they could support their second and seventh cousins and bribe their own superiors—one can imagine at what price. In the higher administration in Phnom Penh, even under Sihanouk, corruption reached well-nigh inconceivable heights. One extremely corrupt provincial representative told me one day that officials with jobs in Phnom Penh amassed more in a day than he did in a year.

This makes it easy to understand how an intelligent propaganda campaign could exploit these injustices by making the peasants aware of the situation and stirring up their hatred of the towns, where both Chinese merchants and administrative officials were entrenched. On the morning of April 18, 1975, I was not surprised to hear one Khmer Rouge cadre explaining that "the enemies of the Khmer people are the Chinese merchants living in our country." Traditionally, the Khmers' foe was the ever invading Vietnamese; but this Khmer Rouge gave me a Marxist analysis of the exploitation of his people, in which historic feuds were relegated to the background; and this is undoubtedly why, according to refugees, Chinese merchants have been even more abominably treated than the rest of the urban deportees.

Many Khmers deplored the abusive practices of the feudal

power, it is true, and longed for some change in their society. But they possessed neither the tools they would have needed for a valid analysis of their situation nor any effective means of altering it. The people in authority were responsible for the injustices; but the masses themselves, used to living under the system, unwittingly oiled the gears of their own exploitation.

Even intellectuals with a Marxist background—of whom there were plenty—performed their public duties with claws as long and grasping as the mandarins of old. To give but one example, there was a minister-parliamentarian who was noted for his progressive, even Communist leanings, and who embarked penniless on his career but was able to retire into exile in France in 1967 with a comfortable fortune under his belt.

On March 18, 1970, the young, the teachers, the army, and many honest people hailed the *coup d'état* which overthrew Sihanouk as the dawn of an era of justice after the rot and filth of a feudal regime. But the republic only trudged on in the wake of the kingdom, and the liberal dream vanished and left nothing behind but corruption, now more widespread than before, since the number of people with access to positions of authority was larger than before. For true democrats among the Khmers, the history of the republic is the history of one long disappointment. Some radical change in attitudes and human relations had become indispensable. But was there no other way to bring it about than by this blood-drenched revolution?

TEN

Thirty Years for a Battle

"The wonderful victory of April 17, 1975, crowns thirty years of revolutionary struggle by the people of Kampuchea. After the period of political struggle, and under the enlightened and just leadership of the Angkar, our people have fought for five years to free the country from the American imperialists and their lackeys."[1] "Just as we drove out the French and Japanese colonialists, our little people, entirely without wealth, have succeeded in driving out the American imperialists, the greatest imperialists in the world."[2] "What the people of Kampuchea have been waiting for for two thousand years has come to pass: at last, they are the masters of their destiny."[3] These are the refrains which Radio Phnom Penh broadcasts repeatedly to the people rebuilding their country in the mud of the rice paddies.

The origins of the Khmer Communist party, which is now run-

---

[1] Radio Phnom Penh (April 15, 1976).
[2] Radio P.P. (October 2, 1975).
[3] Radio P.P. (March 15, 1976).

ning Kampuchea, date from the anticolonialist struggle against
the French. Ho Chi Minh, whose aim was to get France out of
Indochina and set up a Socialist regime there, founded the Indochinese Communist party on February 3, 1930. It was joined by a
newly formed Cambodian section composed solely of Vietnamese
and Chinese nationals living in Cambodia, who could exert no
profound influence on the Khmer people. The first Cambodian
revolutionaries made their appearance in the Khmer minority in
Cochin China, during the first Indochinese war.

The Khmers in Cochin China had always been fiercely political; detached from their motherland since the eighteenth century, they lived under the French-endorsed dominion of the
Vietnamese. Their Khmer honor suffered from this, and from early
childhood they had to defend themselves against the Vietnamese
in order to preserve their own culture. "Ever since we were children," one of them says, "we were taught to hate the monarchy
because it was the monarchy's fault that we had lost our Khmer
identity."

Around 1930 Son Ngoc Thanh began stirring up anticolonialist
feeling in the region. He moved to Phnom Penh as a magistrate
attached to the newly created Buddhist Institute, and started a
newspaper whose progressive ideas were a source of constant
worry to French authorities. In 1943 a teacher at the Buddhist
Institute was arrested and a number of bonzes reacted by
demonstrating against the French occupation; Son Ngoc Thanh,
also slated for arrest, had to flee to Japan. He was an intransigent
nationalist but was never closely involved with the Indochinese
Communist movement.

The prosperous Khmer families of Cochin China sent their
children to school in the homeland. Around 1943 a young Khmer
of fifteen named Kim Trang turned up at Svay Rieng. He came
from a family of landowners held to be relatively wealthy by the
other peasants of Phum Samdech in the canton of Luong Hoa,
Tra Vinh province. Both his parents were originally Khmers,
contrary to what has been written since. His mother died when
he was still a child, leaving him with an older brother. At the
village and canton schools he successfully completed his primary
Franco-Cambodian studies, but he was over the age limit for

admission to the Svay Rieng high school, so he had a false birth certificate made out describing him as younger than he really was. To silence the teasing of his schoolmates, who accused him of being Vietnamese because of his accent and birthplace, he changed his name to Ieng Sary. He was gifted, so he left to continue his schooling at the Sisowath *lycée* in Phnom Penh—then the only *lycée* in Cambodia. The school was run by French teachers supplemented by a few Khmers who taught the national language. Ebullient, talkative, and gay, Sary was always ready to do a favor and made many friends. He was highly critical of society and already strongly attracted to politics. He was very good at mathematics and passed his first *baccalauréat* exams with high marks. He was not indifferent to feminine charm and, in his last years at the school, flaunted Khmer customs by paying court to a shy fellow student of good family named Khieu Thirith, who later became his wife.

In 1946 another Cochin Chinese Khmer arrived in Phnom Penh: Son Sen, a few years younger than Ieng Sary, hailing from Phum Sambuor in the same canton. His parents were also small landowners, comfortably off. Too old to be admitted to the Sisowath *lycée*, he entered the teachers' training school as a boarder, and there acquired a taste for order and discipline. He had rather poor health, was serious and intelligent. More retiring than his compatriot Sary, he never talked politics. After receiving his secondary-school diploma he was sent to France to continue his education.

Also at the Sisowath *lycée*, young Khieu Samphan attracted little attention. Slight and slender, Samphan was a hard-working pupil, but his grades were only average. He was born at Koh Sothin in 1929, the Year of the Serpent, of a Cambodian father and Chinese mother. His father died soon after, and his mother came to live at Tuol Sbeuv, a lower-class district in Kompong Cham, bringing her two sons with her. To keep her little family she sold vegetables in the local market. At the Kompong Cham primary school young Samphan was not very outgoing, and one of his schoolmates remembers playing many a prank at his expense. After completing his primary schooling he also set off to attend the Sisowath *lycée* in Phnom Penh. He lived at the Cambodian Provinces Hostel, where he was regarded as a bourgeois because, unlike the sons of the poor who slept on a plain mat supplied by the hostel, he had brought his own mattress, sheet, and bolster with him. He worked hard and steadily, and passed his examinations without trouble.

The student body of the Sisowath *lycée* contained a good many of those who were to become Khmer revolutionaries: In Sokan, Tauch Phoeun, Ok Sakun, Hou Youn. . . . Hou Youn was a native of Peam Chi Kang and had gone to school in Kompong Cham like his classmate Samphan, who was three years younger than he. A brilliant and voluble boy, he was also a fine football player and was chosen to play on the national school team. The police had already taken an interest in this young man's activities by the time he finished school.

While all these youths were in high school, Cambodia was living through some fateful hours: On March 9, 1945, the Japanese made a surprise attack on Phnom Penh and interned all the French. A few days later the young King Sihanouk, set on the throne by France in 1941, proclaimed the nation's independence. Son Ngoc Thanh had returned to Cambodia not long before, and he was a very popular man; he maintained that the independence proclaimed by the king was only a milder form of control by the French, and with the help of the Japanese police he contrived to get himself named premier a few days before the Japanese capitulation, to the acute displeasure of Sihanouk, who was jealous of his popularity. In October 1945, General Jacques Leclerc parachuted his troops into the country, and Son Ngoc Thanh was arrested. In 1946 France gave Cambodia the status of an "autonomous state within the French Union." Meanwhile, the Nekhum Issarak Khmer, or Cambodian Liberation Front, commanded by Prince Norodom Chantarangsey, went underground; its goal was immediate and total independence.

The young minds at the Sisowath *lycée* followed all these events with the fervor of their years and developed a taste for political discussion about their country's future.

In those days it was the custom to send the top students to Hanoi, for there were no universities in Cambodia. But since the Japanese attack in 1945, followed by the anticolonial agitation of the Vietminh in Tonkin, France decided it would be preferable to train the country's future elite in Paris. Thiounn Mum and Di Phon, who had begun their university careers in Hanoi, were part of the first contingent sent to France. Beginning in 1949, Son Sen, Hou Youn, In Sokan, Ok Sakun, Khieu Komar, Ros Chethor, Rat Samuoeun, Chau Seng, Khieu Samphan, Ieng Sary and others had their turn. Saloth Sar, who had only a technical diploma from his secondary school, joined the group and attended the École du Livre (for typesetters, printers, and book manufacturers) and later a civil engineering school.

When they got to France, most of the Khmer students lodged at Indochina House. They formed the Association of Khmer Students (AEK), in which all political tendencies were represented; but the AEK was quickly transformed into a hotbed of anti-colonialist agitation, campaigning for Cambodia's immediate and total independence. Several times a week the entire group of Khmer students were invited to Indochina House to attend meetings led by Thiounn Mum, Keng Vangsak, Van Molyvann, and In Sokan. Most of the students were nationalist and antimonarchist, and some were enthusiastic followers of Son Ngoc Thanh. In 1952 Prince Sihanouk took offense at these proceedings and cut off the state scholarships of those who had dared to criticize his reign. In 1953 the French government dissolved the AEK because of its anticolonial attitudes.

Little by little, Marxist ideas gained ground. In Phnom Penh, Prince Youthevong, founder of the Democratic party, owned several books of Marxist doctrine, including the *Communist Manifesto*. He was always willing to share his library with the pupils at the Sisowath *lycée* and in particular lent his books to Rat Samuoeun, a close friend of Ieng Sary. During a stay in a French tuberculosis sanatorium Thiounn Mum also had an opportunity to become acquainted with Marxist writings. As the son of a feudal upper-class family from Phnom Penh that had occupied the post of minister of the royal palace for generations, he could not embrace Marxism as a personal rule of conduct, yet became the life and soul of the Communist cell of Khmer students in Paris. He made a point of meeting newcomers at the airport, guided them through their initiation to Paris, and tried to win them over to his ideals. He returned to Phnom Penh in 1955 with a doctorate in physical science, the first Cambodian to graduate from the École Polytechnique (the most exalted of the French *hautes écoles* and a breeding ground for chiefs of state). In Phnom Penh he found it impossible to lead the political life to which he aspired, so he returned to Paris to continue his work with the students. As his lieutenant he chose Khieu Samphan, who had come in 1953 and whose affability soon won over the new arrivals.

In 1956 about two hundred Khmer students, or one-third of all the Cambodians in France, moved into Cambodia House, newly opened and run by Prince Norindeth, founder of the conservative Liberal party. A few months before this, progressive students had set up *l'Union des Étudiants Khmers* (UEK), which became the new cultural medium for revolutionary ideas. They all kept up their studies: In Sokan, chairman of the UEK, completed his medical course and married a French social worker. Hou Youn obtained a doctorate in law and economic science with a thesis, defended in 1955, on "La Paysannerie du Cambodge et ses problèmes de modernisation" and Khieu Samphan received the same degree with his dissertation on "L'Économie du Cambodge et ses problèmes d'industrialisation," defended in 1959. Son Sen successfully completed an undergraduate year in literature but failed his entrance examination to the École Normale Supérieure (the upper secondary teacher-training institution from which Sartre graduated), after which he went back to Cambodia. Ok Sakun also failed his entrance examinations to the École Centrale (an engineering school); he was recalled to Phnom Penh and went to work for the railway. Ros Chethor and Khieu Komar spent two years at the Sainte-Geneviève school in Versailles preparing for the entrance examinations for the École Polytechnique but went back to Phnom Penh without degrees. Rat Samuoeun completed an undergraduate course in history and geography. Saloth Sar obtained no diplomas but fell in love with French literature and began reading the great authors, Marx, and politics. Ieng Sary passed his second *baccalauréat* exam in Paris but went no further. He was completely absorbed in politics and spent all his time reading in the apartment he shared with Khieu Thirith at 28, rue Saint-André-des-Arts. He sometimes berated his compatriots for thinking only of their studies and getting their degrees: "The revolution will never be made by intellectuals!" he told them. He was the UEK's representative to the French Communist party, of which he was a member, and he admired Stalin and the way in which this man had risen to the summit of power by working as party secretary.

Although the majority behaved like conventional carefree university students, some were quite earnest and tried to live according to the austere moral precepts of their Marxist ideology. Khieu Samphan was especially sober, never wasting time on social frivolities and showing absolutely no interest in the allures of the Parisiennes. In those days he was considered "pure, idealistic, thoughtful, remote from material contingencies, with little idea of the practical consequences of his principles."

Alongside the majority of Khmer students in the UEK, there were other Khmer students in Paris meeting in various mini-groups. The most important of these was the CEKOM, or *Comité des Étudiants Khmers d'outre-mer* (Committee of Overseas Khmer Students), which was supported by Prince Sihanouk and was politically right-wing. Its members were surprised every time they went to call on their compatriots Ieng Sary and In Sokan, for instead of photographs of parents, traditionally displayed in every Cambodian household, they saw those of Ho Chi Minh and Stalin.

In 1950, while Khmer students in Paris were beginning to elaborate their ideas, the largely unknown Khmer revolutionaries from Cochin China founded the United National Front led by the mysterious Son Ngoc Minh—a pseudonym of a chief who was said to be the brother of the much-loved Son Ngoc Thanh. The front's prime objective was to assist Vietnam in its national liberation struggle against France. These Vietminh-Khmers, as they were called, sought to destroy France's economic and financial holdings in Cambodia and sabotage communications within Indochina. The front received very little support from the Cambodian people, who had small knowledge of political issues, and they endured the war of decolonization rather than taking any active part in it—to them, it was a Vietnamese affair. However, the front gained some strength by allying itself with the

Issarak Khmers; but after the Issarak Khmers' submission to Prince Sihanouk in 1954, the United National Front sank into obscurity.

Also, in 1950, the early Khmer revolutionaries founded the Cambodian People's Revolutionary party, better known as the Pracheachon.

The Parisian students' cell sent Thiounn Mum, Ieng Sary, and Saloth Sar as delegates to the Berlin youth festival in 1951. There they met a delegation of Vietminh-Khmers from the United National Front, and returned to Paris bearing documents, photos, and a flag portraying the three towers of Angkor Wat on a red background, which has since become the national flag of Democratic Kampuchea. Ieng Sary came back convinced that only armed combat could bring about true independence from France, but he did not really trust the Vietminh-Khmers because he thought they were too much under Vietnamese influence.

On the delegation's return, the cell decided to send some of its members to the Vietminh-Khmers who were working in the Cambodian countryside: Saloth Sar, Ok Sakun, and Rat Samuoeun were chosen. Ok Sakun soon returned to his French wife, and was later suspected of being a spy for Sihanouk in revolutionary disguise. Saloth Sar joined Norodom Chantarangsey, who was commanding the Issarak Khmers, but quickly realized that the prince was a feudalist at heart, whose goal was to restore the rights of the crown rather than fight for independence. So he went to Phnom Penh, where he acted as liaison between the Vietminh-Khmers and the Democratic party until 1956. Rat Samuoeun has vanished without a trace.

In July 1954 the Geneva Conference met to discuss the Indochinese problem. Since the Issarak Khmers' submission had taken place just a few weeks before the conference opened, King Norodom Sihanouk was the only legal representative of Cambodia: the United National Front and its Vietminh-Khmers were not represented, in spite of the demands of the Vietminh delegation. About half of the five thousand men who constituted its military strength went to Hanoi, the remainder stayed underground in Cambodia. Some of the fighters were embittered and felt humiliated at not having been recognized, but the Khmer students in Paris were not too upset by this turn of events, for several of them feared that the Vietminh-Khmers would impose Hanoi's domination on Cambodia. Meanwhile, Ieng Sary's views had shifted in the direction of internationalism: why bother to maintain a frontier between Vietnam and Cambodia?; why keep an independent Cambodia in a Socialist Indochina?

After completing their studies, the Paris students returned to Phnom Penh, and the two tendencies which had already become visible within the UEK now grew more marked: One was the hard line followed by Ieng Sary, Saloth Sar, and Son Sen: they saw Prince Sihanouk as the chief enemy of the Khmer people who was preventing a true revolution from taking place and who must therefore be defeated by armed combat. The other, "softer" tendency held, on the contrary, that they should cooperate with the prince because he was opposed to American imperialism; what they must do was act within the structures of the kingdom, take over the top positions, and then start the revolution from above. Khieu Samphan, Hou Youn, Hu Nim, and Chau Seng were the chief supporters of this more moderate line.

On March 2, 1955, King Sihanouk abdicated because he wanted more freedom to maneuver politically. He founded the Sangkum Reastr Niyum, or People's Socialist Community, in which he hoped to merge all parties and mobilize them for a program of national action; but the movement lacked a clearcut ideology.

Election day was September 11. All parties campaigned furiously in spite of the multiple pressures, provocations, and impediments emanating from Prince Sihanouk. The Sangkum won every seat. The Democratic party, which criticized Cambodian dependence on American aid, received twelve percent of the vote. The Pracheachon, the Khmer Communist party, received four percent of the vote, but in some wards this rose to forty percent.

Because of government repression, the Pracheachon presented only a single candidate in Phnom Penh in the 1958 elections—Keo Meas, who received 396 votes. Having learned what they could expect from parliamentary procedure, and also under pressure from police harassment, the members of the Pracheachon disappeared; most of the Democrats joined the Sangkum, although without abandoning their political convictions.

Khieu Samphan returned to Cambodia in 1959 and became a professor of political economics on the law school faculty in Phnom Penh. He lived extremely simply in a house with no water on the outskirts of the town, and rode a bicycle, later a motorbike. He edited a review, the *Observateur*, which spread progressive ideas through the academic world. In 1960, at the close of a national congress,[4] the royal police, commanded by Kou Roun, arrested him and publicly undressed him as a humiliation for having dared to criticize the regime.

The UEK alumni reassembled on the teaching staff of a private *lycée*, the Kamputh Both, where Ieng Sary, Khieu Samphan, Hou Youn, and Saloth Sar continued their political fight. Ieng Sary is remembered as a competent French teacher, smiling and affable, who never made the poorest students pay for his classes. He lived in a house near Chamcar Mon and rode a bicycle. His students could call on him at home and ask for help with their lessons, for he was unpretentious and hospitable. "Teachers and pupils, we're all equal," he would say, "there are no social classes." Sometimes he expressed disgust with the royalty which had reduced the people to slavery. "How many human lives it must have cost to build Angkor Wat!" he would exclaim, showing his contempt for the kings. He owned many Chinese publications written in French and would lend them to anyone who wanted to read them.

His wife, the former Khieu Thirith, who had a degree in English, taught at the Norodom *lycée*. Saloth Ponnary, her sister and the wife of Saloth Sar, taught at the Sisowath *lycée*. As well as giving a few classes at the Kamputh Both school, Hou Youn also lectured in the law school.

Son Sen continued to teach in a primary school. He married Yun Yat, an extremely shy girl who taught at the Sisowath *lycée*, and slowly made his way up the ladder until he became director of studies at the National Pedagogical Institute. Under his leader-

---

4 The People's Assembly, presided over by Prince Sihanouk, at which citizens could express their grievances or ideas about how to run the country, in a simulacrum of democratic procedure.

ship the primary-school environment also became a breeding ground for revolutionaries. Frail, respected for his intellectual ability, but rather unforthcoming, he remained little known. However, he organized many secret meetings between primary and secondary schoolteachers and students.

Around 1960 Prince Sihanouk began to feel an intense dislike for these intellectuals who were openly opposing his style of government, the corruption of his regime, and the steady rise of the capitalist right wing.

In 1962 fourteen left-wing activists were arrested by the royal police and charged with acting as Communist agents for North Vietnam in Kompong Cham province. One of them was Nong Suon, secretary general of the Pracheachon. In an attempt to propitiate the young left-wing intellectuals, the prince put up Hou Youn and Khieu Samphan as candidates for his party, the Sangkum, and then appointed them to his cabinet.

Hou Youn abandoned his professorship of political economics to become secretary of state for planning. Urged by his friends, Khieu Samphan reluctantly accepted the post of secretary of state for commerce. With his savings, he bought an old Volkswagen and rented a "compartment" near the Chinese embassy, where he lived with his mother. After a few months he was relieved of his duties for refusing a bribe: somebody offered him a new Mercedes in exchange for permission to carry on an illicit meat trade. So he went back to teaching and private political action.

The intriguer Chau Seng, the only intellectual who openly claimed to be a Communist, continued to publish his newspaper *La Dépêche* while holding a succession of ministerial portfolios: education, agriculture, and economy. He placed his own men in each and simultaneously amassed a small personal fortune from various kinds of embezzlement.

During this period the royal police continued their witch-hunt. All left-wing intellectuals were closely watched. In 1963 Ieng Sary and Son Sen joined the underground somewhere around Pursat, to escape arrest.

Under pressure from left-wing opposition, the prince decided to reject an offer of American aid at a special congress held on November 19, 1963. Despite North Vietnam's promise—endorsed by Peking—to leave Cambodia alone, North Vietnamese and Vietcong were beginning to infiltrate Khmer territory. Bribing Khmer officers and the royal family, they set up bases from which to attack South Vietnam. Prince Sihanouk sensed the danger his country was headed for. Could he use diplomatic channels to get the Vietnamese to withdraw? Not easily. Drive them out? With his little army of twenty-seven thousand men? Could he reinforce the army? No money. The American aid he had turned down was to have been replaced by income from an economic reform, but the reform had been almost a total failure. So he slowly reverted to the idea of American aid as a way out of his predicament.

Elections were held again in 1966. The prince proposed that this time the people themselves should choose their representatives, without the official lists that had been issued on previous occasions. The product of this ballot was an extremely reactionary congress. "You are the true representatives of the Khmer people," was the gist of his statement to the opening session of the sixth legislature. "Two dangers are threatening Cambodia: in the West, Thai imperialism supported by the Americans, and in the East, Vietnamese imperialism!" Violating the constitution, he solemnly renounced his prerogative of choosing the chairman of the council of ministers.

Chau Seng, then head of the prince's private office, had prepared a full cabinet to present to the assembly, but right-wing representatives had been busy among the women of the prince's court, with the result that the ladies defeated the scheme. General Lon Nol was elected premier by sixty out of eighty-five votes. For five days he vainly tried to form a government. On the night of October 23 the prince emerged from Calmette Hospital, where he was being treated, to preside in his pajamas over the final meeting, at which the first Lon Nol government was to be appointed. The next morning Sihanouk, as head of state, announced the formation of a "counter-government" with a watching brief over the official cabinet. In this "counter-government" Hou Youn was named minister of the interior and Hu Nim minister of commerce; Phouk Chhay, Khieu Samphan, and other well-known left-wing figures occupied various other positions. However, Sihanouk had taken care to put one of his own men into the "counter-government" in the person of Kou Roun, the chief of police, who would thus be more comfortably placed to keep an eye on the opposition.

It was at this time that the Samlaut *jacquerie* occurred. Samlaut is a small town west of Battambang, in an isolated forest region inhabited by *Pors*, members of a tribe which had somehow been forgotten in Cambodia's march toward modernization. During the first Indochinese war the Vietminh gained a firm foothold in the area, and their cadres had stayed behind after the Geneva agreements, feeding a latent hostility toward the government. There were about two hundred guns hidden in the forest. In 1966, the Battambang provincial authorities decided to build a sugar refinery at Kompong Kol, near Samlaut. They expropriated land for the plant and did not give the peasants fair compensation for their holdings. The Vietminh cadres seized the opportunity to push the people into open rebellion. The government in Phnom Penh overreacted, sending out a military force under Lieutenant Colonel Chhay Lay, while Oum Manorine, Sihanouk's brother-in-law and secretary of state for defense, dispatched units of national police. Both forces were heavy-handed, killing many villagers and burning their homes. The population fled into the forest, with intensified loathing for the unjust administration that was leaving a trail of death wherever it went.

On April 30, 1968, Sihanouk, faced with the failure of his policy, removed Lon Nol as head of the government and put Son Sann in his place. He also discharged the governor of Battambang and appointed In Tam in his stead, with instructions to reconcile the rebels. Oum Manorine did his utmost to make sure that this mission would fail, and In Tam was forced to resign a few months later. Sihanouk then had the disastrous idea of sending in a force combined of army soldiers and club-wielding villagers from Battambang province to put down the rebellion. And they did; but when the Samlaut peasants took to the mountains this time, they were firmly resolved to pay back a hundredfold the evil that had been done to them.

While this rebellion was sputtering in the northwestern part of the country, China was embarking upon its cultural revolution, echoes of which soon reached Phnom Penh. Some of the Chinese experts began brandishing copies of their little red books, and many teachers were following the Chinese experiment with keen interest. The prince, however, alarmed by their fascination, banned the Chinese-Cambodian Friendship Association, which he suspected of supplying material for subversive propaganda, and redoubled his pursuit of those he had by now baptized the Khmer Rouge.

Some teachers, such as Tiv Ol and Koy Thuon, nevertheless continued their open criticism of the government. To celebrate the Khmer New Year in 1967 they held a party at Sangkum University and invited Prince Sihanouk to attend. They presented a program of entertainment consisting of Chinese revolutionary dances and a concert of revolutionary songs. The prince was stung, and insulted them. To save their heads, they were forced to disappear into the forest the next morning.

Then, on April 24, 1967, Hou Youn and Khieu Samphan dropped out of sight. Sihanouk had publicly accused them of instigating the Samlaut uprising. The two men left Phnom Penh under the protection of the Chinese embassy. Radio Peking accused Prince Sihanouk of killing them and even gave out exact details of their execution. A few days later Phouk Chhay, chairman of the Association of Khmer Students in Phnom Penh, was arrested; and on September 4 Lon Nol managed to have Chau Seng sent into exile after accusing him of fomenting a *coup d'état*. Then Hu Nim and Poc Deuskoma went underground in the Kompong Cham region, and were followed by several left-wing teachers. Some stayed in Cambodia and labored to arouse a political consciousness in the peasant masses; others went to be trained in North Vietnam, where they were regarded as fanatics; and still others went to China for a firsthand look at this cultural revolution which was to stamp out the last vestiges of an ever renascent bourgeoisie. It was undoubtedly during this period that the Chinese influence on the Khmer revolutionaries was the strongest, and pushed them over the edge into active revolution.

During this troubled period, a second seat of rebellion was bathing the Cambodian northeast in blood. Prince Sihanouk had decided to install a vast rubber plantation on the Ratanakiri basalt plateaus, as a source of foreign currency to replace American aid. The colonization of these mountainous regions by the "middle Khmers" from Phnom Penh did not please the "upland Khmers," or mountaineers, who were proto-Khmer tribes living on what they could gather in the forest or grow on burnt-over land. A brutal governor named Thung Nhach imposed numerous exactions on the mountaineers to despoil them of the land for the rubber plantation, and had a score of "upland Khmers" put to death. Then their compatriots took their crossbows and went into the forest, where they held the government forces at bay with their primitive methods of warfare. The regular troops were not used to the forest and were rapidly undermined by malaria and general demoralization. Meanwhile, the mountaineers organized and applied for arms and ammunition to the Vietnamese revolutionaries who had infiltrated their territory.

These Vietnamese revolutionaries were becoming a real menace to Cambodia. True, the aid they were giving the Khmer revolutionaries was minimal, because they wanted to keep on good terms with the Sihanouk regime, which was letting them send their convoys of ammunition and equipment overland from the port of disembarkation at Sihanoukville (now Kompong Som) across Cambodia to the frontier. But their numbers were growing, and Sihanouk was finding them increasingly worrying; would they ever leave, once the war was over? Until the great Communist offensive in 1968, he believed the revolutionaries would win in South Vietnam. But when he saw how fiercely the population in the south defended itself he wavered, and began to think the north might be defeated. The cessation of American bombing in North Vietnam and the opening of the Paris Conference could also be seen as a prelude to the end of war in Vietnam. But whichever side turned out to be the victor, he had to find some way of ensuring his country's independence. Its economic and political plight and its right-wing parliament were pushing him to turn to America, and he reestablished diplomatic relations with the United States in 1969. In his desire to stop the infiltration along Cambodia's frontiers, he disclosed the location of Vietcong bases, which were then bombed by the American air force. He called it a scandal and a crime over Radio Phnom Penh, but nobody was deceived.

In 1969, faced with ever greater difficulties, Sihanouk reshuffled his government twice. First, he made Samdech Penn Nouth head of a "last-ditch" government; then, at the beginning of August, he put General Lon Nol in charge of a "salvage" government. Weary with the repeated failure of his policies and bedeviled by increasingly virulent criticism, he went to France for a rest at the beginning of 1970.

Lon Nol had preceded him to Europe a few weeks earlier, leaving the country in the hands of Prince Sisowath Sirik Matak, the deputy premier. He met Prince Sihanouk in Rome, where the chief of state told him his plan: the general should return to Cambodia and organize anti-Vietnam demonstrations, which the prince would use as a pretext to ask Moscow and Peking to persuade their protégés to withdraw from Khmer territory. With these instructions, the general returned to Phnom Penh, and on March 8, 1970, "spontaneous" demonstrations broke out at Svay Rieng. On March 11, the NLF and North Vietnamese embassies were sacked.

Prince Sihanouk, who had stayed behind in Paris, was acutely embarrassed; he had not foreseen such a violent reaction, and accused his government of letting matters get out of hand. He realized that a direct frontal attack on the Vietnamese Communists was a serious political error, and on March 13 he flew to Moscow. The government tried to justify itself and offered to send Yem Sambaur and Prince Norodom Kantol to Sihanouk to explain. This proposal was flatly refused and the refusal accompanied by a threat to shoot the entire cabinet, which was badly rattled. Then, at 1:00 P.M. on March 18, 1970, at the instigation of Prince Sisowath Sirik Matak—presumably backed by the Americans—the parliament voted to depose Sihanouk as chief of state.

This was an unhoped-for stroke of luck for the Khmer revolutionaries. The Lon Nol government tried to negotiate the departure of the Vietcong and North Vietnamese troops, but the talks broke down. Then the Vietnamese were given notice to leave their bases within forty-eight hours.

And they did indeed emerge from their hideouts, but only to extend their invasion of Cambodia; to avoid being caught between the American–South Vietnamese army in the east and the Khmer in the west, they pushed deeper into Cambodian territory. With the support of the Khmer revolutionaries, they incited the frontier peasants to march on Phnom Penh and overthrow the Lon Nol regime.

On March 29, more than forty thousand Khmer and Cham peasants and mountaineers poured into Kompong Cham, looting all the houses which were not displaying Prince Sihanouk's portrait, burning the courthouse, killing two representatives sent to restore calm, encircling the prefect's offices, and requisitioning all means of transport to take them to Phnom Penh. The army, visibly without orders, did nothing. The buses and trucks crammed full of peasants came within sight of Phnom Penh during the night; in the south they were halted at Koki by the army, which opened on them with cannon fire. To the north the convoy met with the same reception six kilometers outside the city. The next morning, near Skoun, air force planes let off several bursts of machine-gun fire over a convoy of peasants traveling toward the capital, killing about forty people. At Kompong Cham the army fired into the crowd: sixty dead. Equally devastating scenes took place in the southern part of the country. The peasants, humiliated and shocked to find themselves the victims of their own national army, returned home and swore to avenge their dead.

The Vietcong and North Vietnamese, taking advantage of the confusion that followed Prince Sihanouk's deposition, invaded two-thirds of Cambodia. In the countryside they wore badges representing the deposed prince, whom they swore to restore to power. Armed with tape recorders, they played tapes of the prince's call to rebellion, which had been broadcast over Radio Peking. The peasants wept with joy and greeted the Vietnamese as their liberators. Provincial administrations either went over to the revolutionaries or fled. Civil servants, schoolteachers, and students, who were blamed for the prince's deposition, were hunted out and executed.

The government then tried to stir up the Khmers' ancient hatred for the Vietnamese, hoping to unite the people against these foreigners who happened to be supporting the prince but were also invaders. Every Vietnamese living in Cambodia at that time was suspected of being a Communist or aiding the Vietcong aggressors, with the result that thousands of them were assassinated in the first half of April and their bodies thrown in the Mekong. The small and overworked government army had to be everywhere at once. To halt the advance of the Vietnamese revolutionaries, the government ordered a general call-up. Thousands of young men enlisted enthusiastically, eager to fight the hereditary foe. The newly recruited Cambodian elite were far out of touch with reality, however: having deposed Sihanouk with a few demonstrations and massacred a few unarmed Vietnamese civilians, they imagined it would be just as easy to drive out the Vietcong. Some even dreamed of going on to reconquer Cochin China. They soon had to face the unpleasant facts, however: defeat followed defeat, people were dying, the government was entangled in internecine quarrels, and corruption was rampant.

In the first few weeks, the North Vietnamese divided the zones they had "liberated" into squares and put Vietnamese residents in Cambodia into all key positions, sweeping up young Khmers to be trained in revolutionary warfare. The Vietminh-Khmer cadres who had been living scattered about the countryside since 1954 reappeared on the scene, and those who had been in training in Hanoi or Peking quickly returned. Political commissars began circulating propaganda, but at that time their language was still incomprehensible to the peasants.

With their customary political realism, the North Vietnamese did not forget that the feelings of Khmers of all political persuasions were fundamentally hostile toward them. After organizing the countryside and training a few troops, they gradually withdrew from Cambodia and returned to their conquest of South Vietnam. Beginning in 1971, the Khmer Rouge were in control of the entire administrative organization of the "liberated" zones, but they let the Vietnamese take the lead in military operations. After 1972, government troops found themselves fighting an army composed almost entirely of Khmers—their brothers, men of their own race—and their morale began to melt like ice in the sun. Why go on spilling Khmer blood? Often, however, they were pitted against troops recruited among the ethnic minorities of Cambodia, the Brao mountaineers, the Tapouons, Jarais, and

Chams, who fought fiercely alongside the Khmer revolutionaries, revenging themselves for centuries of domination and harassment with the blood of an innocent population.

The revolutionaries were becoming increasingly well coordinated as far as their internal organization was concerned: on March 26, 1970, Khieu Samphan, Hou Youn, and Hu Nim signed a declaration of "unreserved support" for Prince Sihanouk. In Peking, on May 5, 1970, the prince founded the RGNUK. This government, headed by Samdech Penn Nouth, gave several ministries to revolutionaries Khieu Samphan, Hou Youn, Hu Nim, and Thiounn Mum. It was reorganized on May 13, again on August 20 of that year, and once again on March 23, 1972, and each time the revolutionaries gained more ground, until they could begin appointing their own ministers and gradually eliminating Prince Sihanouk's supporters. The last Sihanoukists lost their positions when the government of Democratic Kampuchea was formed on April 14, 1976.

Beginning in 1973, tension became visible in the revolutionary camp, between the Khmer Rouge, whose allegiance was to the Communists, and the Khmer Rumda, or Liberation Front Khmer, who supported the prince. The two groups formed an alliance. In February 1973 Prince Sihanouk, flanked by a team of associates, made a secret trip to Cambodia. He took the Ho Chi Minh trail from Vietnam and went through the "liberated" provinces of Stung Treng, Preah Vihear, and Siem Reap. He visited Angkor Wat and attended a mass meeting in Phnom Koulen, at which the main leaders of the resistance were also present. But there was dissension among the rebel leaders—the revolutionary army encircled Phnom Koulen and turned away all the cadres who had been invited to the meeting. After this, the tone of revolutionary propaganda in the countryside changed, and Sihanouk became the target of criticism at least as violent as that aimed at Lon Nol and his regime.

This dissension in the underground was also perceptible in Peking, where the visiting Khmer lived as two separate groups. The prince, with about forty close associates who formed his court, was housed on his private estate. The second group, the

Khmer Rouge, lived at the Sino-Khmer Friendship Hotel, and the Chinese had far less contact with them, considering them too independent and possibly subject to Soviet influence because of their early training in the French Communist party.

From the outset of the Cambodian crisis, China decided to back Prince Sihanouk all the way, and welcomed him in Peking on March 19, 1970, with all the honors accorded to a chief of state. On March 25, Chou En-lai urged him and Pham Van Dong, North Vietnamese minister of foreign affairs, to form a "United Front of the Three Indochinese Peoples"; this led to the Canton Conference, held on April 24 and 25, over which Chou En-lai came to preside in person. On this occasion Prince Sihanouk, Prince Souphanouvong (of Laos), Pham Van Dong (of North Vietnam), and Nguyen Huu Tho (of the South Vietnamese NLF) decided to join forces at military and diplomatic levels in order to drive the American imperialists out of Indochina. On May 1 Chairman Mao Tse-tung made an official statement expressing China's total support for Prince Sihanouk, who was seated during the announcement on the Chinese leader's right. This support was not only moral, it also took the form of financial assistance—"an interest-free loan to be repaid after the victory"—and abundant military aid. In the ensuing years it was displayed at the diplomatic level as well, when China attempted to get the UN to recognize the RGNUK instead of the Khmer Republic.

The United States was not sure what attitude to adopt in the Cambodian crisis. Sihanouk's downfall was bad news, for the prince had moved much closer to America during the last months of his reign, and his departure upset the balance the United States had begun to establish in the Indochinese peninsula. After a few hours of hesitation, America decided to back Lon Nol, for if he fell it would mean the end in Vietnam. Immediately after the *coup d'état* of March 18, 1970, GIs and military equipment began landing at Phnom Penh airport by night. In view of the government troops' repeated setbacks in their attempts to curb North Vietnamese infiltration, President Nixon authorized the American–South Vietnamese forces to launch a cleanup operation extending forty kilometers inside Cambodian territory and lasting from April 30 to June 30. The South Vietnamese took advantage of this official blessing to avenge a hundredfold their compatriots who had been massacred by Lon Nol's men the month before; their savagery drove a number of Cambodian peasants over to the Khmer Rouge.

After the agreements concluded with North Vietnam on January 27, 1973, America undertook to restore peace in Cambodia by detaching the Khmer Rouge from Sihanouk and launching the idea of a coalition government to be formed after negotiation with all parties concerned. Faced with a recrudescence of Communist attacks, Lon Nol asked the American air force to intervene "to compel the other party to negotiate." Between March 7 and August 15, forty thousand tons of bombs fell on Cambodia every month, causing the deaths of two hundred thousand persons, according to the revolutionaries' calculations. Chou En-lai supported Prince Sihanouk's rejection of the "American peace," which would mean a cease-fire maintaining the frontiers at the line of battle and a division of the country. On April 11, 1975, after a final appeal to the prince to return to his country, the United States abandoned Cambodia. Flanked by an absurdly large deployment of troops, the American ambassador climbed into a helicopter on April 12, with the Stars and Stripes under his arm.

The USSR and France, in contrast with the Chinese and American positions, sat on the fence for five years and tried to make friends in both camps. On March 18, 1970, the Soviets made a determined attempt to dissuade Sihanouk from going to Peking. In May of the same year they accused Chinese leaders of trying to sabotage the Indochinese national liberation movements. The USSR was unable to adopt a consistent policy in relation to China and maintained diplomatic relations with the Lon Nol regime until March 27, 1975, while simultaneously tolerating the presence of an RGNUK ambassador in Moscow. After the Paris agreements on Vietnam and Laos, the USSR opted for an American-style solution to the Khmer problem, with cease-fire and negotiations, and abstained from the UN vote on the admission of the RGNUK. Moreover, the USSR waited three and a half years before recognizing the RGNUK as the sole legitimate representative of the Cambodian people, so it is not surprising that it should now stand high on the list of enemies of the Khmer people, coming right after France and America.

On April 17, 1975, Prince Sihanouk was informed of the revolutionaries' victory at a reception in the embassy of an Arab state. When the news became official he displayed the appropriate enthusiasm, but privately he was badly shaken. He awaited news from the interior of Cambodia, at length and in vain. Foreign journalists were plying him with questions that he was unable to answer. He gave the state of health of his mother, Queen Kossomak, as a reason for postponing his return to Cambodia, but the queen died in the last days of April and the prince's position was no clearer than before. "My presence in Cambodia is not indispensable. By remaining at a distance from our capital I wish to show my determination not to be associated with the affairs of the Khmer Rouge," he told an Algerian newspaper on May 8. He decided to "go into voluntary exile at Pyong Yang, capital of North Korea, to live at peace far from indiscreet questions." At the end of May, convinced that he would never set foot on his native soil again, he even wrote a song called "Farewell Cambodia."

However, the revolutionaries had one last favor to ask of him: to legitimize their regime both at home and abroad. But before doing so, they took care to organize the country in such a way that there could be no turning back to the old regime.

On July 18, 1975, Sarin Chhak, the RGNUK minister of foreign affairs, and Thiounn Prasith went to Pyong Yang and asked the prince to return, but he refused. On August 19 Samdech Penn Nouth and Khieu Samphan again went and asked him to come home. He was promised that he would remain head of state for life, and agreed. Back in Peking, the prince went to bid farewell to Chou En-lai, who congratulated him from his hospital bed and said he was very pleased with the wise decision Sihanouk had made. By returning to Cambodia the prince was fulfilling the policies of the Chinese premier, who had given his all to this end; a billion-dollar loan which was granted to Kampuchea at the same time may not have been entirely unrelated to this political victory. "My decision to return to Cambodia," Sihanouk told his close friends, "does not mean that I approve the cruel policy of the Khmer Rouge, but I must sacrifice my own views out of consideration for China and His Excellency Chou En-lai, who have done so much for Cambodia and for myself."[5]

After a short stay in Hanoi the prince reached Phnom Penh on September 9. All was in readiness at the airport: red carpet; college of bonzes to recite victory psalms; girls scattering flower petals; armed revolutionary soldiers on parade, others disguised as civilians. When the plane door opened the prince paused a moment and drew back, then plunged into the unknown.

His first days in Phnom Penh brought many disappointments: he found a dead city, in which even he was not allowed to go where he pleased. He was taken to see a work site for dike and canal construction ten kilometers south of the capital, and to visit a textile mill in the suburbs. When he walked into the factory several of the women workers began to weep at the sight of "Monsignor Papa," whom they had been awaiting like a savior. A few managed to slip him bits of paper describing their misery. He wanted to take his mother's ashes to Angkor, but was not allowed to. He sat in the chairman's seat at cabinet meetings but had no power of decision. If one member of his entourage can be believed, "in the obscurity of his palace, the prince wept."[6] A true patriot, he could not remain unmoved by his people's unhappiness or the condition of the city he loved.

After a stay of three weeks, which was enough to convince the population that the new power was legitimate, the prince was appointed to represent Cambodia at the UN, where he had lost his seat in 1970. There, cheered by the representatives of the third world, he made an important speech against the American imperialists, the greatest imperialists in the world, who had been stopped in their tracks by little Cambodia. He returned home by way of Paris, where he was received by the president of the republic on October 9. "The number one ambassador of Cambodia" spoke of himself as "a little more than the Queen of England or the King of Sweden," something comparable to Albert Lebrun in

---

[5] Associated Press (October 17, 1975).

[6] Agence France-Presse (October 17, 1975).

the French Third Republic or Vincent Auriol in the Fourth. Apparently satisfied with his stay, he said he would "make a good report to his government." However, the prince's visit unleashed a campaign of protest in the press against the nonchalance with which he seemed to treat the sufferings of the Khmer people.

The prince returned to Cambodia, remained a few days, then set off on November 15 for an official tour of eleven countries. Kampuchea's new authorities let him go, convinced that he would remain a power-loving, honor-courting feudalist forever, and would certainly still want to be head of state when he returned.

Back from his travels on December 31 of that year, he found that the atmosphere at the airport had changed, and he was greeted like an ordinary citizen. At the beginning of 1976 he was asked to recall his sons from abroad. When they returned, they were separated from him and sent to build the country like the rest of the population.

The prince, meanwhile, living confined in his palace, was finding life in this Asian Sparta very little to his taste, so he did not much mind when he was asked to resign in March 1976: he was hoping he would be able to go abroad. He wrote a statement in French in his own hand which he read out over the radio on April 2. In contrast to the bombastic tone of his past speeches, his voice on this occasion expressed painfully restrained emotion. Then, when he read the Khmer translation of the same text, his distress was audible.

On April 4, "The Council of Ministers . . . expressed its regret at this request for retirement by Samdech Norodom Sihanouk" and proposed that "the following decisions be submitted to the People's Representative Assembly": that the "title of Great Patriot" be conferred upon the prince and that a monument be built in honor of his good deeds. In addition, "the Government of Democratic Kampuchea will fully guarantee and bear the living expenses of himself and his family" at the rate of "$2,000 quarterly or $8,000 per annum . . ."[7]

Since that time various rumors have circulated regarding the

---

[7] Text issued, without references, by the RGNUK. See Appendix.

prince's fate; important political figures have made anxious
enquiries. Some claim he is dead, others that he has been injured,
and still others that he is sequestered. The official voice, however, affirms that he is writing his memoirs and is consulted on all
major issues of international policy. It is symptomatic that he did
not sign the book of condolence at the Chinese embassy in Phnom
Penh after the death of Mao Tse-tung, who had done so much for
him. It seems that the prince may be living under surveillance
somewhere south of Phnom Penh, working to earn his keep.
Khieu Samphan said in an interview taped for Radio Phnom Penh
on April 4 that the prince had resigned in order to "look after the
needs of his family himself."[8] Having abandoned his position as
head of state, he is just an ordinary citizen and must live like
everybody else.

The inconsistency of this "red prince"—"the first prince to be
named chief of state of a Communist regime" as he put it himself
—may be found hard to believe. He undoubtedly felt no great
love for those he baptized the Khmer Rouge and had ruthlessly
persecuted after 1966. "Mad, but mad with a streak of genius,"[9]
he had, through his acrobatic diplomacy, kept his country at
peace for seventeen years in the midst of a blazing Indochina. His
words gave new energy to his people and renewed their national
pride, but at no great cost. He wanted to see social justice but
could not part with his courtiers, and thus sacrificed any chance
of carrying out badly needed reforms. Morbidly introverted, he
judged men and events solely in terms of the personal glory he
might derive from them. A demagogue himself, he had little desire to educate his people, for anyone rising to prominence might
later become an enemy.

He knew perfectly well that his alliance with the Khmer Rouge
could never last: "The Khmer Rouge detest me and I feel the
same about them. When they have no more use for me they will
spit me out like a cherry pit." But he would go to any lengths to
revenge himself on those who had deposed him.

---

[8] April 5, 1976 transmission.

[9] General Paul de Langlade, quoted in Norodom Sihanouk, *L'Indochine vue de
Pékin* (Paris: 1972), p. 54.

In the early days after the *coup d'état* of 1970, the fallen prince was planning to return to France and end his days in peace and quiet in his house at Mougins. But his Khmer pride was stung by the insults and unfounded calumny heaped upon him by people who had been singing his praises the day before. At the time, observers were amazed at the total lack of psychological tact of the new leaders who hoped, by dragging Sihanouk through the mud, to turn people away from him. Their tactics achieved the exact opposite. "If it is necessary to attribute some personal motive to my efforts, I would say that I want to avenge myself for having been calumnied, insulted, and humiliated in such a cowardly, base, and wicked manner by my enemies on the extreme right. I cannot accept injustice and shall fight the Lon Nol clique without any thought of drawing back. If they had simply taken the power without stooping to abase me, I should probably have been content to live peacefully in exile in France."[10]

He expressed the same feelings in his declaration of April 2, 1976:

. . . the traitorous clique criticized me harshly and soiled my name with slanderous statements and contempt.

For the rest of my life I shall remain grateful to the Kampuchean people, Kampuchean heroes and heroines, and the Kampuchean revolutionary Angkar for clearing my name so fully in the eyes of the world and history.

It is here, no doubt, more than in any ideological consideration, that we must look for the source of the energy deployed by this prince during his five years in exile. To avenge his lost reputation and wash away the affront he had suffered he was prepared to destroy himself and the people he loved along with him. That the Khmer Rouge victory was hailed so eagerly by a war-weary population and that the troops surrendered with such alacrity, was due to the prestige of their beloved prince, whom they longed to see at home again. Presumably, he did not realize that

---

[10] Quoted by Charles Meyer, *Derrière le sourire khmer* (Paris: 1971), p. 372; see also Norodom Sihanouk, *L'Indochine vue de Pékin*, pp. 159–60.

in hiding behind his name the new authorities had avenged his honor in a sea of blood. Will history rehabilitate him as easily as he says?

Since April 14, 1976, a new government has been running Democratic Kampuchea. Khieu Samphan, chairman of the state presidium, is assisted by two previously unknown vice-chairmen, So Phim and Nhim Ros. They are probably revolutionaries who went underground in the early days of the movement. At the meetings he attends and on his travels through the country Khieu Samphan is called Met Hem. It is he who officially represents Cambodia abroad. He is taciturn, seldom shows his feelings, and is a thinker. However, at mass meetings such as the one held in Phnom Penh on April 17, 1976, to celebrate the first anniversary of the liberation, he shows an oratorical style capable of rousing the public.

Nuon Chea, always mentioned second in official texts, seems to be the number two man of the regime. Since the war began he has been "vice-chairman of the military high command of the PNLAFK[11] and chief of the army political directorate."[12] After April 14, 1976, he officially became chairman of the standing committee of the People's Representative Assembly.

Pol Pot, premier since April 14, 1976, was "authorized after September 27, 1976, to relinquish his post temporarily for reasons of health."[13] Nuon Chea has been standing in for him, combining the premier's job with his own. However, Pol Pot would still seem to be head of the government, for his name and title are always given alongside those of Khieu Samphan and Nuon Chea as the coauthors of letters to foreign governments.

Little is known of Nuon Chea and Pol Pot. Several observers think that Pol Pot is merely a pseudonym for Nong Suon, pillar of Khmer communism from the 1950s; for others, he is really Rat Samuoeun, one of three students sent out to work as liaison agents

---

[11] People's National Liberation Armed Forces of Kampuchea.
[12] Ieng Sary, *Cambodge 1972* (distributed by RGNUK), p. 5.
[13] Radio P.P. (September 27, 1976).

with the Vietminh-Khmers; and yet others believe he is a former rubber plantation laborer. However, a comparison of photographs indicates that Pol Pot is really Saloth Sar. A native of Prey Sbeuv in the Kompong Thom region and the son of peasants, Saloth Sar took a technical course in Phnom Penh and then went to France to study at the École du Livre. He is married to Khieu Ponnary, was vice-chairman of the military high command of the PNLAFK during the war years, and has allegedly been secretary of the Khmer Communist party since September 30, 1972.[14]

Ieng Sary, the number four figure in the regime, is deputy premier in charge of foreign affairs. He is called Met Vann. His job as foreign minister has brought him much more before the eyes of international circles than his colleagues, so that many people take him to be the strong man in the country; and he undoubtedly is one of the top people, but not the foremost. He is married to Ieng Thirith, Khieu Ponnary's sister; this makes Ieng Sary the brother-in-law of Saloth Sar, alias Pol Pot. Ieng Thirith is minister of social affairs, and her brother is Khieu Tham, formerly Lon Nol's ex-ambassador to Berlin.

Von Vet is deputy premier in charge of economy. He too has presumably come straight from the underground, for nobody knows anything about him.

Son Sen, nicknamed "the Old Man with the Glasses" or Comrade Khieu, is deputy premier in charge of defense. His wife, Yun Yat, is now minister of culture and education.

Hu Nim is nicknamed Comrade Phoas. He is minister of information and propaganda and has been since 1970.

Thiounn Thioeun, former physician-in-chief at the Khmero-Soviet Friendship Hospital in Phnom Penh, has been minister of health since 1970.

Tauch Phoeun is minister of public works.

In addition to the ministries there are six committees that are subsidiaries of the deputy premiership of economy: agriculture, industry, commerce, communications, energy, and rubber plantations. The chairman of each has ministerial rank in the govern-

---

[14] Associated Press (October 10, 1976).

ment of Democratic Kampuchea, and their high position in the government shows how much importance is attached to economic problems. Some of their names are known: Mey Pran heads the communications committee, Chey An the industry committee, Chea Doeun the committee on commerce.

Official statements make no mention of a central committee of the politburo of the Angkar or a secretary general of the Communist party, such as one might expect to find in the organizational setup of a Socialist country. Some refugees say that a central committee exists, however, and has five permanent members: Saloth Sar, nicknamed Comrade Pol; Comrade Nuon; Ieng Sary; Son Sen; and Comrade Yann. The former names of comrades Nuon and Yann are unknown. This committee is said to make all important decisions.

Refugees who left Kampuchea in 1977 report serious dissension within the revolutionary army and the country's leadership. There may even have been an aborted *coup d'état* in February 1977. It is hard to learn more about these internal events, but conflict certainly does exist, for a large number of refugees speak of sporadic fighting between rival factions of the army. The names of Von Vet, Hu Nim, and Premier Pol Pot had not been pronounced over the radio since the beginning of 1977. In late September 1977, however, Pol Pot reappeared on the political scene and made an official visit to Peking, on which occasion he was described as secretary of the Khmer Communist party. Does this mean the disagreements on high have now been settled?

It may be worth pointing out that Democratic Kampuchea is being governed by a family clan—a fairly frequent occurrence in Asiatic tradition. Most of those now in power were initially teachers of one sort or another. Their lives, like those of the Khmer people, hold more than one secret; but just as it is in silence that births are prepared, so silence is what remains behind, sole master of the field, when the fighting is over.

ELEVEN

Happiness for All?

The leaders of Democratic Kampuchea, like those in every other country on earth, whatever its regime or ideology, are fond of proclaiming that their one ambition is to build a nation "overflowing with harmony and happiness." One could hardly criticize them for that. But although the present authorities may be firmly convinced that the sufferings being endured at this moment by the Khmer people contain within them the seeds of happiness for generations to come, the population does not unanimously share this vision.

Since April 1975, thousands of Khmers have fled into voluntary exile. About thirty-five thousand have gone to Thailand, and at least another fifty thousand to Vietnam—not counting the two hundred thousand or so Vietnamese who had been living in Cambodia and returned to their homeland after April 17, 1975. Many of these did not need to be told to go; the prospect of returning to Vietnam meant liberation to them. In addition to the refugees, there are the real or supposed "reactionaries," for whom "liberation" has been final.

179

Thus the total number of citizens who have refused, in one way or another, to be "liberated" is relatively large. Moreover, the refugees say that a large proportion of the population now living in Cambodia is awaiting another liberation, and finding it long in coming. Resistance groups are already engaged in armed opposition.

In the months before the fall of Phnom Penh, the number of departures for France and Hong Kong rose at a dizzying rate. Airplane seats cost a fortune, not because the air fares were so high but because of the exorbitant taxes officially levied by the state and the no less exorbitant bribes which had to be paid at every step of the procedure. More and more people were wanting to go, and seats had to be reserved long in advance. Most of those who left at this time came from the Chinese merchant class or the Khmer civilian and military administration, who were attempting to provide for their families and futures in some other part of the world.

In the days immediately before and after the capture of Phnom Penh, other "refugees" crossed the border into Thailand; for the most part, these were middle-class families living near the frontier, who wanted a quiet place in which they could wait to see which way the wind was going to blow. A good many of them were military leaders or corrupt high-ranking officials too deeply involved in the old regime, with too much to lose in the new. The Thai government was acutely embarrassed by this drove of undesirables; even if the Thais felt themselves ideologically remote from the new Khmer regime, they were anxious to avoid anything that might spoil their future relations with it. The presence of American soldiers and aircraft on their territory was bad enough —not to speak of the training grounds for republican troops— without anything more coming along to aggravate the situation. Officially, therefore, there were no Khmer refugees in Thailand.

Three months after the fall of Phnom Penh, however, the truth began to leak out: tens of thousands of Khmers had escaped from their country, and more were coming every day. Upon reaching Thailand they were parked in abysmal conditions in ten or a dozen camps set up along the border; and the news they brought of life in Kampuchea was terrifying but unverifiable.

These refugees came from every class of society, ranging from a few senior officials or high-ranking officers to laborers from the factories of Phnom Penh and peasants from Preah Vihear. They also represented every political tendency: some were unconditional supporters of Sihanouk, others were loyal to Lon Nol, and there were even some Khmer Rouge among them; but the majority held no strongly defined views. After months of misery under the new regime, they had simply risked everything and run. At the end of 1976 they were still coming, in a thinner but steady stream.

Even if he lives in the city, the Khmer is primarily a peasant who loves his land and his race and does not take readily to the idea of emigration; so the motives that impelled so many people to choose the wrench of exile must have been powerful ones.

For the officials and military, the most common reason was the simple dread of physical elimination. Several had been eyewitnesses to the massacres of their comrades-in-arms or fellow office workers, and had only saved their skins by changing identities. They knew, from the inquisitorial methods of the new regime, that sooner or later they would be discovered and killed off in turn. "I went to Phum Srok," one captain reports, "where I met people I had known before, and I ran away because I was afraid they would denounce me." "If we had stayed," said a customs officer from Battambang, "we would certainly have died: denunciation, sickness, or hunger would have made an end of us."

Some lesser officials and white-collar workers chose exile out of disgust with the methods employed by the new regime. Pon Sampiech was an office employee in a small firm in Phnom Penh; in January 1975 he went to work near the Thai frontier, leaving his wife and children behind in the captial. The "liberation" overtook him far from home. He wanted to stay in Cambodia and work to rebuild his country, for, like many others, he had been revolted by the corruption of the republic. He asked to go back to his family. "After the plowing," replied the Angkar. A month later he was told, "after the plants have been set out," then, "after the harvest." When he understood that he would never see his wife and children again, he left the country in despair, swearing to return, gun in hand.

Many laborers and peasants left their native land for similar reasons. Lao Bun Thai thought the Socialist regime would increase his country's prosperity by developing its agriculture:

"What they're doing is good."

"So why did you leave?"

"I was in the army from 1970 to 1972. If they found out they would shoot me. And I'd had more than one affair with girls: that's something they don't forgive!"

Phat Saren also had no complaints about his work in the country: "It was very hard," he said, "but we were living outdoors in the fresh air. Even so, death was never far away because of the shortage of food and medicine. The reason why I decided to go was because I was suddenly followed for a week; they were spying on me in order to find out who I was. I wasn't guilty of anything, but when they start to follow somebody like that it's very dangerous!"

The workers in the Battambang textile mills say the same thing: "We learned, from comments let slip by Khmer Rouge friends, that they meant to kill everybody who had held an important position in the factory, so we fled on February 19, 1976."

On April 7, 1976, we were in a prison at Thap Se [Thailand]. The Thai officials brought in a Khmer who had just arrived from Cambodia. His name was Vinn Sokha and he was the owner of a garage in Pailin. One day the Khmer Rouge had come and bound him to the wall of his house. Then they left, saying they would come back to kill him at dawn. During the night Sokha scraped his hands against the wall and suddenly the rope gave way. So he escaped through the forest and mountains, and had nothing to eat but leaves and fruit for a month. We saw the marks of the ropes in the flesh of both arms. He was very thin and his clothes were in rags.

This was told by Chan Dara, the court clerk from Pailin.

So for a large number of refugees terror was the deciding factor. Other reasons given as often are hunger and lack of hygiene. "Sooner or later we all would have died." Many believed that the entire population which had been officially "liberated" on April 17 was meant to die, except for the children and young people who could be reclaimed. So in that case, why stay? Why work

oneself to death building the country, if one could not live to see
the fruit of one's labors?

Compulsory hard labor is seldom mentioned as a motive for
escape. Obviously, many of the people from Phnom Penh were
not too enthusiastic about working with their hands like the peasants they despised. They were not given time to complain,
however, but were quickly turned into "fertilizer" for the land
they were supposed to be cultivating. The men who had to pull
the plows do not speak of their agricultural stint as a time of great
happiness, but if they had been decently fed and less harshly
treated they would have stayed and gone on working, because
it was their own land they were cultivating.

Now, after the initial months of indecision and reorganization,
living conditions in the country are still driving villagers to flee
abroad. For many, the country's conversion to the cooperative
system at the end of 1975, entailing the compulsory displacement
of hundreds of thousands of people, was the last straw. At har-
vesttime in December 1975, the workers were bitterly disap-
pointed: "We were hoping to eat the rice and vegetables we had
grown, but the fruit of our work was taken away from us!" Even
the "old" people in the zones that had been "liberated" years
before could no longer bear the relentless pressure: in late February 1976, 114 peasants from the village of Kaun Kreal, fifteen
kilometers from Preah Vihear, fled to the Lumpuk camp. They
had been living in a "liberated" zone for five years, growing rice
in forest clearings and making their own carts, which was their
special trade; but they left "because," as one said, "we couldn't go
on living in continual fear."

Since January 1976, even Khmer Rouge soldiers—about two
hundred of them—have begun to leave. Bitterness was infecting
the ranks: the soldiers had been promised an era of happiness,
which was to have begun immediately after the victory, and
nothing had changed; there was still the same tension, still
bloodshed.

Most of the Khmer refugees who came to Thailand in the first
months after the capture of Phnom Penh had traveled hundreds
of kilometers on foot, crisscrossing the country in every direction
at the whim of events. They had traveled by the main highways,

on trains, and even in Khmer Rouge trucks. When I expressed my amazement at the ease with which they had been able to move about, Sam Suon explained:

It was simple. To get from one place to another we had to have a mission order or a *laissez-passer*. A lot of the Khmer Rouge didn't know how to read and those who could write did so very badly, so we wrote out our own *laissez-passers*, trying to make them as illegible as possible. At Prek Kdam I showed mine to a Khmer Rouge who was on guard there. He looked at it upside down, glared at me, and said. "All right, go on!"

These methods were not always successful, however, because the new administration quickly armed itself with printed forms and rubber stamps, which greatly increased the risks, and those bold enough to brave them had to be prepared for the worst.

Two brothers, Nan Pun and Nan Pon, and their two cousins, hit upon a rapid and easy solution. The four young men had been requisitioned to learn how to operate a camera and develop film. For this purpose they lived in Phnom Penh from July to November 1975 near the Sorya cinema. Now and then they were sent out to the country to take photographs, and they noticed that big cars driving important officials were left strictly alone on the roads; nobody dared to stop them.

In a garage near the cinema stood the abandoned Mercedes of some professor. The young men remembered it, and somehow managed to lay hands on some fuel. Around midnight on December 19 they wheeled the Mercedes through the empty streets of Phnom Penh, then drove hell-for-leather to Battambang, which they reached at dawn. They showed faked orders and drove on to the Thai border without mishap. Loaded down with cameras, they said they had been sent by the authorities in Phnom Penh to make films and take pictures of Cambodia from the Thai side. Escorted by guards, they crossed the frontier bridge, which they photographed from every conceivable angle—because the guards were always watching them. There seemed to be no way to get rid of them. Their hearts in their shoes, the team of photographers reentered Cambodia. Suddenly one exclaimed, "I've lost my lens cover!" "Go look for it yourselves," said the guards. "We've got too much to do already with all these Thais coming to buy and sell!" Without further ado the four men drove back over the bridge and disappeared.

By means of similar subterfuges, some other people made their way across the border without too much trouble. One refugee from Kampot had been working as a mechanic on a boat. Drop by drop, he too saved up fuel until he could make his getaway on a motorboat, taking his whole family with him. One young man from Koh Kong, who used to fish with the Khmer Rouge in the open sea, escaped in a rowboat after carefully noting the revolutionaries' lookout posts.

For most, however, the voyage was long and perilous. First, they had to escape the vigilance of their guards, which was no easy matter in a system as thoroughly policed as that of the new Khmer society. Then they had to walk for weeks through forest and over mountain, living on roots and leaves. They were eaten alive by mosquitoes and bloodsuckers, and they also had to reckon with panthers and wild elephants. There were patrols in the forest, too, and revolutionary soldiers' camps. Tripping over a mine at the frontier could be fatal. Keum Chaom, a doctor, was escaping with his family; he stumbled into a mine and died with his own two children, leaving his heartbroken wife to march on alone for nine more days and nights with their nephews.

Often, macabre encounters took place: according to refugees, the forests were littered with corpses. "Around midnight," one reported,

we were approaching a deep stream. It was cold and the banks were covered with bamboo. We decided to sleep there and look for a way across the next day. At dawn I climbed a tree to get my bearings: there was a Khmer Rouge command post on the other bank, just a few yards from the stream! Luckily we hadn't tried to cross during the night. I woke up my companions and we went on to the east, where there was a little bridge over the stream. New mosquito netting hung just nearby, which meant that there were guards around. We moved off to the left and almost fell over a pile of corpses stacked up like logs. It took our breath away. They hadn't even spread them apart!

It is easy enough to understand that the Khmer authorities are
not overjoyed by this hemorrhage of refugees. In an attempt to
staunch the flow, they tried to convince the population that flight
was impossible:

They said that everybody who ran away was recaptured and shot.
One day a customs officer from Thmar Puok escaped with his family.
He was pursued and hid in a thick-leaved tree in the forest. The Khmer
Rouge caught his wife and children, brought them back to the village,
and killed them in front of the whole population, to serve as an example.
The Khmer Rouge used to say the frontier was mined and there was a
soldier patrolling every five meters, so it was impossible to escape. Sometimes they bragged that they had captured the Thai province of Chanta-
buri, so it was no good trying to get into Thailand.

Despite these dissuasive tactics, the refugees continued to
escape. Late in 1975, in the region of Sdau (Battambang), families and even couples were separated in the hope that a single
member of a family would not want to go alone. But the result
was exactly the opposite: if people were going to be parted from
their nearest and dearest, they might as well make a break for
freedom! In other places, the families of those who fled were
punished: a boy who reached Ta Praya in January 1976 learned in
the course of a resistance raid on Cambodia that his parents had
been executed after his departure.

In 1975 everybody caught trying to get away was killed on the
spot; since 1976, however, they are apparently being sent to
reeducation camps.

After braving every obstacle, the refugees reach Thailand in a
state of total exhaustion. One needs to have seen a new arrival
with one's own eyes to imagine the sort of life he has led. Sary,
whom I met immediately after his arrival on June 15, 1976, was a
hunted man with haggard eyes, his face and limbs swollen with
beriberi. He could only speak in monosyllables. The impression
he gave me was of a man who had escaped from an insane
asylum.

As a finishing touch to their ordeal, the refugees are often met
at the border by gangs of bandits who despoil them of the little
they have left, and sometimes even take their clothes. Others

come up against soldiers or frontier police, whose attitudes vary
widely from one post to another. Sometimes they treat the refugees kindly, but more often, like the gangs, they fleece them.
Then—or at least that has been the rule since February 1976—
refugees entering the country illegally spend a week or more in
prison before being sent to one of the camps for Khmer
refugees, where they live in tin shacks put up by the UN high
commissioner for refugees, and are fed increasingly short rations.
The atmosphere in these camps is that of every refugee camp the
world over: under a leaden sky, crowded together in conditions of
terrifying promiscuity, with a diet and sanitary arrangements that
are less than mediocre, the refugees live without work, without
hope, and without a future. Some have tried to find work outside
the camps, but the Thai government is not eager to employ this
source of manpower, which it regards as politically compromis-
ing. Of course there are always a few unscrupulous employers
ready to take advantage of such a defenseless labor force, paying
ridiculously low wages and sometimes none at all. On top of that,
the refugees have to offer some token of gratitude to the camp
guards for letting them out to look for work.

There is little hope in them. They live with their memories,
constantly reliving the horrors they have witnessed. Each one
recounts what he saw or heard, his imagination and homesickness
tending to exaggerate and distort the facts.

The International Red Cross, the high commissioner for refugees,
and a few private bodies—often more efficient than the more
highly publicized ones—are helping the refugees within the limits
allowed by the Thai government. They all long to return to their
country one day, but they know that going back now means death.
Their great fear is that the UN will abandon them and they will be
forcibly sent back to Cambodia.[1] They know that those who have

---

[1] This fear is not entirely groundless. On November 23, 1976, the Thai authori-
ties sent twenty-six Khmer refugees home blindfolded and with their hands tied.
These twenty-six, including one child of eleven, had their throats cut at Mongkol
Borei three days later. On November 28 six Khmer Rouge who escaped into
Thailand that same day were also handed back to the authorities of their home
country.

gone back have died. In June 1975, eighty-eight airmen being trained in Thailand asked to return home; their request was granted, but as soon as they crossed the frontier the Khmer Rouge stripped and shot them. "We can't weigh down the earth with people like that," the cadres explain to the peasants at their daily meetings. About the same time, a group of about two hundred soldiers returned to their country and met with the same fate.

We may also wonder what has become of the four hundred or so Khmers who were living abroad and have chosen to return since the end of 1975. Most were students or trainees in various trades who had gone to France before the fall of Phnom Penh. With no news of their families and nothing to keep them in France, refusing to believe the apocalyptic tales they were hearing about life in Kampuchea, most of the students set off full of enthusiasm. Not all: one man of about forty, who had come to France for a six-month training course, was to go home on April 17, 1975—but that day the regime changed. A few months later he decided to return anyway. Before leaving, he came to see me, for we had known each other a long time:

"Are you really familiar with the situation in your country?"

"Yes."

"Then why are you going?"

"In France I'd be an outcast all my life. If I go back, I might be able to see my wife and children again. I know I don't have a chance in a hundred of finding them but I want to try anyway. If I don't find them this year, maybe I'll succeed later."

Those four hundred or so Khmers returned to Phnom Penh via Peking, either by plane or Trans-Siberian Railway. Little news of them has filtered out since. One eyewitness saw the first group to land in Phnom Penh:

When they got out of the airplane you could see how worried they were because their families weren't there to meet them. One girl burst into tears because all she saw were men in black. The group was taken to the Khmero-Soviet Technical School, where the newcomers were taught how to grow vegetables for two months. Then they were sent to the country, but I don't know where.

Many of those who have fled to Thailand would rather stay there than move on, because the sunshine and way of life make their exile less harsh. But in addition to an ancestral animosity between Khmers and Thais, there is the political tension. The Thai authorities would gladly be rid of these unwelcome guests, who are a potential source of conflict in their relations with their neighbor. The UN is short of money and has cut the daily refugee allowance to the Thai government from eight bahts (forty cents) per person to four bahts; and the organization is contemplating withdrawing its aid altogether. If it does, and the authorities adopt the radical solution of sending the refugees back to Cambodia, who will stand up for them?

"Besides," they say, "if we stay in Thailand and the regime does change, we'll be killed by our compatriots who will come to get us."

For most of them, the only real solution is to go somewhere else. About four thousand Khmers have been taken by America; Australia and Austria have admitted a few hundred. France, conscious of its responsibilities to its former protectorate, had admitted nearly nine thousand by October 1976 and planned to take a few thousand more.

But many of the refugees know now that they will not be able to leave Thailand for Europe or America; they will have to sit and rot in the camps for long years, idle and abandoned. From time to time they get letters from friends who have gone to France or elsewhere: good news, of course, but already tinged with disillusionment, for life in their adopted countries is not easy, the sun there is wan and the work hard, and human relations tend to be strained. Beyond all doubt, the refugees appreciate what France has done for them: in a period of economic difficulty the country is spending an average of sixty francs (twelve dollars) per refugee per day for food and clothing during the six months following their arrival. Many public and private charities show prodigious ingenuity in their efforts to help; but in spite of their good intentions, their assistance is often tinged with paternalism. It is fine to provide clothing, shelter, and employment; but it is not enough. Few organizations are making any real attempt to integrate the refugees in their new country, by teaching them the language, customs, and social code and giving them enough political awareness to avoid being exploited once again.

The most effective service anyone can render them is to educate them, and it may sometimes mean taking a firm line, to prevent them from becoming permanent "welfare cases." In all likelihood these people are going to spend the rest of their lives among us. They may never hear from their families again; and to have any sense of the tragedy they are living through now, one must know how strong are the ties that bind an Asian family.

Some give up the fight, and dream of returning to Cambodia gun in hand to reconquer some morsel of Khmer earth and put down new roots. Are their dreams completely utopian? A resistance movement does exist, but . . . :

In the early months after the defeat of the republic, some of its officers tried to carry on the fight. Others, under a mask of patriotism, were simply hoping to perpetuate their former lives. One former governor employed his men to collect and sell logs, supposedly to obtain funds for the resistance forces. The same man sent out commandos to recapture a Khmer banker who was the sole signatory of his bank account in Bangkok, where he had deposited a portion of misappropriated American aid. Also, allegedly, to further the resistance, other commandos went to rob the caches of precious stones which had been mined and hidden by the inhabitants of the Pailin region. After robbing them, the commandos murdered the mining families and blamed the Khmer Rouge. Even in France there are tiny groups embroiled in various questionable political schemes, inspired less by patriotism than by personal interest. And personal rivalries continue to divide the Khmer community both in France and in Thailand so sharply that one begins to wonder whether five years of war followed by total defeat have taught anybody anything.

Yet there are armed resistance movements of real patriots, who do not care for publicity. They are few in number but efficient, and they have learned some lessons from the past. They receive no help from any foreign country, which is their weakness but also their strength: American aid, after all, caused the downfall of the Khmer Republic by leading to a proliferation of corruption rather than the reinforcement of an ideal. Their main activity is to increase the "awareness" of the population, to give a little nudge here and there. They are counting on a change of loyalty within several revolutionary units with which they have already made contact.

Inside Kampuchea, too, there are a few centers of resistance, but their strength is hard to evaluate and they are hard to pin down. Kompong Speu, Kompong Chhnang, and Battambang have been the scenes of disturbances caused by resistance forces of unknown origin. Peasants have rebelled in a few places, only to be ruthlessly exterminated. In Siem Reap province several village cadres were assassinated during the opening months of 1976 by groups of four or five resistants dressed in black like Khmer Rouge. Groups of mysterious "White Khmers" have control of part of the area near Staung (Kompong Thom). They were first heard of in 1972; they are neither Sihanoukists nor republicans nor Communists and their leader and goals are unknown, but they are distinctly effective and definitely feared. These local incidents have led the revolutionary authorities to redouble their vigilance and surveillance of the population.

At this point, resistance both within and from without presumably does not represent a real threat to the government. With their long fighting experience, the Khmer Rouge are past masters of the art of guerrilla warfare, and they hold the people in an iron fist. Nevertheless, these movements are the sign of a refusal, a living hope that the Khmer soul may not be utterly crushed. The future will tell whether they can confirm the words of Mao Tse-tung: "One small group, with no resources at all, can free itself from the yoke of any oppression if it wants to badly enough."

TWELVE

Year Zero

On April 17, 1975, a society collapsed; another is now being born from the fierce drive of a revolution which is incontestably the most radical ever to take place in so short a time. It is a perfect example of the application of an ideology pushed to the furthest limit of its internal logic. But the furthest limit is too far, and "too far" is akin to madness—for in this scheme of society, where is man?

Immobility and corruption have given way to a frenzy of production and a hysteria of purification. Individualism and chaotic license have been replaced by radical collectivism and perpetual conditioning. Using class inequality and racial animosity as tools, a handful of ideologists have driven an army of peasants to bury their entire past. To learn a new art of living, many of the living have died.

Revolutionary ideas excite young students who long to see justice done and have a share in the government of their countries. But in this new regime, in which all possessions have been abolished and knowledge confers no privilege, the one thing that is not shared is power: it remains wholly concentrated in the hands of a very small number. The credulity of the people has been used to drive them out of towns, eliminate objectors, keep whole populations constantly on the move, and treat them as instruments of production. The irony of talking about the "people's happiness"!

The Khmer revolution has shown how woefully ill informed the French were. In April and May 1975 French newspapers gave most of their coverage to the fate of the foreigners interned in the French embassy in Phnom Penh. Nothing could be more natural than that the press should rise up to denounce violations of human rights in Spain, Latin America, and South Africa. But nothing could be less justifiable than that so few voices should be raised in protest against the assassination of a people. How many of those who say they are unreservedly in support of the Khmer revolution would consent to endure one hundredth part of the present sufferings of the Cambodian people?

Even organizations whose sole aim is the defense of man, like the French League of Human Rights, have never answered the cries of distress from the Khmers or their friends. Even the UN has turned a deaf ear. On Christmas Day 1975 one of my Khmer friends remarked to me with some bitterness: "In France there are societies for the protection of animals and factories which manufacture special food for dogs and cats. The Cambodians must be less than animals, then, since nobody can be bothered to defend them."

The smile of the Leper-King has frozen into a grimace of death.

Appendixes

A FEW MILESTONES

NEOLITHIC:
Lacustrian cities.

GRAECO-ROMAN PERIOD:
Cambodia is the "Chersonesus Aurea" of the Ancients.

1ST–4TH CENTURIES:
Fou Nan period, a kingdom in the southern part of the Indochinese
peninsula.
Economy based on water control (swamp drainage).
Indian influence in the 1st and 4th centuries; Brahminism.

5TH–7TH CENTURIES:
Tchen-la period, a kingdom northeast of the lakes. Economy based on
water control (irrigation by canal and dam).

7TH–8TH CENTURIES:
Javanese domination.

9TH–14TH CENTURIES:
Angkor: Union of Fou Nan and Tchen-la.
Introduction of Theravada Buddhism.
10th Century: Angkor Thom ("the Great City"), embellished in the
11th century.

12th Century: Angkor Wat ("the Temple City").
Late 12th Century: Greatest geographical expansion, in the reign of
   Jayavarman VII, the "Leper-King" (1183–1201).

14TH–19TH CENTURIES:

Decadence. Cambodia torn apart by Thais and Vietnamese, aided by
   palace intrigues.
First appearance of the West: Portuguese, Spanish, Dutch.
1394:   Capture of Angkor; followed by a hundred-year war.
1431:   Capital moved to Longvek, then, in 1593, to Oudong.
1841–45:   Cambodia a province of Vietnam.

FRENCH PROTECTORATE (1863–1953)

1863:   King Norodom accepts the protectorate.
1884–89:   Peasant uprisings provoked by the regulations enacted by
   Charles Thomson during the Jules Ferry government.
1907:   King Sisowath recovers the provinces of Battambang, Siem
   Reap, and Sisophon, previously annexed by Siam.
1941:   Prince Norodom Sihanouk ascends the throne.
1953:   Independence of Cambodia.

KINGDOM OF CAMBODIA (1953–70)

1963:   Nationalization laws, rejection of American aid.
1965:   Departure of Americans.
March 18, 1970:   Prince Sihanouk deposed.

KHMER REPUBLIC (1970–75)

October 9, 1970:   Proclamation of the republic.
June 1972:   Marshal Lon Nol elected president of the republic.
April 17, 1975:   Phnom Penh taken by revolutionaries.

DEMOCRATIC KAMPUCHEA (1976–PRESENT)

January 5, 1976:   Constitution of Democratic Kampuchea.
March 20, 1976:   First elections.
April 2, 1976:   Prince Norodom Sihanouk resigns.

CONSTITUTION OF DEMOCRATIC KAMPUCHEA

The sacred and fundamental aspirations of the people,
workers, peasants, and other laborers as well as those of the
fighters and cadres of the Kampuchean Revolutionary Army

Whereas a significant role has been played by the people, especially the workers, poor peasants, lower-middle-class peasants, and other strata of urban and rural working people, who account for more than ninety-five percent of the entire Kampuchean nation, who assumed the heaviest responsibility in waging the war for the liberation of the nation and the people, made the greatest sacrifices in terms of life, property, and commitment, served the front line unremittingly, and unhesitatingly sacrificed their children and husbands by the thousands for the battle at the front line;

Whereas great sacrifices have been borne by the three categories of the Kampuchean Revolutionary Army who fought valiantly, day and night, in the dry and rainy seasons, underwent all kinds of hardship and misery, shortages of food, medicine, clothing, ammunition, and other commodities in the great war for the liberation of the nation and the people;

Whereas the entire Kampuchean people and the entire Kampuchean Revolutionary Army desire an independent, unified, peaceful, neutral, nonaligned, sovereign Kampuchea enjoying territorial integrity, a national society informed by genuine happiness, equality, justice, and democracy, without rich or poor and without exploiters or exploited, a society in which all live harmoniously in great national solidarity and join forces to do manual work together and increase production for the construction and defense of the country;

And whereas the resolution of the Special National Congress held on 25, 26, and 27 April 1975 solemnly proclaimed recognition and respect for the above desires of the entire people and the entire Kampuchean Revolutionary Army;

The Constitution of Kampuchea stipulates as follows:

CHAPTER ONE

The State

ARTICLE 1

The State of Kampuchea is an independent, unified, peaceful, neutral, nonaligned, sovereign, and democratic State enjoying territorial integrity.

The State of Kampuchea is a State of the people, workers, peasants, and all other Kampuchean working people.

The official name of the State of Kampuchea is "Democratic Kampuchea."

CHAPTER TWO

The Economy

ARTICLE 2

All important means of production are the collective property of the people's State and the common property of the people's communities.

Property for everyday use remains in private hands.

CHAPTER THREE

Culture

ARTICLE 3

The culture of Democratic Kampuchea is of a national, popular, forward-looking, and healthful character such as will serve the tasks of defending and building Kampuchea into an ever more prosperous country.

This new culture is absolutely opposed to the corrupt, reactionary culture of the different oppressive classes of colonialism and imperialism in Kampuchea.

CHAPTER FOUR

The Principle of Leadership and Work

ARTICLE 4

Democratic Kampuchea applies the collective principle in leadership and in work.

CHAPTER FIVE

Legislative Power

ARTICLE 5

Legislative power is invested in the representative assembly of the people, workers, peasants, and all other Kampuchean working people.

This Assembly shall be officially known as the "Kampuchean People's Representative Assembly."

The Kampuchean People's Representative Assembly shall be made up of 250 members, representing the workers, peasants, and other working people and the Kampuchean Revolutionary Army in the following proportions:

Representing the peasants	150
Representing the laborers and other working people	50
Representing the revolutionary army	50

ARTICLE 6

The members of the Kampuchean People's Representative Assembly are to be elected by the people in direct general elections by secret ballot, held throughout the country every five years.

ARTICLE 7

The People's Representative Assembly is responsible for legislation and for defining the various domestic and foreign policies of Democratic Kampuchea.

CHAPTER SIX

The Executive Body

ARTICLE 8

The government is a body responsible for giving effect to the laws and political lines laid down by the Kampuchean People's Representative Assembly.

The government is elected by the Kampuchean People's Representative Assembly and must be fully answerable to it for all its activities both inside and outside the country.

CHAPTER SEVEN

Justice

ARTICLE 9

Justice is administered by people's courts, which represent and defend the people's justice, defend the democratic rights of the people, and punish any act directed against the people's State or violating the laws of the people's State.

The judges at all levels shall be chosen and appointed by the People's Representative Assembly.

ARTICLE 10

Actions violating the laws of the people's State are as follows:

Hostile and destructive activities that threaten the popular State shall be subject to the severest form of punishment.
Other cases shall be handled by means of constructive reeducation in the framework of the State or people's organizations.

CHAPTER EIGHT

The State Presidium

ARTICLE 11

Democratic Kampuchea has a State Presidium chosen and appointed by the Kampuchean People's Representative Assembly once every five years.

The State Presidium is responsible for representing the State of Democratic Kampuchea inside and outside the country, in keeping with the Constitution of Democratic Kampuchea and with the laws and policies laid down by the Kampuchean People's Representative Assembly.

The State Presidium is composed of the following: a president, a first vice-president, and a second vice-president.

CHAPTER NINE

The Rights and Duties of the Individual

ARTICLE 12

Every citizen of Kampuchea is fully entitled to a constantly improving material, spiritual, and cultural life. Every citizen of Kampuchea is guaranteed a living.

All workers are the masters of their factories.

All peasants are the masters of the rice paddies and fields.

All other working people have the right to work.

There is absolutely no unemployment in Democratic Kampuchea.

ARTICLE 13

There must be complete equality among all Kampuchean people in an equal, just, democratic, harmonious, and happy society within the great national union for defending and building the country.

Men and women are equal in every respect.

Polygamy and polyandry are prohibited.

ARTICLE 14

It is the duty of all to defend and build the country together in accordance with individual ability and potential.

CHAPTER TEN

The Capital

ARTICLE 15

The capital city of Democratic Kampuchea is Phnom Penh.

CHAPTER ELEVEN

The National Flag

ARTICLE 16

The design and meaning of the Kampuchean national flag are as follows:

The ground is red, bearing a yellow three-towered structure in the middle.

The red ground symbolizes the revolutionary movement, the resolute and valiant struggle of the people of Kampuchea for the liberation, defense, and construction of the nation.

The yellow building symbolizes national tradition and the people of Kampuchea, who are defending and building the country to make it ever more glorious.

CHAPTER TWELVE

The National Emblem

ARTICLE 17

The national emblem consists of a network of dikes and canals, which symbolize modern agriculture, and a factory symbolizing industry, framed by an oval garland of rice ears with the subscription "Democratic Kampuchea."

CHAPTER THIRTEEN

The National Anthem

ARTICLE 18

The national anthem of Democratic Kampuchea is the "Dap Prampi Mesa Moha Chokchey" ["Glorious Seventeenth of April"].

CHAPTER FOURTEEN

The Kampuchean Revolutionary Army

ARTICLE 19

The three categories of the Kampuchean Revolutionary Army—regular, regional, and guerrilla—form an army of the people made up of men and women fighters and cadres who are the children of the laborers, peasants, and other working people. They defend the power of the people of independent, unified, peaceful, neutral, nonaligned, sovereign, and democratic Kampuchea, which enjoys territorial integrity, and at the same time they help to build a country growing more prosperous every day and to improve and develop the people's standard of living.

CHAPTER FIFTEEN

Worship and Religion

ARTICLE 20

Every citizen of Kampuchea has the right to worship according to any religion and the right not to worship according to any religion.

All reactionary religions that are detrimental to Democratic Kampuchea and the Kampuchean people are strictly forbidden.

CHAPTER SIXTEEN

Foreign Policy

ARTICLE 21

Democratic Kampuchea is firmly determined to maintain close and friendly relations with all countries sharing a common border and with all near and distant countries throughout the world in conformity with the principles of mutual and absolute respect for sovereignty and territorial integrity.

Democratic Kampuchea is committed to a policy of independence, peace, neutrality, and nonalignment. It will permit absolutely no foreign country to maintain military bases on its territory and is resolutely opposed to all forms of subversion and aggression from outside, whether military, political, cultural, social, diplomatic, or so-called humanitarian.

Democratic Kampuchea refuses all intervention in the domestic affairs of other countries, and scrupulously respects the principle that every country is sovereign and entitled to manage and decide its own affairs without outside interference.

Democratic Kampuchea adheres entirely to the great family of non-aligned nations.

Democratic Kampuchea strives to promote solidarity with the peoples of the third world in Asia, Africa, and Latin America, and with peace- and justice-loving people the world over, and to contribute actively to mutual aid and support in the struggle against imperialism, colonialism, neo-colonialism, and in favor of independence, peace, friendship, democracy, justice, and progress throughout the world.

DECLARATION

by Samdech Norodom Sihanouk

April 2, 1976

On March 20, 1976, the Kampuchean people were very happy and proud to hold general elections in the country and to select democratically their representatives who are to be the male and female members of the Kampuchean People's Representative Assembly.

This sovereign Assembly, whose members were chosen by the people on the basis of pure patriotism and their important contribution to the complete victory in the struggle for national liberation and for the revolution in Kampuchea, will elect the patriots who are to be members of the government of Democratic Kampuchea and the State Presidium of Democratic Kampuchea.

Thus the government bodies and political institutions of the state will be set up in conformity with the provisions of the Constitution of Democratic Kampuchea, which is the great achievement of the heroic men and women fighters of the Kampuchean revolutionary army and the peasants and workers and other laboring patriots, to whom Kampuchea owes its total liberation from the clutches of U.S. imperialism and the regime of the traitorous clique, its revolution, and its authentic democracy.

As far as I personally am concerned, it has been my great pride and honor from March 1970 to this day to accompany my most beloved

Kampuchean people on the great and prestigious historical march that is now leading Kampuchea into a new era, in which the people are the only true masters of their destiny and of the nation and the fatherland; a new era which, beyond all doubt, will be the most radiant and glorious in the two thousand years of our national history.

When the *coup d'état* of Lon Nol and his clique took place in Phnom Penh on March 18, 1970, I swore to myself and to the Kampuchean people that after I had accompanied my countrymen to complete victory over U.S. imperialism and the traitorous clique and after the opening of the new revolutionary era, I would retire completely and forever from the political scene, for my role would logically come to an end.

Today, my dream that Kampuchea would recover and strengthen forever its independence, sovereignty, territorial integrity, and neutrality, and acquire a system capable of giving the people and the nation true sovereignty and perfect social justice, and a national life that is absolutely clean (without stain, corruption, and other social ills) has been fulfilled beyond anything I could imagine, thanks to our fighting men and women, peasants, laborers, and other working people, under the enlightened leadership of our revolutionary Angkar.

Thus, all my fondest wishes have come true. Better yet, our Kampuchea has achieved, thanks to its heroic revolutionary men and women, splendid exploits of great significance, which are among the greatest in the history of all mankind, such as being the first to overcome completely the arrogant and allegedly "invincible" U.S. imperialism, the most powerful, cruel, and tenacious imperialism the world has ever known.

As for myself, shortly after the liberation of the fatherland, our people, our revolutionary Angkar, and revolutionary army solemnly honored me as a patriot and member of the resistance and spontaneously renewed my term of office as head of state of Kampuchea; they then invited me to return officially to Kampuchea and, just as they had welcomed me in March 1973 during the war, gave me a solemn, extremely cordial, and warm welcome and extended to me a hospitality filled with affection, respect, and consideration, and with understandably great pride they showed me their wonderful and innumerable achievements, most thrilling among them being the new irrigation systems, which will assuredly make our country one of the most advanced and highly developed agricultural nations.

My content is therefore greater than can be imagined.

As head of state since 1941, I have now completed thirty-five years of service.

From March 18, 1970, the day of the antinational *coup d'état* by Lon Nol, until April 17, 1975, the historic day of the complete victory of the Kampuchean people and the Kampuchean Revolutionary Army over the U.S. imperialists and their lackeys, the traitorous clique criticized me harshly and soiled my name with slanderous statements and contempt.

For the rest of my life I shall remain grateful to the Kampuchean people, Kampuchean heroes and heroines, and the Kampuchean revolutionary Angkar for clearing my name so fully in the eyes of the world and history.

It is with this sentiment and with the conviction that our people and revolutionary Angkar understand me as one of their fellows that I request them to permit me to retire [Khmer: *chol kan nivath*] today. I wish to assure you that everywhere and under all circumstances I shall remain a valiant supporter of the Kampuchean people, the revolution, the People's Representative Assembly, the government, the State Presidium, the revolutionary Angkar, and the revolutionary army of Democratic Kampuchea.

Long live the most heroic and glorious people of Kampuchea!

Long live Democratic Kampuchea!

Long live the Constitution of Democratic Kampuchea!

STATEMENT BY THE GOVERNMENT
OF DEMOCRATIC KAMPUCHEA

In response to the request for retirement of
Head of State Norodom Sihanouk

After receiving the request for retirement of Head of State Samdech Norodom Sihanouk dated April 2, 1976, the Council of Ministers met on April 4 and held an exhaustive discussion of the question, led by Premier Penn Nouth.

The Council of Ministers considers that Samdech Norodom Sihanouk is an eminently patriotic prince who has actively contributed to the struggle for national liberation in the most barbarous war of aggression conducted by the American imperialists and their lackeys. Part III of the resolution of the National Congress dated April 27, 1975, clearly defines the services rendered by Samdech and solemnly proclaims that he should continue to act as Head of State in the new phase of Kampuchea's history and in the new Kampuchean society. However, Samdech has expressed his wish to withdraw from active life to devote himself to his family after thirty-five years of political activity.

The Council of Ministers has expressed its regret at this request for retirement by Samdech Norodom Sihanouk; however, out of respect for his highest wishes it has decided to accept his withdrawal and, at the same time, to propose that the following decisions be submitted to the People's Representative Assembly:

(1) In recognition of the services rendered to the Kampuchean nation by Samdech Norodom Sihanouk, who took an active part in the

national liberation during the most barbarous war of aggression waged during the last five years by the American imperialists and the traitors Lon Nol, Sirik Matak, Son Ngoc Thanh, Cheng Heng, In Tam, Long Boret, and Sosthenes Fernandez, the Council of Ministers unanimously wishes to confer upon Samdech Norodom Sihanouk the title of Great Patriot.

At the same time the Council of Ministers proposes to build a monument in honor of the services rendered by Samdech Norodom Sihanouk;

(2) The Government of Democratic Kampuchea will fully guarantee and bear the living expenses of himself and his family in recognition of his honor and status as former Head of State and former chairman of the NUFK. Also, the Government of Democratic Kampuchea proposes that a retirement pension of $2,000 quarterly, or $8,000 per annum, be paid to Samdech.

The government will submit these proposals to the Kampuchean People's Representative Assembly for consideration and approval.

THE GOVERNMENT OF DEMOCRATIC KAMPUCHEA

Phnom Penh, April 4, 1976

François Ponchaud was born in 1939 in Sallanches, a small village in the French Alps. As a member of the Society of Foreign Missions, he spent ten years in Cambodia. For the first five years he shared the life of the Khmer peasants (he himself is the son of peasants), learning their language, customs, and religion. In 1970, after Sihanouk was deposed, Ponchaud headed a student center in Phnom Penh and a committee for translations. He was forced to leave Cambodia with the last convoy of foreigners on May 8, 1975. He is presently living in France, where he has been working with Cambodian refugees.

Nancy Amphoux was born in Rockford, Illinois, in 1935 and was educated at Vassar and Carnegie Institute of Technology. Since 1960, she has lived in Europe. Ms. Amphoux is the translator of Henri Troyat's biographies of Tolstoi, Pushkin, and Gogol, and Edmonde Charles-Roux's biography of Chanel, among other books.